Defying Corruption

One Man's Quest to Expose

DEFYING CORRUPTION

ONE MAN'S QUEST TO EXPOSE

R Gopal Sharma

Bigfoot Publications
Because, there's a writer in everyone.

Defying Corruption: One Man's Quest to Expose
Author : R Gopal Sharma

First Published by
Bigfoot06 Publications (OPC) Pvt. Ltd.
1st floor, BSR Building near Vishal Mega Mart,
Daultabad Flyover, Laxman Vihar Phase 3,
Gurugram, Haryana (122001)
Website: www.bigfootpublications.in
Email: info@bigfootpublications.in

First Edition : November, 2023

ISBN Print Book : 978-81-19512-56-0

Printed in India

Dedicated to the coming generations who are expected to be wiser after going through the omissions and commissions of their fore fathers.

Road not to contradict and confute;
Nor to believe or take for granted;
Nor to find talk and discourse;
But to weigh and consider.

- Francis Bacon

Introduction

When thousands are against me but God is with me, I definitely have the divine majority.

- Emerson

What has inspired me to pen this memoir, after spending twenty-three long years in these institutions? It is an exceptional step. But for me, it is a journey of passing from one significant phase of my life to another. This is just an attempt to disclose the hitherto hidden activities inside he enclosures of the organizations. In my own humble way, but empowered by my spiritual Guru Ji himself, my aim is solely the reformation of these institutions; to enable society to have peep into the panoramic but veiled ocean, like the seashell that holds a few drops of sea water. So that the book should in no way hurt those inside the iron curtain. Let the fresh breeze enter the closed walls and purify its stinking corners.

It may be considered by some that this account is unduly critical but closing of eyes and ears would have been at the cost of truth. And the truth, however bitter, should not upset this group of people.

In sum, the objective of the book is to expose those who are corrupt by choice and some others who are forced to conduct acts of corruption under the influence of their seniors.

Everyone is aware of the fact that if you are honest and raise your voice against corruption in the system, you are either gone with the wind or you are stopped by the influential people in the government whose interests you are hurting, by hook or by crook. Ultimately, what has to happen will happen and there is no point in getting perturbed over it because honesty pays in the long run.

I am indebted to the individuals and institutions with whose selfless help the study material and rare information could be made available. I am morally bound not to disclose their identity for obvious reasons.

I express my profound gratitude to Colonel Jawed A Mir and Sushant Sharma for taking trouble to read the manuscript and making valuable suggestions.

I remain beholden to members of my family specially Lily and Rose who maintained a congenial atmosphere for the work at the cost of their inconvenience.

I wish to thank all my foes who continue to throw stones at me, misunderstanding the vision of truth I seek to accomplish through "Defying Corruption".

Benjamin Franklin said," Either write something worth reading or do something worth writing'. I can't claim to have done something remarkable that is worth writing about. I am certainly not in the league of stalwarts such as Kuldip Nayyar, Balraj Puri, Khushwant Singh or Joginder Singh but I have tried to write something that is worth reading. I hope that readers not just enjoy the narration but also take back some lessons from my experience.

R Gopal Sharma

Lily-Rose
254/G, Sainik Colony
Jammu (J&K)
Nov. 10, 2023

Foreword

Corruption is a disease that has swept like a tidal wave through few of our government institutions. The book offers insight into the rampant corruption that exists in certain government departments, notably the National Cadet Corps and Sainik School in the Union territory of Jammu and Kashmir. It has only left a trail of negligence by the competent authority and inefficiency of the concerned department to investigate the serious allegations to a logical conclusion. The author has raised disturbing questions which are a cause of concern, if not addressed by the concerned authorities. The book is a wakeup call for all of us to clean up the system plagued with corruption.

Jai Hind!

Col Jawed A Mir, Sena Medal

Table of Contents

CHAPTER – 1

During my childhood era, there existed only one private academy within the Mendhar tehsil of the Poonch district that was dedicated to provide pre education to the toddlers. This institution was known as the Gandhi Seva Centre. After completing three years of foundational education at this establishment, children continued their studies at government schools. The Gandhi Seva Centre was overseen by a Punjabi couple (Shree Amar Nath Bhardwaj and his wife) who, having no children of their own, regarded all the toddlers and staff as their extended family. Within this Centre, two teachers by the names of Kiran Dutta and Champa were instrumental in shaping the educational experience of the little minds.

In 1970, I got enrolled in the Gandhi Seva Centre, an experience that deeply influenced me with Gandhi's principles and ideals. Kiran Dutta in particular stood out as my favorite teacher. Even in the KG (Kindergarten) class, she appointed me as the class monitor. Kiran Dutta must have been approximately 15-16 years old when she began her teaching journey at the Gandhi Seva Centre. She possessed a naturally simple and pure disposition and was also remarkably beautiful. While teaching the toddlers with great affection, she consistently emphasized the value of honesty. Today, as the Centre has evolved into a Middle school and later an *Anganwadi*, Kiran ji remains closely associated with this institution.

Although I was deeply influenced by Gandhi's ideology, I never adopted a defensive stance but instead confronted every situation with unwavering determination. In 1972, I was enrolled in Government Primary School, Mendhar, where Master Khadim Hussain served as the head teacher. He possessed a stern and principled demeanor. Following an assessment, he appointed me as the class monitor, a role of significant responsibility at that time. In this capacity, the monitor functioned like a teacher within the class, responsible for overseeing studies and managing various aspects when the teacher was away.

Master ji often referred to me as the ‘Cheetah’ due to my agility and quickness. I stood out as the sole student in the school who had transitioned from the Gandhi Seva Centre. My aptitude owed much to the nurturing care of Kiran Dutta Madam, who had lovingly nurtured my talent.

As the time passed, I was now in the fifth grade when an incident occurred that left an everlasting impact in my life. I was bitten by a snake. Unfortunately, the healthcare services in Mendhar were not as advanced as needed for immediate treatment. Consequently, a *Nambardar* and his son, Master Jagdish Lal ji, resorted to traditional methods by chanting mantras to heal me. Regrettably, I had inadvertently aggravated the wound by scratching it before their intervention. It took me a considerable 3-4 months to make a full recovery. Despite this setback, I persisted in my studies, and hard work rewarded me well as I achieved the top position in my class.

Upon completing the fifth grade, I was awarded a scholarship of Rs 60(sixty), a reward for securing the first position in my class. This performance continued, and in the sixth grade, Master Omkar Nath ji once again appointed me class monitor. By this point, I had become the teacher's favorite student due to my exceptional academic performance. Excelling in both studies and other responsibilities, I maintained my position as the top student in the class as I topped in seventh grade and eventually reached the eighth grade.

During my eighth-grade year, the school's headmaster, Ved Vyas Dutta ji, approached me with a request. He informed me that his son needed to sit for the combined examination of both the seventh and eighth grades and asked if I would tutor his son. Recognizing my academic prowess, he extended an invitation for me to stay at his residence until the exams concluded; assuring me that attendance at school would not be an issue. When I discussed this opportunity with my family, they too agreed, seeing it as a valuable life experience for me. The following day, I began teaching the headmaster's son, dedicating day and night to cover the entire eighth-grade syllabus while managing my own studies at the same time. Despite this additional responsibility,I was confident that I would maintain consistency in my academic performance..

Finally, the day of results arrived, and I approached school with high hopes. However, my confidence crumbled when I saw my result. This time, I did not secure the top spot but was placed fourth. Later, I discovered that some teachers had cheated and disclosed the question papers to their own children before the examination, resulting in one teacher's son securing the first position followed by the headmaster's son who was second and another student ranking third, while I found myself in fourth place. Furthermore, during the paper evaluation process, I faced discrimination, receiving only 33 percent marks in Hindi language paper. Dissatisfied with this outcome, my demeanour turned assertive, prompting me to bring my father to school the following day. I demanded re-evaluation of my papers. This news spread rapidly throughout Mendhar since my father was a well-known figure in the village, due to which villagers knew me as well.

This incident sent shockwaves through the school administration, wherein two teachers from the institution responsible for conducting our examinations had engaged in unethical practice. Notably, one of the teachers happened to be the headmaster's sibling, while the other student who secured the top position was the accused teacher's son. These two individuals along with another teacher named Master Vidya Sagar, came to our house in an attempt to dissuade us from raking up the issue against them. Master Vidya Sagar cautioned us that pursuing this matter could lead to a backlash from all the teachers of the school. He also assured us that such an incident would not happen again in future. Satisfied with his assurances, my father explained the situation to me and advised me to move on. He used to enjoy conversing with me in English and commended my proficiency in the language.

I also left these incidents behind and found myself in the ninth grade. I had enrolled in Government Boys Higher Secondary School, Mendhar, where our English teacher was Chandra Mohan Puri. Once again, I was appointed as the class monitor due to my abilities. On one occasion, when I made a minor mistake in English subject, Puri Saheb scolded me so severely that I fell ill and had a fever for several days. However, I persevered and dedicated myself to my studies, eventually scoring an impressive 149 out of 150 marks in the English subject in examination. My English teacher, pleased with my success, proudly displayed my paper and showed it to all the teachers, attributing my achievement to his strictness. It was during this time when I realized that I owed big thanks to him which helped me in later years that I became a journalist and writer.

Every year, a fete was organized at the memorial of martyrs in Mendhar on the occasion of the Baisakhi festival, which falls on April 13th. In 1978, Major General MS Cheema, the then GOC of the 25th Infantry Division, attended the function as the chief guest. I was also present in the function. During his address to the public, Major General Cheema shared a sentiment he had once heard from a sage during his time as an ascetic in the forest: "*Sabse bada hai banda, lekin isme hai mehnat ka dhandha* (He is the greatest person, but it is a matter of hard work)." He recounted the challenges he had faced in his life and how his dedication and hard work had propelled him from a soldier in the army to the rank of Major General. His words left a profound impact on me, reinforcing my commitment to excel in my studies.

Coming from a humble family background with no political connections, my father's strong aversion to bribery and corruption instilled in me the values of hard work and honesty. With this lesson in mind, I resolved to diligently pursue the top position in the 11th grade. My aspiration was to pursue a B.Sc. in Agriculture and become an officer. With this objective, I opted for the non-medical stream in the 11th grade and began working tirelessly.Ultimately, my unwavering effort bore fruit, as I not only secured the first position in my school but also ranked first in both the Rajouri and Poonch districts. I stood as the sole student in these districts to pass with first division honors, a significant achievement.

In those days, gaining admission to a professional college hinged on successfully passing a written examination. Immediately following the 11th-grade exams, I commenced rigorous preparations for the written test, dedicating myself to study day and night. Consequently, I clinched the top spot in this written examination as well. With this achievement in hand, I proceeded to navigate the application process, duly filling out the B.Sc. Agriculture form, which required submission by August 16, 1982.

During that era, there existed a lingering apprehension that individuals with less marks but with approach and acquaintances might tamper with form submission and even may attempt to cause disruption on examination day. A similar incident involving a doctor named Rakesh Sahni served as a stark example, as he had consumed tea that left him unwell. Nevertheless, he persevered and eventually became a doctor.

Following the completion of my form and its attestation, I approached my family for some financial support to travel to Poonch for form submission. However, they declined this request and suggested two alternatives:

either send the form by mail or hand it over to Sham Lal, a clerk in my father's office, who was scheduled to go to Poonch the next morning. Adhering to their counsel, I entrusted the form to Sham Lal on August 6th. Regrettably, when he returned on August 13th, he returned the form to me, revealing that Gurcharan Singh, a clerk at the DC office in Poonch, had refused to accept it. Sham Lal voiced concerns that the clerk may have been susceptible to bribery from students with lesser scores, resulting in only four forms being submitted, one of which belonged to the headmaster's son, whom I had personally tutored. I relayed this situation to my family, but they persisted in their advice to send the form by post. Left with no other recourse, I dispatched the form through the mail.

It was at this juncture that the reality hit me hard – the saying, "*Bure waqt mei saya bhi sath chhodh deta hai* (In bad times, even your own shadow leaves you)," became evident. During that time, I couldn't even secure a ten-rupee loan to travel to Poonch and submit my form, despite the widespread belief in Mendhar that I would undoubtedly secure a spot in the course.

Throughout my life, I've been fortunate to receive encouragement from various individuals, including some girls who interestingly shared a common trait—the initial letter of their names, "M". Among these girls, one M was my senior, another my junior, and the third was a classmate. The senior girl held the closest place in my heart, forming a strong friendship with me. All three of them were renowned throughout the school for their exceptional beauty and impeccable manners, while I had earned the reputation as a top-performing student. These girls were confident that I would secure a spot in the agriculture course, and their unwavering support served as a powerful motivator, driving me to intensify my studies. Additionally, upon my family's insistence, I also got enrolled in the 12th grade.

However, unbeknownst to me, the clerk at the DC office, Gurcharan Singh, had taken an unusual step—he had sent all the students' forms to the Training Branch of the Secretariat except mine. During that time, the Board of Professional Entrance Examinations (BOPEE) did not exist, and all examinations were conducted by the Training Branch of the Secretariat. In the absence of BOPEE, a limited number of eligible students were selected, while the majority gained admission through recommendations from politicians and officials. My awareness of this issue arose when ten students from my class were granted admission on the recommendation of MLC Sabar Saheb and MLA Rafiq Hussain, bypassing the need for a written examination. Among the selected lot was Sabar Saheb's own son. IAS Sonali Kumar also highlighted this matter in her book, "Unmasking Kashmir: A Bureaucrat Reveals," describing her efforts, alongside then Governor of erstwhile state of Jammu and kashmir,Mr Jagmohan to establish BOPEE, which would enable students to seek admission to the professional colleges based on their merit.

It was during my 12th-grade year that the date for the written examination for B.Sc. Agriculture was announced, with GGM Science College designated as the examination Centre for students in the Jammu division. On the appointed date, I arrived at the examination venue with my documents in hand, only to be taken aback when I discovered that my name was conspicuously absent from the list of candidates. Immediately, I approached the examination committee, presenting my marks sheet and explaining my predicament.

Recognizing the excellence of my academic performance, they issued me a provisional roll number 535, and granted me permission to take the examination. Following the completion of the exam, the examination manager summoned me and advised me to visit the DC office in Poonch to investigate why my form had not been forwarded. He also mentioned that if I passed the written examination, I would need to undergo an interview to secure admission.

The following day, I made my way back to Poonch from Jammu, heading directly to the DC office to meet the then DC, Mohinder Singh ji. I recounted the entire sequence of events, sharing my entire ordeal with him. Without hesitation, he promptly summoned the clerk, Gurcharan Singh, and proceeded to inquire about the situation. Gurcharan Singh attempted to justify the delay in processing my form by claiming that it had arrived late. However, the DC remained resolute and unswayed by this excuse. He reprimanded the clerk firmly and instructed him to hand over my form, enabling me to proceed with the mandatory interview required for course admission. Following this encounter, DC Sahib offered me words of encouragement, serving as a profound source of inspiration.

Approximately two months after this pivotal meeting, the results of the written examination were officially released, and successful candidates were summoned for interviews. Nevertheless, mirroring the previous episode, my name was conspicuously absent from the list due to the mishandling by the clerk throughout the entire process. Recalling the counsel of the written examination manager, I retrieved my form and presented myself for the interview. Fortunately, the interview panel comprised the same individuals who had conducted the written examination. Unfortunately, they were compelled to adhere to their earlier stance, refusing to conduct my interview, as students not listed were not permitted to be interviewed.

Understanding the gravity of the situation, I accepted their decision without much protest. However, the interview process was scheduled to span 4-5 days, affording me an opportunity to advocate for my rights. I reached out to Ministers Lal Mohammad Sabar and Rafiq Hussain but was left disheartened, as both were entangled in matters pertaining to individuals seeking admission through recommendations.

Unable to find a solution through these channels, I made my way to the Training Branch of the Jammu Secretariat, where I met with Secretary Mohammad Amin, an IAS officer. I meticulously explained the entire incident to him, and upon comprehending my predicament, he promptly contacted the interview committee and provided me with his business card. In haste, I returned to the Circuit House, where the interviews were being conducted.

Eventually, they scheduled me for an interview on the final day. On the designated day, I arrived thoroughly prepared. I confidently and accurately responded to every question posed by the interview panel. Impressed by my performance, they assured me of my selection. The following day, I departed for Mendhar with a strong sense of certainty that I would be chosen, given my exceptional scores and top rankings in both the written and interview phases.

In the meantime, I continued my studies through the 12th grade and subsequently enrolled in a college to pursue my B.Sc. degree. While I was immersed in college life, one day I received news about the release of the selection list for

B.Sc. Agriculture. With eager anticipation, I promptly checked the list, only to be met with astonishment. To my dismay, all my classmates had been selected, but my name was conspicuously absent. Determined to find answers, I made the journey to the Srinagar Secretariat to seek clarification from Mr. Amin. He explained to me that, due to political interference and the delayed arrival of my form, my selection was impossible. This revelation left me devastated and I resolved not to accept a position within my district, as it would relegate me to a junior status among fellow students with lower marks, which was utterly unacceptable to me. However, I harbored a steadfast belief that if I improved my circumstances, I would undoubtedly secure selection in future. Additionally, I made it my mission to make those politicians understand the consequences of their corruption, a goal I later achieved when I became a journalist and interviewed them, serving as a poignant reminder of this incident.

Meanwhile, Operation Blue Star had commenced in Punjab. Within my family circle, it was assumed that after completing my graduation, I would take up teaching as my profession, given that, at that time, 12th-grade students were being employed as educators. Many of my friends had already embraced teaching careers but my resolve remained steadfast in avoiding confinement to the village. Immediately after my exams, I returned to Mendhar.Here I frequented a government library located near my house and I avidly read newspapers, periodicals and various other books.

At home, I had the responsibility of tending to two buffaloes and gathering fodder from the fields. During my trips to fields, I would carry my books along, allowing me to study while the cattle were grazing. It was during this period that I spent time with my senior colleague Miss M.. I affectionately named her Lucy due to her resemblance to Lucy Gray. In our shared pursuit of knowledge and dreams, we studied together, oblivious to any distinction between a boy and a girl. Our dedication to our studies fueled our ambitions—Lucy aspired to become a doctor, while I aimed to secure an officer's position after completing my B.Sc. Agriculture degree.

Our homes were separated by a river, connected by a wooden bridge that people used to cross. During the rainy season, when the river swelled, I would swim across to reach Lucy's fields. My father had taught me to swim during my childhood, so navigating the river posed no significant challenge. Many boys from our village frequently swam in that river during such times.

During my 10th-grade year, we had science practicals held in Poonch, and Lucy and I would frequently make the journey there. We typically stayed with our relatives during these times, and coincidentally our relatives' residences in Poonch were in close proximity to each other. After one set of practicals, Lucy expressed her desire to watch the movie "Noori," along with her friends which was being screened in the cinema hall. She invited me to join her, but I staunchly declined, citing discomfort in being the sole male among a group of girls. However, the underlying reason was my lack of funds to purchase a movie ticket. Lucy grasped this situation and attempted to offer me money, which I declined, insisting that I would wait for her outside the theater while she enjoyed the film. Upon its conclusion, she recounted the entire movie to me and remarked that it would have been more enjoyable if I had been there with her.

The following day, Lucy and I had an NCERT scholarship exam, and I waited outside her examination Centre for her to finish the examination. When she emerged after completing her paper, she was in tears. Her eyes and face were red, and she appeared to have a fever. Inquiring about her well-being, I learnt that she was suffering from homesickness. Without hesitation, I took her to a doctor and procured medication for her. Subsequently, I dropped her off at her relatives' house, where she was staying. The next day, we all returned to Mendhar. Lucy had a peculiar habit of occasionally becoming upset with me without any apparent reason, refraining from speaking to me for several months, and then eventually reconciling on her own.

Approximately, two months after this examination, I received an invitation for a scholarship interview. My interview was scheduled at the Jammu University campus, which was situated on Canal Road at that time. Following the interview, I was granted a scholarship worth Rs 50. Unfortunately, on the day of her interview, Lucy fell ill and was unable to qualify for the scholarship. This marked the continuation of our shared educational journey, spanning from the eighth to twelfth standard. Despite our diligent efforts, Lucy was unable to fulfil her dream of becoming a doctor, while I still awaited selection for the B.Sc. Agriculture program. After completing the 12th grade, Lucy entered into marriage, while I pursued my college admission, transitioning from Degree College, Poonch, to commence my AMIE (Electrical) studies in Jammu.

CHAPTER – 2

During this period, our village's former minister in Jammu and the then-Member of Legislative Council (MLC), Lal Mohammad Sabar Saheb, held a prominent position. His son was a fellow student of mine, pursuing civil engineering at Polytechnic College and residing in a hostel. Around this time, I had also secured admission to NITS. Unfortunately, a tragic accident occurred in which Sabar Saheb and his younger son Mahmood was involved while traveling to Mendhar. Sabar Saheb sustained minor injuries but Mahmood suffered a fractured right arm. Consequently, Mahmood had to be admitted to Shalamar Hospital in Jammu, with his Class 12 exams just a few days away. Leveraging his connections, Sabar Saheb arranged for Mahmood's examination Centre to be set up within the hospital premises and obtained permission for someone else to write Mahmood's papers. Despite Sabar Saheb's elder son having recently completed his engineering studies, both Sabar Saheb and his elder son chose me to write Mahmood's papers. This decision was based on my reputation as the most promising student in the entire Mendhar area at that time. Although Mahmood was a medical student and I was enrolled in the non-medical stream, I wrote all of his papers, and he achieved commendable marks. Subsequently, Mahmood pursued a law degree and went on to become a judge in the lower judiciary in 1998, currently serving as a session judge.

In the midst of these events, my family, particularly my father, expressed disappointment that I had not pursued a teaching job, which made me feel like a burden on them. In 1986, while residing in Jammu for a year, I decided to alleviate this perceived burden by taking up employment as a security guard in NCC. My rationale was that working as a guard during the night would allow me to dedicate my daytime hours to study and achieve some self-sustainability. Additionally, government accommodation was provided. However, upon learning about this job, my father and mama ji paid a visit to my office and requested my commanding officer Lieutenant Colonel AK Soparkar, to terminate my employment. Their stance was understandable, given that my family had a high level of education, and my father held a respectable profession. Thus, this job did not align with their expectations for my career. Concurrently, certain individuals in my village, motivated by jealousy, spread rumors that I was working as a watchman. Nonetheless, external opinions and judgments did not sway my determination.

My commanding officer had a conversation with my father and my mama ji about the situation, and as they departed, my father made it explicitly clear that I should not return home until I had achieved something significant in my life.

As my job continued to progress smoothly, our office underwent relocation from Canal Road to Trikuta Nagar, resulting in improved living conditions for me. My daily routine consisted of attending college in the morning and working afterward. Colonel S.S. Kataria, our NCC Group Commander, resided with his family in the officers' mess, not far from the office. He had two daughters whom Colonel Kataria requested me to tutor. Upon observing my tutoring sessions with Colonel Kataria's daughters, Major DS Rana, who also lived in the mess, sought my assistance in tutoring his sons. Consequently, I began providing lessons to them as well. These opportunities generated envy among other employees in the office as they were all individuals with a 10th-grade education, while I was studying in a private engineering college. My interactions with my colleagues in the office were limited during this period. As my probationary period neared its conclusion in 1989, Colonel Kataria, Major Rana, and our Officer Commanding, Major RC Katoch, were transferred from Jammu, and Lieutenant Colonel VM Wahi assumed the position of Officer Commanding in J&K Armd Sqn NCC, Jammu.

I was juggling my studies, tutoring responsibilities, and my job, all while preparing for a career in journalism. This commitment was reflected in my choice of attire, often seen in lounge suits, boots, and ties, projecting an air of pride and professionalism. Some clerks in my office became envious of my appearance and decided to file complaints against me with the commanding officer. Since my duty hours were during the night, the officers' options were limited, so they decided to instruct me to vacate the government accommodation I was residing in. Initially, I made a plea for reconsideration and even presented government orders to support my case. However, when that approach failed, I served them with a court notice and promptly sent a copy of the notice to higher-ranking officials.

Shortly after this incident, a heated argument erupted between Colonel Gurcharan Singh, Brigadier Kapila and Colonel Wahi in the officers mess, revolving around financial matters. In a bid to teach Colonel Wahi a lesson, both individuals used my court notice as the basis for their argument. Consequently, Colonel Wahi was transferred to Madras. Although Colonel Wahi had been stationed in our region for only six months and was nearing his retirement.

With Colonel Wahi's departure in 1989, Lieutenant Colonel Vikram Singh assumed the role of Officer Commanding of J&K Armd Sqn NCC Jammu. He began encountering issues with Brigadier Kapila and expressed a desire to reside in the office. However, Group Commander Colonel RS Char firmly denied this request, citing inconvenience to the cook and the Havaldar working in the mess. In response, Colonel Vikram started inviting constables from the Madhya Pradesh Police, who were in Jammu for VIP security, to stay in the mess. When Brigadier Kapila raised objections, Colonel Vikram transformed the office into a venue for alcohol consumption. When we reported this situation to the Group Commander, we were scolded, as it was deemed inappropriate for an army officer to take such actions. At this point, my only recourse was to gather evidence of Colonel Vikram's misconduct to hold him accountable.

I began by instructing the NCOs responsible for procuring liquor from various units to provide me with copies of the bills whenever they procured liquor for Colonel Vikram, and they complied. However, Colonel Vikram was involved in corrupt and fraudulent activities in several other areas as well. He had installed the parts and engine of the official Bullet motorcycle into his personal one. Additionally, he was engaged in fraudulent activities such as misusing railway warrants and embezzling funds allocated for fuel for an armoured vehicle that came for cadet's training, among other offences. Unfortunately, an office clerk was also involved in these fraudulent activities.

Amidst all this, another officer Col Raghubir Singh was embezzling NCC funds. The money designated for NCC-organized camps was being diverted for the personal luxuries of the officers in the mess. Despite the precarious security situation in Srinagar where camps could not be conducted at battalion and Group level, continuous camp arrangements were documented in files, accompanied by significant financial transactions, with connections reaching all the way to Delhi. Previously, outside contractors had been entrusted with the Republic Day camp contract, but now office clerks were securing these contracts and paying substantial commissions in return. It wouldn't be an exaggeration to describe NCC as a breeding ground for corruption.

Colonel Satpal Singh of the 2nd J&K Girls Battalion NCC, Jammu too was engaging in improper celebrations by inviting women into his office and mess. During this period, the battalion had acquired a new vehicle, which Colonel Satpal started using for personal convenience. On one occasion, while traveling to Vaishno Devi with his family in the same vehicle, an accident occurred involving a bus. Although the accident was severe, thankfully no one sustained serious injuries. However, the battalion vehicle suffered significant damage. Subsequently, a cover-up court of inquiry was conducted, justifying that uniforms were being transported for NCC cadets in that vehicle. All of this was happening with the cooperation of Colonel RS Char, although NCC Deputy DG Brigadier Kapila remained unaware of these matters. I wanted to expose these issues but was not sure if any action would be taken. Therefore, I discreetly documented all of this in my diary. While I couldn't initiate inquiries into other battalions, I did manage to initiate one for the battalion I was serving in, the 1 J&K Armd Squadron NCC in Jammu. Notably, Colonel Vikram Singh would bring women in the office during my absence and engage in immoral activities in the officers' mess too.

I shared a room with my colleague, Havaldar Premchandra Joshi. It was December 31, 1991, and after performing the Chabarasi ceremony for my late grandmother, I returned to the officer's mess. I did so because Premchandra Joshi, who was serving as the mess Havaldar at the time, had the room key. Premchandra had organized a small New Year's Eve party and insisted that I return promptly to celebrate the occasion. On that evening, Lieutenant Colonel Vikram Singh was also present in the mess. I had previously heard that he would invite female friends to the officer's mess for entertainment and spend the entire night with them in his room. I had been wanting to catch him in the act for a while, and on this particular day, I got that opportunity.

As soon as I entered the officer's mess, Lieutenant Colonel Vikram Singh ushered me into the drawing room, where SP Kaul from the CBI was already present. Colonel Singh introduced me to SP Kaul, possibly with the intention of intimidating me. However, this attempt failed when I recognized Kaul Sahib. After some time, I got up and went to interact with Premchandra. He had prepared a cake of my favourite choice strawberry and laid chicken on the table.

Apart from us, two assistants of Brigadier A Kapila, a cook and a watchman were also present in the room, eating and drinking separately. Prem got up and joined me, and we had cake together, followed by chicken. During our conversation, Prem informed me that a girl had entered Lieutenant Colonel Vikram's room with a boy who was drinking. I cautioned Prem that we needed to tread carefully and plan our actions, as Lieutenant Colonel Vikram could potentially accuse us if we didn't handle the situation correctly. We continued to enjoy cake and chicken for some time, while Colonel Vikram and SP Kaul consumed whiskey.

Internally, I was devising a plan to enter Colonel Vikram's room. I instructed Prem to keep watch and explained that once Colonel Vikram dropped off SP Kaul at the gate after their drinks, I would enter his room to expose them. Everything unfolded as planned. When Colonel Vikram and Kaul Sahib left, I knocked on their room's door. The young man inside opened the door and I observed that he, too, was enjoying whiskey while the young woman was on the bed. He invited me for a drink but I declined. Instead, I lied and made a false excuse that I had given 500 rupees to Colonel Vikram for some private time with the girl. Upon hearing this young man left the room.

Now, I was faced with a dilemma about my next course of action. If I did nothing at this point, Colonel Vikram could accuse me of intruding without permission and misbehaving with their guest. While I weighed my options, Colonel Vikram returned and when he saw the young man outside the room, he was astonished. His shock grew when the young man informed them that Captain Sharma from the transit camp was inside with the girl. Upon hearing this, Colonel Vikram entered the room and asked me what kind of drama this was, and I immediately suggested to call the police and report. In response, Colonel Vikram asked me to leave the premises. The manner in which he made the request seemed more like he was imploring me to depart. I returned to my room, but after the incident, Colonel Vikram physically assaulted Prem and manhandled him. The next day, news of the entire incident spread rapidly throughout the NCC fraternity. When asked about it at the office, I provided a detailed account to Head Clerk Balkrishna, BL Dutta, and RC Pandey. In the meantime, Colonel Vikram also visited the office and narrated the entire episode to Subedar Lakhbir Singh, explaining how I had attempted to misbehave with his guest in the officers' mess the previous night. Subedar Sahib responded that given the circumstances, there was nothing that could be done now. This particular matter concluded within the office, but it later emerged during a Court of Inquiry, where I provided evidence that certain officers had turned the Officer's Mess into a Centre for illicit activities. As a result, I faced several life-threatening attacks.

Some time following this incident, Lieutenant Colonel Vikram Singh, in collaboration with Colonel RS Char, devised a plan to harm me and dispatched individuals to carry out this task. On that particular night, I was in the kitchen with another NCO named RN Singh, engaged in food preparation. We noticed some people standing at the gate and calling out to us. I approached and inquired about their identity, and they claimed to be from the Srinagar office, seeking overnight accommodation. I declined their request, explaining that they needed to obtain permission from the officer commanding first. Returning to the kitchen, I urged RN Singh not to go to the gate, but he did not heed my advice. As a result, when he approached the gate, the attackers assaulted him. He sustained injuries and fell to the ground, prompting me to grab an iron rod from the kitchen and give chase to intimidate them. However, my injured colleague stopped me, wisely noting that there were too many of them, and it would not be prudent to follow them. Our office was in close proximity to the Trikuta Nagar Market, which was regularly patrolled by the police, so we reported the incident to the police. Regrettably, when the police arrived, the assailants had already fled the scene.

I promptly informed not only to Colonel Vikram but also Brigadier Kapila about the incident. Brigadier Kapila was already aware of Colonel Vikram's actions, and he assured me that a thorough inquiry would be conducted into this incident, including a police report. Brigadier Kapila directed Colonel Vikram to initiate the investigation, but to my dismay, Colonel Vikram neither commenced an inquiry nor filed a police report. Over time, I came to learn that this attack had been orchestrated at Colonel Vikram's behest, but I had been spared because the attackers couldn't identify me and had mistakenly targeted my companion.

When Colonel Vikram's scheme failed, he arranged for my transfer to Poonch, but I managed to thwart that plan as well. I sought the assistance of Major Kamal Bhalla, the staff officer of Brigadier Kapila, to have the transfer order revoked. In fact, I submitted an application calling for an investigation into Colonel Vikram's activities, presenting all the evidence I had gathered. Brigadier Kapila assured me that not only would there be an investigation into Colonel Vikram's actions, but he would also face consequences following the inquiry. Subsequent to these events, Colonel Vikram openly began issuing threats to have me harmed. A month later, the investigation commenced, with Colonel Gobind Aale as the lead investigator and Colonel PD Sharma and Colonel MK Raina as members. This inquiry began at the Group Headquarters Jammu and encompassed the entire staff of our office. Given that I was leading an inquiry against a colonel, I spent my nights poring over army regulations whenever I had the opportunity.

Colonel Vikram had become increasingly convinced that he would face severe consequences, possibly a court-martial. Consequently, he openly declared his intent to have me harmed in the office on a daily basis. Fellow staff members advised me to stay away from the office due to these threats, but I was not one to be intimidated. The office staff also provided testimonies in my favour, further bolstering the ongoing inquiry. I also lodged a complaint with the State Vigilance, where I met DIG Masood Chaudhary, who happened to be the elder brother of my close friend. He understood my predicament and referred me to CBI Deputy SP Satish Gupta. Deputy SP Satish Gupta collected my written complaint and all the supporting evidence. Within 15-20 days, he submitted the internal inquiry to higher authorities.

In 1993, Brigadier Kapila got subsequently transferred, and Brigadier AS Behl assumed the appointment as his relief. Upon his arrival, Brigadier Behl initiated strict actions against all the officers at NCC Group Headquarters Jammu, resulting in a widespread crackdown. During his brief stay at the officers' mess, other officers were compelled to curtail their festivities. To avert this crisis, a collective decision was made to persuade Colonel Vikram to file a complaint against Brigadier Behl in Delhi. When the inquiry began, Brigadier Behl presented the previous Court of Inquiry against Colonel Vikram and also summoned me as a witness in this matter. Colonel Vikram was now attached to

Station Headquarters Jammu, and the new Officer Commanding, PC Parmar, took over as his reliever.

The inquiry eventually concluded, leading to Colonel Vikram Singh's transfer to 180 Brigade, where he assumed the role of a duty officer. However, he did not cease his fraudulent activities. There he was engaged in embezzlement by selling the petrol allocated for the brigade at a civilian petrol pump. On one occasion, a dispute arose over a transaction, necessitating the involvement of both civilian and military police. When this matter reached higher authorities, a comprehensive inquiry was conducted, which found him guilty. Subsequently, he faced a court-martial. Following the court-martial proceedings, he received a sentence and was incarcerated in Tihar Jail, where he breathed his last and passed away after a year.

It was during this time that I learnt about Colonel Vikram's privileged background. His father and father-in-law held significant influence in society. Interestingly, Colonel Vikram had suffered a head injury from a fall during a horse riding incident, which seemed to have played a role in his subsequent behavior. I even learnt from his wife that this injury had prevented his promotion, while his younger brother had been promoted to the rank of Colonel. This injury had also contributed to his deteriorating mental condition, which in turn led him to engage in such abnormal behaviour.

In 1993, I successfully completed a Bachelor of Divine Theology course at a local church, establishing strong connections with the staff of St. Mary's Convent School, particularly the school principal and the church father. At that time, our new Officer Commanding, Lieutenant Colonel P.C. Parmar, faced challenges securing admission for his daughter in a convent school through the efforts of Colonel RD Verma, the Commanding officer of the 2 J&K Girls Battalion NCC Jammu. However, obtaining admission proved to be quite difficult. Nevertheless, Colonel Parmar became aware of my capability to assist in such matters. The principal of the school had a reputation for not considering recommendations, and my past association with Colonel Vikram, the former commanding officer, may have cast a shadow on my reputation. However, when Colonel Parmar inquired about me with several individuals in the Officers' Mess, he received consistently positive feedback. Subsequently, he invited me for tea in the officers' mess, during which we had an opportunity to get to know each other better. During our conversation, Colonel Parmar came to understand that my previous actions were not my fault. He discussed his daughter's admission with me, and I provided him with the assurance that she would be admitted to St. Mary's Convent School. My commitment and assurance boosted his confidence, leading him to entrust me with the education of both his children. Without delay, I successfully secured admission for Colonel Parmar's daughter at St. Mary's Convent School in Jammu the very next day.

Colonel Parmar was a person of integrity and a cheerful disposition. Given my frequent visits to Shimla and other hilly areas of Himachal Pradesh during the summers, Colonel Parmar suggested that I pay a visit to DPS Dalhousie where his son was studying. In accordance with his recommendation, I traveled to DPS Dalhousie and had the opportunity to meet Captain GS Dhillon, the Principal and the Chairman of the school, during my month-long stay. I took the opportunity to explore the nearby tourist attractions and even had the privilege of meeting the Buddhist guru,His Excellency the Dalai Lama. My connection with the DPS principal continued, and I made it a point to visit him whenever I visited Dalhousie.

Under the competent supervision of Lieutenant Colonel Parmar, office operations ran smoothly. Bal Krishna Sharma, the head clerk of the same office, was a kind and supportive individual who also worked part-time as an Advertisement Manager for a newspaper in Jammu. He brought to my attention the fraudulent activities of certain clerks in the office who had manipulated employment exchange stamps to secure jobs for specific individuals. Bal Krishna Ji supported my efforts to expose these wrongdoings and introduced me to the crime reporter of his newspaper. With his assistance, I also became the President of NCC Jammu Kashmir Association in 1993, although I later resigned from that position. In the meantime, Bal Krishna and another clerk were transferred, and they were replaced by two corrupt individuals, Ved Prakash and Ramesh Chandra. Their level of corruption was so egregious that during a camp, Colonel Parmar had to pay from his pocket to rectify the situation. Bal Krishna Ji had apprised me of their misconduct, and I was engaged in the process of collecting evidence regarding the fake stamp case.

CHAPTER – 3

In 1995, Dogra College of Education was established in Jammu, enrolling male and female students from other states for B.Ed. I shared a good rapport with the college owner, Gulchain Singh Charak. The appointed principal of the college had previously served as a professor at my college, which led me to occasionally visit the college to meet him. One day, Havaldar Ratan Lal informed me that some guests had arrived. Upon entering the office, I found two young men and two young women. One of the young women introduced herself, mentioning that her father was a doctor, and she had come to Jammu for admission to the B.Ed. program. Another young woman had already secured admission, and the two young men were her brothers. As there was no hostel available, they intended to rent a place near the college. They requested that I accompany them to Colonel Parmar's house, to which I agreed. As we set off, they followed in their car, but for some reason, one of the young women, whose name also began with 'M,' chose to sit behind me on my motorcycle, as if we were old friends. I affectionately began calling her "Honey" due to the sweet way she spoke.

Upon arriving at Colonel Parmar's residence, Honey discovered that I also provided tutoring to Colonel Parmar's children, which further left a positive impression on her. Given my extensive social connections, Colonel Parmar had entrusted me with the responsibility of finding suitable accommodation for the two girls within a reputable family. In the meantime, I offered to transport them to and from the college on my motorcycle. For some reason, upon hearing this, Honey wore a sweet smile. After ensuring that their sister and Honey were comfortably settled, the boys returned home, and I made my way back to my office.

Within a span of two days, I managed to locate a pleasant room available for rent close to my office. We collected some essentials from the market and furnished the entire room to make it suitable for habitation. On the second day, as I reached Colonel Parmar's house to accompany them to college, I found Honey already waiting for me at the gate. The college had afternoon to evening classes, so I informed Colonel Parmar that we would be dining out that evening. On that particular day, I also introduced both of them to the college principal, who had previously been my professor.

When I arrived at the college at 5 o'clock in the evening to pick them up, both girls were famished. We first headed to a restaurant, where we enjoyed coffee and snacks before proceeding to Hotel Asia for dinner. Following our meal, I dropped both of them off at Colonel Parmar's residence.

After a short while, Honey and her friend settled into a rented room close to my office and started using a minibus for their daily commute to college. We frequently visited each other's homes and shared meals together. In those days, mobile phone service wasn't available in Jammu, but I had access to a STD phone. This led Honey to often use my phone to keep in touch with her family. As a result, I became familiar with her family members. I engaged in conversations with Honey's mother, a government doctor, on a regular basis. In no time, the three of us developed a comfortable rapport, as if we'd known each other for ages.

Honey's friend had attended St. Bede's College, which lent her a sharp wit. Honey, on the other hand, exuded grace, manners, and cultural refinement. Whenever I met the college principal, he would consistently remark on Honey's exceptional character, even going so far as to suggest that I should consider marrying her. Nevertheless, I held steadfast to the promise I had made to my father, vowing to achieve something significant.

It had escaped my notice that Honey's friend had developed feelings for me. Later, Honey disclosed that her friend had harboured doubts about the platonic nature of my relationship with Honey. This arose from an occasion when she had encouraged Honey to pursue a closer friendship with me, prompting Honey to reprimand her. This incident, Honey confided, had led to a cooling off in their interactions after returning from Jammu. While I treated both Honey and her friend with equal respect, I shared a more open dialogue with Honey.

We celebrated numerous festivals together. Although I hadn't been much of a celebrant of festivals with my family since leaving the village for Jammu, I had forged close friendships with doctors and engineers in the city. Previously, during festivals, I'd often attend gatherings in hotels or partake in weekly gatherings with friends. However, this had ceased prior to Honey's arrival in Jammu. On one occasion, Honey inquired about this change, and upon learning that I had adopted a strict vegetarian lifestyle, she expressed great joy. She admired my dedication to my goals, even in a new environment far from home, oblivious to these personal details. Honey hoped that I would leave Jammu to pursue a journalism career in her home state, suggesting that I depart from the NCC position as well.

Honey, in fact, had aspirations of becoming a teacher after completing her B.Ed. She envisioned a life where both of us would secure an academic profession in her home state and plan our future life together. Her family's open-mindedness contributed to her forward-thinking mindset. However, despite being aware of Honey's aspirations, I remained oblivious. I had sensed the affection she held for me deep within her heart, yet I lacked the courage to reciprocate her love. Responsibilities surrounded me from every direction. As the sole child of my parents and the only brother to my sisters, my primary goal was to achieve something substantial in life, which meant sacrificing Honey's love in pursuit of my passion. Moreover, during that period, my parents had received a marriage proposal for me.I couldn't find the strength to break the trust, and the promise I had made to my father.

Time swiftly passed, and only a few months remained for Honey to complete her B.Ed. She had begun her teaching practice, which required her to wear a saree. In the saree, Honey's beauty shone even more brilliantly. During this phase, I often dropped her off and picked her up on my motorcycle. We would take leisurely strolls together. Honey felt a profound sense of security with me and frequently sang my praises to her family. I maintained close ties with her family members' including her two sisters, the elder one was married to a doctor, while the younger one was still pursuing her studies.

One day, during a conversation with Honey, I casually mentioned that she would marry a doctor. Upon hearing this, she grasped the reason behind my lack of response to her love. She knew me well and comprehended that a considerable amount of struggle still lay ahead in my life's journey. I too understood that Honey deserved a brighter future, and I didn't want to complicate her life for my own sake. Our relationship retained its purity, and with that purity in mind, we eventually reached a mutual understanding of parting ways.

Time elapsed, and in 1996, an unexpected situation arose that prompted me to leave Jammu for a few month periods. Upon sharing this news with Honey, her eyes welled up with tears. Yet, both she and her friend expressed happiness. Prior to my departure, I offered Honey words of encouragement, urging her to devote herself to her studies and excel in college. I was confident that Honey would channel her focus towards academics, leaving everything else behind. After my departure, I returned to Jammu in November, only to discover that Honey had also left the city. I learned that she was pursuing her M.A. in English and simultaneously working as a teacher in a private school.

During my stay in Jammu, a childhood friend from my village would frequently visit me. Together, we would visit our minister from Poonch Mushtaq Bukhari and contribute a portion of our earnings, which he would distribute among the less fortunate, seeking their blessings. On one occasion, Bukhari Sahib recommended that I visit Darvesh Ishaq Sahib. I followed his advice and went to meet Darvesh Sahib. In Darvesh Sahib's presence,I felt an unusual energy enveloping me. I humbly touched his feet and got his blessings. Darvesh Sahib encouraged me to visit him daily, and one day, he presented me with a ring. Darvesh Sahib's fame had spread far and wide, attracting even high-ranking officials who sought his blessings. Notably, Jammu and Kashmir Chief Minister Dr. Farooq Abdullah and several ministers attended his court. During my visits to Darvesh Sahib, he graciously offered solutions to all my problems without much of an effort on my part.

In the second week of December, Honey's exam results were announced, and as I had anticipated, she secured the top position. The college principal conveyed this news to me, prompting me to immediately call Honey and share the joyful tidings. Upon hearing the news, Honey's father reached out to me from Delhi the following day, requesting that I visit his home with his daughter's marks sheet. Instead of going in person, I immediately sent her marks sheet through the mail along with a New Year's greeting card. My action caused her to become upset with me, and she remained angry for about six months. Although I was saddened by her displeasure, I was determined not to let it distract me from my objectives.

I continued to seek guidance from Guruji. His blessings inspired me a lot and continued to be a source of strength for me. Although I contemplated leaving my NCC job, Guruji advised me against it, emphasizing the importance of conducting oneself with integrity and avoiding ill-gotten gains, thus safeguarding one's life from harm.

These principles became the guiding light of my life, and their impact was unmistakable. My writing began to find its way into newspapers, one after another. Witnessing this, the people of my village extended their compliments to my father. During this period, I also conducted an interview with a senior minister from our region. The publication of the interview filled my father with immense pride. Encouraged by my progress, he visited me in Jammu a few days later, gifting me a plot of land and overseeing the construction of a house for me in Sainik Colony, one of the most posh colonies in Jammu. The atmosphere in my village home was filled with joy. I proudly acquired the title of being the first journalist from my village. My writings were not only being read across the nation, but also in foreign lands as well, marking a significant milestone in my life.

As time passed, Parmar Saheb got transferred in 1996. He handed over to Lieutenant Colonel OP Verma, a person known for his unwavering honesty and deep spirituality. He hailed from Udhampur and was a doting father to a son and a daughter. He requested my assistance in expediting the process of obtaining state subjects for his children, a task I accomplished within a matter of days. At that time, Mr Khalid Hussain served as the ADC of Jammu, a close associate of my mentor. With his support, the task was swiftly completed.

My schedule now entailed monthly trips to various other states for research, a responsibility I embraced wholeheartedly. One day, while seated at the Press Club in Delhi, I received news of Honey's engagement. Without delay, I reached out to convey my congratulations. In a playful moment, she remarked, "Gopal, tell me something else, so it too comes true." It warmed my heart to know that she still remembered our old conversations. I had assured her she would excel in her college, and she did. Additionally, I had predicted that she would marry a doctor, a prediction that had now come to fruition. She was engaged to one. I chuckled and brushed it off, expressing how fortunate the young man was going to have her in his life. I wished and prayed for her happiness and blissful life. On February 27, 1998, I made my final call to her, bidding farewell for good.

Thanks to the abundant blessings of Guruji, my life had taken a positive turn. I had comfortably settled into my new environment. My father would frequently reach out to me, occasionally visiting me in Jammu. My life had undergone a complete transformation, with my old friends gradually fading away. Guruji and his invaluable guidance were my sole companions. Prayer and meditation had become an integral part of my daily routine, with several hours dedicated to these practices. One day, my parents approached Guruji and requested his assistance in arranging my marriage. In response, Guruji instructed me to consider marriage, a proposition I accepted wholeheartedly. On February 6, 1999, my parents orchestrated a grand wedding ceremony for me with a girl of their choice.

During the wedding ceremony, as I began to garland my bride, a sense of surprise washed over me.I had not seen her prior to the marriage, although our telephone conversations had taken place. Yet, inexplicably, it felt as if I had encountered her before, as if I knew her. It then dawned on me that she was the same young woman who had attended my sister's wedding. Her captivating beauty had prompted me to invite her to dance with me at that event. Several years had passed since that encounter, and she had forgotten about it. But when I reminisced about it and asked her, we shared a laughter-filled moment. Both of us were immensely content with this union, as we had embarked on a love marriage, all thanks to Guruji's blessings despite our initial reservations. Due to her rosy complexion, everyone in our household affectionately addressed her Pinky.

After the wedding, Pinky and I, accompanied by my mother, sought Guruji's blessings before embarking on a honeymoon to Shimla, one of my favored destinations. Following our visit to Shimla, we explored Goa and Ooty, immersing ourselves in our own world, detached from the hustle and bustle of everyday life, for a blissful two months. Initially, Pinky found my passion for reading books somewhat unexciting, but over a period of time, she grew used to it and accepted the fact that my life revolved around books.

I became engrossed in my work and was in pursuit of financial stability, while Pinky capably assumed the responsibilities of managing our home. Everything was progressing smoothly until the day Guruji unexpectedly departed from this world for his heavenly abode on 29 June 1999. His departure left emptiness in my life, yet his blessings continued to guide me, ensuring that his absence was never truly felt. Thanks to his blessings, I advanced from being a security guard to a clerk in NCC, constructed a new home for myself in Sainik Colony, and gained recognition in the field of journalism.

Upon my return from a two-month honeymoon, the Kargil war had erupted, necessitating my assignment in Kargil. After a 15-day deployment in Kargil, Colonel OP Verma was transferred, and Lieutenant Colonel Khullar assumed his position. Before this, Khullar Saheb had held the role of Administrative Officer at NCC Group

Headquarters Jammu, known for his strict demeanour but also tainted with corruption. Given my penchant for punctuality, I was punctual and ensured that I arrived at the office a little early to avoid any unpleasantness.

Colonel Khullar noticed this during his initial days in office that upon his arrival, only the cleaning staff and I were present, while others consistently arrived late. In a fit of anger one day, he chastised the entire office staff, including a senior clerk known for his bluntness. This clerk, always eager to find fault with me,would seize opportunities to undermine my reputation in Colonel Khullar's eyes. Despite facing salary delays and attempts to tarnish my name, Colonel Khullar recognized my integrity and punctuality, eventually bringing me along with him to NCC Group Headquarters. Moreover, he provided me with a government motorcycle to enhance my office efficiency.

Working in Group Headquarters afforded me insight into the activities of all NCC units and I could expose various forms of malpractice. I began to gather information about irregularities spanning from the canteen to the officers' mess. Surprisingly, the wife of a training officer stationed at NCC Group Headquarters operated an academy that illicitly used NCC vehicles to transport academy children in the afternoons. Many office clerks had become contractors embroiled in such scandals. There were also officers who not only were engaged in corruption but also indulged in inappropriate behavior, inviting women to the officers' mess and partaking in debauchery. One such officer was Colonel AK Mandhok, newly transferred to the area. Following the death of his first wife, he had wedded his younger sister-in-law. Mandhok struggled with alcoholism and occasionally viewed porn films within the office premises.

During that period, promotions for fourth-class employees had commenced within NCC Group Headquarters Jammu. Given the presence of numerous corrupt individuals, it was almost certain that these promotions would be manipulated. Some of those who received promotions had connections to the Education Minister, while others were relatives of officers. However, conspicuously absent from the list of recipients were the deserving candidates, approximately 15 individuals, including me. Despite the silence of others, they were aware of my intent to speak out and get initiated legal action, a move that would ultimately benefit everyone.

As anticipated, I took the matter to court, making it abundantly clear that I would unveil the entirety of the fraudulent scheme. This marked the first instance within Jammu and Kashmir NCC where the pervasive corruption within the organization was exposed nationwide, all due to the unethical conduct of Lt. Col V K Khullar. Officer JS Chaudhary, the Commander of the 2nd Jammu Kashmir Girls Battalion, a person of knowledge and principles, offered unwavering support to me throughout this crusade. Despite being a Sikh, he adhered to a strict vegetarian diet and openly voiced his opinion.

Corruption within NCC Group Headquarters Jammu was so deeply entrenched that even during the annual arms/ammunition inspection in 1999, the name of JD (1) Company NCC Nagrota had been omitted from the roster, a revelation I brought to light in 2014. Officers deliberately delayed the construction of the NCC Battalions accomodation in the NCC Camping Ground to lease kothis/buildings to NCC units for personal gain.

Subsequently, Colonel Khullar was transferred from NCC, and I too, was relocated from Jammu to NCC in Sainik School, Nagrota.

CHAPTER – 4

In 2001, during my posting at Sainik School, Nagrota NCC, there was a clerk by the name of Sitaram. Y N Sahni, had been posted out to Poonch, leaving a vacant junior assistant position in the office. Before my arrival, Officer Commanding Lieutenant Commander Kanchan Mukherjee and the Principal of the Sainik School Nagrota had received directives to keep me in check. Unbeknownst to the Infantry Officers, the Education Corps personnel treaded cautiously when targeting someone. So they initiated an secret inquiry against me, about my role as a journalist. Bharat Singh Chib, who served as a PA to the Principal at the time, informed Mukherjee about my dual role and my endeavours against unjust treatment and corruption within the NCC. Mukherjee was already aware of my background, but the school Registrar, Amulya Dayal, a young officer in the Indian Air Force, may have initially had some reservations. However, after Chib's persuasive efforts, he too became acquainted with my mission.

Within a very short span of one week, I had familiarized myself with the entire environment of the Sainik school and the NCC office. Everything that IG Masood Chaudhary IPS had mentioned was turning out to be accurate. With the exception of a few employees, nearly everyone was entangled in some form of corruption and sought ways to curry favor with the principal. Some even engaged in activities like bringing women for sexual favours to appease the principal. Conversely, employees who were mistreated by the principal confided in me with their grievances. The school's lab assistant, JN Sharma, had also become aware of my intentions, which led him to develop a close bond with me. He often told other employees that I aimed to revolutionize the school.

One of the school's clerks, Lal Chand, stood out for his remarkable integrity. Upon learning that he hailed from Kishtwar, I sought a meeting with him. During our conversation, I discovered that he had been a student in my Guruji's class, and Guruji had bestowed his blessings upon Lal Chand too, ultimately helping his son become a doctor. Encouraged by Lal Chand's support, I shared my aspiration to combat corruption in the school. He advised me to persevere in my battle and entrust the rest to Guruji. His words served as a profound inspiration, prompting me to intensify my efforts in gathering evidence against corruption for the further action.

I had to embark on a two-hour journey from my residence in Sainik Colony to reach Nagrota School, usually taking a minibus to commute. Throughout this journey, I found solace in reciting Guru Gyan, which not only fortified my mental resilience but also alleviated my anxieties. My connections with various individuals, ranging from the school peon to members of the Delhi Society, had grown significantly. Consequently, I received tidbits of information from a diverse network of people. At school, I often found myself spending more time in the main office or the PA's office than at my own designated workspace.

During these days, I also held a role as a crime reporter for a prominent newspaper in Jammu, despite not receiving any financial compensation for my work. This dual life was not without its challenges. There were issues related to electricity, water, and road infrastructure in Chib Saheb's locality. When Chib Saheb sought my assistance in arranging a press conference to address these problems, I promptly organized it the very next day. In the ensuing months, I nurtured valuable relationships with the school staff, which eventually led me to uncover a disturbing revelation: the school principal had terminated ten staff members, all of whom had secured a court-issued stay order enabling them to continue their employment within the school.

The principal's conduct was marked by corruption and moral impropriety, and a number of clerks and teachers were complicit in unethical activities such as admitting their own relatives' children and engaging in various fraudulent activities. Despite bearing witness to these transgressions, I chose to remain silent, discreetly amassing evidence to bolster my fight against corruption. My paramount concern was to ensure that the integrity of my anti-corruption efforts remained uncompromised by the corrupt elements entrenched within the school.

During the same year, our NCC Office received a sizable umbrella valued at Rs. 6000 from the headquarters for use in the garden. Clerk Sitaram had taken it as charge to, and it was stored within the confines of the NCC office. However, temptation gripped the principal, leading him to order the relocation of the umbrella to his residence. In military circles, it is customary not to refuse the requests of senior officers, hence the umbrella was promptly dispatched to his home. Sitaram, who had meticulously documented the umbrella 's procurement, risked losing his job if it went missing. To avert such a scenario, Mukherjee Saheb, at personal expense, procured an identical umbrella for Rs. 6000/- and placed it in the store. Part of his motivation was driven by the impending prospect of his promotion, and he harbored concerns that the principal might draft an unfavorable report about him. Upon learning of this incident, I diligently recorded it in my diary.

During my commute from Jammu to Nagrota, I often shared the journey with two female teachers from the Sainik School. One of them hailed from Jammu and was named Mandeep Kaur, while the other, Monica, was from Uttar Pradesh. On numerous occasions, we collectively traveled in Monica's father's vehicle, who served as a military officer.

As previously mentioned regarding the principal's behavior, there was an incident when he summoned Mandeep Madam to his office and acted inappropriately towards her. Witnessing this, Madam became infuriated and even gestured by showing her slipper to the principal. Following this distressing incident, Madam chose to resign from her position at the school. The news of this incident quickly circulated throughout the school, but a pervasive fear of the principal kept everyone silent, inadvertently bolstering his audacity. When I suggested to Monica Madam that I should publish this incident involving the principal to the newspaper, she cautioned me against it, remarking that getting involved in such a situation might only result in tarnishing our own reputation, akin to throwing a stone into the mud. I found this incident deeply unsettling, as it seemed that within the school, there was a notable absence of individuals willing to speak out against the principal. The Principal's driver, Havaldar Puran Singh, confidentially shared information with me about the principal's escapades, including his encounters with various women at Jammu's *Bagh-e-Baahu*. I meticulously recorded all these details in my diary for future reference.

Amidst these developments, a team from the Delhi Society arrived in Sainik School Nagrota, Jammu for an inquiry. It was revealed that the school Registrar, Amulya Dayal, had lodged a complaint against the Principal, prompting the team's visit. Approximately two months later the principal was transferred and Captain VK Verma assumed the role of the new school Principal. His arrival marked a turning point in the school's atmosphere. Under his leadership, the school received the Defense Minister's trophy that year, with some students also earning placements in the prestigious National Defence Academy. Nonetheless, the culture of corruption persisted within the Jammu NCC Group Headquarters.

When the NCC Directorate in Jammu and Kashmir performed poorly during the Republic Day Camp, I decided to expose their corrupt activities. My report on their misconduct made it to the front page of the renowned newspaper 'State Times' on February 10, 2002. Although an investigation ensued, it appeared to be cursory in nature. Nevertheless, my efforts had shed light on their wrongdoings, revealing to the public that even an organization like the

NCC was immune to corruption. This marked my debut as a crime reporter. The editor expressed satisfaction with my work, encouraging me to persevere. The entire NCC community in Jammu and Kashmir became aware that I was the individual who had unveiled their corrupt practices. Mukherjee Saheb also expressed his appreciation, calling to congratulate me and urging me to persist in my battle against corruption.

Mukherjee Saheb had concluded his tenure at the school and was reassigned to INS Chilka. Taking his place, Major DB Kar assumed the role of our NCC Officer Commanding. Under the leadership of Vice Principal Mukherjee, Principal VK Verma, and School Registrar Amulay Dayal, the school maintained discipline, and the overall atmosphere was positive.

However, Major DB Kar's arrival brought disruptions to this equilibrium. Some teachers would frequent his office and engage in activities such as smoking cigarettes. In the evenings, they would visit his residence for alcohol consumption. When the Principal became aware of these occurrences, he got Major Kar transferred back to the Education Corps, ensuring that he would never be assigned to any Sainik School again. Major Kar's stint at the school lasted only six months.Following his departure, the school's environment gradually began to improve once again.

During this period, I continued my crusade against corruption within the NCC, speaking out openly against it. On July 30, 2002, I took the significant step of forwarding the same news that had been published in the newspaper to the Central Vigilance Commission of the Central Government, situated in New Delhi. In my letter, I formally requested an investigation and also sent a copy to the

Defence Secretary and Director General of National Cadets Corps (DGNCC) in New Delhi.

As mentioned previously, the NCC Directorate had been closely monitoring my activities from Jammu and Kashmir to Delhi, eagerly awaiting an opportunity to terminate me if I made any misstep. This time, DG NCC in New Delhi issued an order for my expulsion, accusing me of directly contacting the Central Vigilance Commission and breaking the chain of command. However, they overlooked the crucial detail that I was a state government employee and thus could not be terminated by the Central Government.

The adage "birds of same feather flock together" proved true when, on August 31, 2002, the NCC Group Headquarters Jammu initiated a Court of Inquiry against me, following orders from Deputy DG Brigadier Anil Sharma of NCC Directorate Jammu and Kashmir. I was summoned to appear on September 10, 2002. Given my extensive reading of books on CSR, DSR, and law since 1990, this inquiry didn't present a significant challenge for me. I had already filed a legal case against NCC Group Headquarters Jammu in which they were deeply implicated. In this order, they mistakenly used the term "court" instead of "board." I pointed out this error and reminded them of their true status, particularly the clerks who were subordinate to the officers. I filed a case in the High Court against the inquiry order, and when the judge inquired which court holds authority higher than the High Court, they had no response. The court annulled the inquiry order, asserting that I, Ram Gopal, am a civil servant and cannot be investigated under the Army Act of 1953. Through this experience, I imparted such a lesson to these corrupt employees and officers that they refrained from using terms like "court" or "investigation" ever again. Those involved in this matter completed their work discreetly and did not attempt to hinder me further.

NCC Day is an annual celebration observed by the NCC on every fourth Sunday of November. In 2003, on the occasion of NCC Day, the NCC Directorate Jammu and Kashmir invited the then State Defense Minister, Shri Chaman Lal Gupta, to serve as the chief guest. The entire management of the event was entrusted to Headquarter 16 Corps situated at Nagrota, which in turn, delegated the responsibility to the army Brigade located at Meeran Sahib. The Meeran Sahib Brigade efficiently managed all aspects of the event, including tents worth lakhs of rupees. NCC Day was celebrated with great grandeur. However, merely three days after the event, the 2nd Girls J&K Battalion NCC, in collusion with fraudulent actors and NCC Group Headquarters, submitted counterfeit bills totaling Rs. 2.5 lakh and withdrew the funds from the treasury. To this day, this money remains unaccounted for, as its entry still exists in the withdrawal register.

In 2003 Colonel SS Bagga assumed the position of the new Group Commander at NCC Group Headquarters Jammu. He upheld stringent principles but was an individual of utmost integrity. Upon his appointment, I provided him with a comprehensive briefing on the prevailing situation so that he could gain insight into the state of affairs within NCC in Jammu and Kashmir.

It had become customary that when honest officers were assigned to Sainik School for a three-year term, corrupt officers would be dispatched to NCC, and vice versa. I didn't object to this rotation because, in such a scenario, I could effectively combat corruption. During this particular instance, honest officers had assumed roles at the NCC Group

Headquarters. However, the Principal of Sainik School, Nagrota, Captain SB Ray, and Registrar Squadron Leader Balwinder Singh were both deemed inept and lacking in moral character.

As our Officer Commanding Major DB Kar had been transferred, the responsibility for NCC fell upon the Registrar. Several other corrupt employees at the school, notably AK Tripathi, AK Handu, and BK Sood, had ingratiated themselves with these two officers and were embroiled in various forms of malpractice at the school. Some teachers even rushed to secure enrolments for students. In 2003, when the then Deputy Chief Minister contacted the Principal to admit a child, the Principal falsely asserted that there were no available vacancies. In response, the Deputy Chief Minister got sanctioned 15 new vacancies. While one of the students was known to the Deputy Chief Minister, the school administration filled the remaining 14 slots at their discretion. Corruption within the school reached its zenith, and the school's computer assistant, AK Tripathi, took advantage of the situation. Without informing any higher authorities or the Delhi Society, he secured a promotion and assumed the role of a computer teacher, despite there being no such position in any Sainik School at the time. In Sainik School, Nagrota, no decisions could be made without the approval of certain teachers and BK Sood. I closely observed these developments, biding my time for an opportunity to expose these irregularities in the newspaper.

I was associated with newspaper writing for eight years and was currently serving as a bureau chief for a magazine called "Street Voice." This magazine had a wide readership not only in India but also in the United States, Canada, and Malaysia. It boasted correspondents in these countries as well. Since my appointment as Bureau Chief, I frequently stayed with the Editor in Chief and was assigned to various regions of India, occasionally even traveling to Nepal. During this period, I established connections with influential figures in journalism, including Balraj Puri, Kuldeep Nayyar, and retired CBI director Joginder Singh. I also extended invitations to them to serve as guest editors for the magazine and published their articles on a monthly basis. My network within the journalism field continued to expand.

'Street Voice' held the distinction of being the top magazine in Jammu and Kashmir, where I honed my skills in crime reporting. During this period, we welcomed our new Officer Commanding and Vice Principal of Sainik School Nagrota, Wing Commander A Sudarshan. Upon his arrival, a truck transporting his belongings accidentally collided with the school's main gate, resulting in minor damage. Consequently, the school administration imposed a deduction of five thousand rupees under the pretext of gate repair.

Principal Ray had made a series of questionable appointments, recruitments, and promotions within the school, all of which came to Vice Principal Sudarshan's attention. He initiated actions against BK Sood due to discrepancies in the accounts. Principal Ray had appointed his driver as the hostel superintendent, but the driver continued to serve as the principal's chauffeur. During the annual stock audit, Wing Commander Sudarshan exposed all instances of manipulation and issued warnings to those implicated. However, given the collusion among the school Registrar, accountant, certain teachers and the Principal, the Principal instructed them to disregard any directives from the Vice Principal. They were even told to ignore the Vice

Principal's bell, and this directive extended to the peon as well.

At this juncture, only four of us NCC personnel remained in support of Sudarshan. He wrote numerous letters to the Chairman and the Society, expressing his earnest desire for transfer to escape the pervasive corruption. Regrettably, his appeals fell on deaf ears, as corruption had permeated every level of the institution. The Principal went so far as to remove the computer from Sudarshan's office, prompting me to lend him my personal computer for his work. Even after these concessions, the corrupt individuals remained unsatisfied. In a desperate move, the Principal enlisted the assistance of a former surrendered insurgent who happened to be the father of a student. This individual was instructed to threaten Sudarshan. Fortunately, I was present in his office at that critical moment and was able to de-escalate the situation, escorting the individual out of the office.

In response to these egregious injustices, I took the step of publishing all these details in the magazine and sent copies under a covering letter to authorities ranging from the President of India to the Defence Ministry. Approximately 8-10 days later, investigative teams from various quarters descended upon the school. Simultaneously, Air Headquarters transferred Wing Commander Sudarshan back to the Air Force. The investigation proceeded, yielding the typical outcome often observed in the army, where senior officers receive preferential treatment, and lower-ranking employees are shielded through false testimonies provided by Principal Ray and the corrupt staff.

Following these events, the responsibility of NCC reverted to the Registrar, who seized any opportunity to subject me to harassment. School teachers NK Sharma, Sanjay Bahl, and AK Handu also initiated threats and hostilities. After approximately 3-4 months, our new Officer Commanding, Lieutenant Commander Sanjay Nirmal took over. The school's environment gradually ameliorated under his stewardship. Sanjay Nirmal introduced yoga in the school, sending some teachers to Mount Abu for yoga and meditation training. He was a principled officer who reposed considerable trust in me. On one occasion, when he needed to take sudden leave, he entrusted me with signed blank papers to oversee office responsibilities during his absence.

It is often remarked that excessive honesty and integrity can become a burden, as exemplified by the case of Hindi teacher Sangeeta Choudhary. She was terminated from Sainik School, Nagrota, a mere 18 months after her appointment, simply because she had reprimanded Principal Ray. Principal Ray and Registrar Balwinder saw no fault in this action and even forcibly locked her residence. Sangeeta Choudhary, hailing from Bihar and unfamiliar with Jammu, contacted her husband to convey the situation. She subsequently filed a lawsuit. Although Sangeeta and I were not acquainted, she reached out to me upon a recommendation and requested a meeting at Raghunath Temple in Jammu. Coincidentally, I was in the vicinity at the time, so my cameraman and I met with Sangeeta and her husband. Sangeeta sought my assistance in approaching the Delhi Society, but I explained that it was going to be futile. The society had vested the Principal with the authority to terminate individuals, and they were all interconnected within the same network. Disheartened, Sangeeta accepted my advice. Nevertheless, I assured her that one day I would certainly remove Principal Ray, Handu, and Tripathi from the school. Following this incident, I consulted Vice Principal

Sanjay Nirmal on how to penalize these corrupt individuals. He concurred that Principal Ray should be targeted, believing that others would subsequently rectify their conduct.

Unable to contribute multiple articles to the same magazine, I approached a newspaper editor and asked if they could publish several articles shedding light on corruption within Sainik School Nagrota. They agreed to my proposal, and I subsequently penned numerous articles for their publication. In these pieces, I also exposed the involvement of Major General B.S. Jaiswal, who held the position of chairman at the school during that period. Fortunately, during this time, Major General GS Gumman, a senior officer in the Education Corps, visited Nagrota School and came across the newspaper articles exposing Principal Ray's misconduct. Just one month later, Principal SB Ray decided to voluntarily retire, despite having several years left in his tenure. Witnessing Ray's departure, teacher Sanjay Behl also chose to retire. The school environment remained stable for the next three years.

However, in 2008-09, a teacher named AK Handu was involved in an incident where he molested a class 11 student. The student reported the incident to the Principal, who promptly expelled Handu from the school. Handu's wife then came to the school, pleaded with the Principal and the girl's father.She requested her husband's pension to be secured despite Handu still having 16 years of service left. The Principal consented to her request. She acknowledged the consequences of Handu's actions, and he received the pension he was due to him. When I inquired about this incident with the school Principal Group Captain Ajay Kumar, he explained that if the student's life had not been in danger, he would have handed Handu over to the police authorities.

In 2004, upon my return from Nepal and while I was in Delhi, I met with some police officers who informed me that IGP PK Nayyar was carrying out research on the topic of girl trafficking in India. I had already completed approximately 75 percent of my work on this subject. I learned that Dr. Promila Kapoor had already written a book on this matter, so I decided to focus on publishing my book on Sufism, for which the work was already completed. After arriving in Jammu, I completed all the necessary formalities for getting my book printed and contacted a local printer who managed to produce the book within 15 days. We were contemplating how to release the book when, with Guruji's blessings, DSP Jamil Mir from the office of Jammu IGP MA Anjum IPS noticed a copy of my book featuring Guruji's picture. DSP was aware of the special connection between IGP and Guruji and thought of presenting this book as a gift to IGP. When he requested a copy of the book from the printer, he contacted me and sought permission to give it to IGP, a request which I gladly obliged.

Upon receiving the book from the DSP, the IGP promptly reached out to me and he extended an invitation for a meeting. The very next day, I visited the police headquarters to meet him. He was genuinely pleased to discover that we both hailed from the same district, Poonch. During our conversation, he mentioned that his family had received blessings from saints and sages, and interestingly his younger brother held the position of IGP with several other family members serving as senior police officers. When he inquired about the book's release, I proposed that it would be most fitting if he were to officiate the event as I preferred not to have any politician, regardless of their stature, unveil my book. He embraced this suggestion, and in the subsequent week, he introduced my book at the Police Headquarters in Jammu. The ceremony was attended by senior police officials and esteemed members of society, generating significant attention from the media and the press.

Following the book's release, I dispatched a copy to the then President, Shri APJ Abdul Kalam. In response, a letter arrived from his private secretary, RK Prasad, confirming that the Honorable President had received the book and intended to peruse its contents. On January 20, 2006, we received a call from RK Prasad, who conveyed the Honourable President's deep admiration for my book. He also shared the news that the President would use reference to the first chapter of my book in his address to the nation on the evening preceding Republic Day, on January 25. I was not only overjoyed by this announcement but also eagerly appreciated by the editor of my magazine. Finally, that memorable evening arrived when President Abdul Kalam ji highlighted a section of my book where I had discussed the lessons derived from the life of Sheikh Abdul Qadir Jilani. My happiness knew no bounds, as the number 11 digit holds special significance for me, coinciding with Kalam Saheb being the 11th President, and Sheikh Abdul Qadir Jilani is also known as the 11th Pir.

Now, back at the NCC Group Headquarters Jammu, both officers and clerks had reignited the flames of corruption. My intention was to expose their misconduct spanning over the past two to two-and-a-half decades in the print media, with the hope of triggering a Crime Branch investigation. Initially, I met DSP Tabassum, an exceptionally honest and astute police officer responsible for the state's crime structure. I briefed her on the entire situation. She advised me to write about the clerks who had facilitated the employment of their favored individuals in NCC through forged documents. I accordingly published an article in the newspaper detailing all fraudulent appointments from 1986 to 1999. Upon this revelation, DSP Tabassum initiated an inquiry based on my report. As the investigation began, the Crime Branch apprehended Ramesh Chandra Sharma and Ved Prakash. Their capture threatened to expose the entire scheme, prompting a collective effort to shield these two individuals. Nevertheless, DSP Tabassum remained resolute in spite of a lot of pressure.

Subsequently, military officers from NCC Group Headquarters Jammu wrote a letter to the IGP Crime and also had a meeting with him. This led to an order for DSP Tabassum to cease the investigation and close the case. The inquiry came to a standstill, and the corrupt elements emerged victorious once again. This outcome disheartened DSP Tabassum since it involved a major recruitment scam in NCC, wherein a Brigadier and some ministers were involved. Therefore, she handed me that letter and urged me to obtain a court order from the High Court. My cameraman, Naresh Dutt, filed a case against NCC and the Crime Branch in the Jammu and Kashmir High Court, requesting that the investigation be conducted under the court's supervision. Over time, the case got stalled, and by then both clerks, Ramesh Chandra Sharma and Ved Prakash Sharma had retired. This case lingered until 2017, and in the interim unbeknownst to us, our lawyer had also been influenced. Our lawyer failed to inform us of the final hearing. He preferred to attend it himself, resulting in the judge dismissing the case.

When I began writing this book, I reached out to the lawyer's son regarding this case. It was then revealed that the lawyer had passed away two months prior. We have now reopened this case, with the hope that truth will ultimately prevail and corruption within NCC will be rooted out.

Sainik School Nagrota
Jammu-181221

SSN/20098/pers 30 May 05

Registrar
Sainik School Nagrota

CREDIT BILL : SILENCE ON IMPROPER FINANCIAL TRANSACTIONS : REPLY AWAITED

1. Refer credit bill of Apr 05.

2. With reference to SSN/20098/pers dated 26 Apr 05, 17 Mar 05 and 28 Feb 05, no replies have been received so far. In addition, areas, where clear grounds for recovery of improper and unethical expenditure exist, were brought out through a note attached with the previous telephone bill of phone number 2673023. It's learnt that this bill, with a note addressed to you, has also joined the long list of financial documents that have vanished/disappeared from their original files/folders into cupboards (as skeletons?).

3. When the Accounts Section is not interested (or instructed?) to recover tens of thousands of rupees of school money misappropriated through unethical means as brought out in one of the letters mentioned above, its misplaced priorities need to be checked before it goes off the rails. Such disinterest on the part of the Accounts Section in forgoing school money should've been conveyed to the LBA during its recent meeting for its 'approval' so that the 'benefits' of living off public resources could be extended to others as well like parents not paying fees, not refunding scholarships after withdrawal, etc.

4. Further please refer SSN/913/Accts dated 07 May 05 regarding missing financial documents in the Accounts section that were essential for taking over the duties of the Registrar. When auditable documents are not kept in the Accounts section, it's clear that the staff have strayed from their basic duties in the maintenance and safe custody of books of accounts.

Under such pathetic state of affairs, your Accounts staff may first be advised to set their own house in order before venturing into unknown areas. The attention of the Accounts staff may also be drawn to various provisions in the SSS Rules & Regulations by which collusion of staff in illegal and unethical activities, that would be construed as violation of the Conduct Rules, would be disastrous for them.

5. A cheque for Rs.542.78p/- (No.477266) dated 30 May 05 is enclosed as full and complete payment of the Apr 05 credit bill. Please acknowledge receipt.

(A Sudharsanan)
Wg Cdr
Headmaster

Encl:- Cheque No.477266 dt 30 May 05

Sainik School
Nagrota, Jammu.
Pin : 181 221

07 May 2005

No.SSN/913/Accts/

The Principal
Sainik School
Nagrota, Jammu.

RETURN OF REMOVED VOUCHERS

1. Reference is made to SSN/101/MO dt. 02 May 2005.

2. While taking over, it's seen that some vouchers, especially those pertaining to the Principal's TDs, are not available in the voucher folders. When the Accountant was asked about them, he has informed that they were removed quite some time back and kept with the Principal.

3. All such vouchers removed may please be returned for checking before taking over as Registrar.

(A Sudharasaran)
Wg Cdr
Headmaster

Sainik School
Nagrota,Jammu
Pin : 181 221

14 May 2005

No.SSN/32/MO/

The Quartermaster
Sainik School
Nagrota,Jammu.

A.S.T.B : EQUIPMENT VOL I

1. Reference is made to letter No.SSN/32/MO dated 01 April 2005.

2. A check of items was carried out of 'Equipment Vol I'. It's seen from the ledger that of the three ACs, one is shown as fitted in the Principal's Office and two in the Guest House. However, on physical check, it is seen that only one is in the Guest House and the other is in the Principal's residence.

3. You are to give the following details :-

(a) Proof of authority under which the Guest House AC was shifted to the Principal's residence.

(b) Date of installation of AC in the Principal's residence.

(c) Date of installation of separate meter for AC in the Principal's residence.

(d) Amount recovered on account of use of AC in the residence.

(A Sudharasanan)
Wg Cdr
Presiding Officer

<u>CONFIDENTIAL</u>

Sainik School Nagrota
Jammu-181221

14 May 05

SSN/20098/pers

Principal
Sainik School Nagrota

<u>REPEATED INDIGNITY TO RANK & SERVICE</u>

1. Reference is made to SSN/913/Accts dated 07 May 05.

2. The request for return of financial documents for checking before taking over as Registrar has met with resounding silence. Further, shameful instructions to the clerical staff to deny access to official documents to their own Officer-in-Charge give rise to speculation and serious suspicion on the leitmotiv behind the stashing away of these vouchers and documents. With the lower level employees getting sucked into the vortex of deceit and deception, it's once again reiterated that little can be expected from the other staff and cadets on ethics, morality and discipline. If there's even a modicum of seriousness in trying to achieve the aims of the Sainik Schools in preparing cadets for NDA, the least that one should strive for is to provide an ethically and morally clean atmosphere for officer-like qualities and values to be nurtured.

3. When the government has already moved the Right to Information Bill empowering all citizens of this country to get any information from the departments, agencies and bodies of the central, state and local bodies besides government aided institutions, as long as public interest in disclosure

<u>CONFIDENTIAL</u>

2

CONFIDENTIAL

outweighs the harm to the protected interests, if any, which in this case is not applicable, it can only be pointed out that skeletons in the cupboard cannot be prevented from tumbling out by sweeping things under the carpet in Sainik School Nagrota.

4. With reference to SSN/850/QM dated 07 May 05, car diaries required for checking while taking over as Registrar and for retention with the Quarter Master (QM), have also not yet been received. All this while, the vehicles continue to be used of which the QM is completely in the dark to brief the undersigned. On checking with the drivers regarding the usage during this period, it's sadly brought out that they have been resorting to telling blatant lies which can be easily made out when compared with what's been seen (by the undersigned also) and reported by different people regarding the movement of vehicles, including time, driver, occupants, destination, purpose, etc.

5. In this connection, it's brought to your notice that while you were on leave and gone out of station to Lucknow, the school Bolero was seen going outside the school driven by Shri. Harbajan Singh, the driver-turned-Hostel Superintendent. When the chowkidar tried to stop the vehicle for checking the occupants since you were on leave to Lucknow, by waving it down, the driver swerved to the outside of the road, under the half lifted barrier and went outside the school. On his return, when the same chowkidar stopped him and told him to speak to the undersigned, he noticed that your wife and also your dog were inside the vehicle.

6. Explanations were promptly sought from both the driver and the chowkidar. However, on your return from leave, you sent a letter 'cancelling' such explanations as they were 'disturbing and harmful' to the employees and that 'no action/reply is to be expected from the individuals.'

CONFIDENTIAL

3

CONFIDENTIAL

7. While enquiring about the incident, it became amply evident that the driver-turned-Hostel Superintendent was uttering lies and concealing facts, clearly under instructions. It is well known and seen by all that the casual labourer working as a driver, has been driving the school Bolero. However, when the QM tried to find out his movements with the vehicle, he not only resorted to untruths but even told him that he was officially employed in the Mess. With the reliability of such drivers under a cloud and the non availability of vehicle diaries with the QM, the responsibility of the Registrar in ensuring the proper use and maintenance of vehicles and records (vide Rule 17.02 & 17.03) has been reduced to a near farce.

8. When sincere attempts to streamline the working of drivers and others have been stymied through obfuscation and skullduggery, with a driver-turned-Hostel Superintendent performing the duties of a driver to the neglect of his 'primary' duties for which he's been pulled up on quite a number of occasions and a casual labourer working as a driver, obviously being instructed to utter blatant untruths, even when their jobs could be on the line, I'd like to express my reluctance to persist with performing the pared down job of a Registrar, which I've been doing till now in the larger interest of the organization, since tolerance beyond a point of absurdity is no more a virtue but cowardice, an unworthy and undesirable shame, no honourable Service officer worth his salt would desire to bring upon himself or his Service.

(A Sudharsanan)
Wg Cdr
Headmaster

Copy to:-
1. Maj Gen BS Jaswal VSM
COS HQ 16 Corps & Chairman LBA

2. Honorary Secretary - W.r.t. my application of 23 Mar 05,
Sainik Schools Society may I request you to impress upon
New Delhi IAF to expedite my posting.

CONFIDENTIAL

CONFIDENTIAL

JD Indep Coy NCC
Sainik School Nagrota
Jammu-181221

SSN/501/A/NCC // Jun 05

Gp Hq NCC (Attn Gp Cdr)
Gandhi Nagar
Jammu

HARASSMENT OF PI STAFF

1. Reference is made to discussions held with you on the subject some time back.

2. In consequence of the decision taken to de-link PI staff from the mundane activities of the school not related to NCC training, there's been a step-motherly treatment of the PI staff. During the inspection of the school by Col Choudhary (AEC) , the Inspecting Officer (IO) from Sainik Schools Society (SSS), New Delhi, the undersigned was asked regarding the 'non-involvement' of the PI staff in the day-to-day activities of the school and their not taking orders from the school Principal directly. Even after he was categorically told that the school Principal was no more their Group Commander as was the case in yesteryears and that the PI staff were under the OC who was answerable to the Gp Cdr at Gp HQ for NCC activities and that in case of any ambiguity on this, the Gp Cdr be contacted, the IO made it known that they were to be under the Principal. Apparently, no efforts were made to visit or contact the NCC Gp HQ for discussion or clarifications.

CONFIDENTIAL

CONFIDENTIAL

3. The NCC JCO Sub Vijay Singh was also summoned by Col Choudhary and questioned about his 'non-involvement' in the activities of the school and for not taking orders from the Principal directly. It was also inappropriately pointed out to him that he (IO) would be taking up this matter with the DG NCC at New Delhi to which of course a JCO could only listen without any reply.

4. Immediately after the departure of the IO, the Principal informed me that as the JCO was under the OC and not under him, he had decided to remove the JCO's son from the school for which he had obtained the IO's concurrence and that I was to initiate the necessary paper work for this and put up the JCO's son's file to him. In view of the cruel and inhuman nature of such a decision, I had my qualms in being a party to such malevolence. The file was then taken directly by the Principal who then informed me that the JCO's son's was no more eligible for a seat under the day scholar's quota and that he was sending his case to the IO for withdrawal from the school.

5. Since it was the end of the academic year when admissions in most schools had closed, the JCO's plight could only be pitied especially when the ill treatment meted out to him was ironically not from a civilian but from someone from the Services. He promptly withdrew his son immediately to run from pillar to post for admission in some school at that belated stage.

6. It may not be out of place to mention that ill-treatment by the Principal of even Army officers is not unknown to the Gp HQ. My experience over the past year had been thoroughly demoralizing and de-motivating that I found myself a fish out of water in an ethically debased work culture. The utter disdain for Service norms and conventions and repeated attempts to desecrate military traditions had been brought out by me time and again to the notice of ~~SSS~~ which elicited only deafening silence.

CONFIDENTIAL

CONFIDENTIAL

7. While I'd shortly be handing over charge to someone who'd be officiating in my place (Registrar), vituperative vindictiveness targeted at the NCC staff, especially the PI personnel, can't be ruled out in the light of what's been brought out in the earlier paragraphs and needs to be guarded against. It's therefore my earnest request that suitable morale boosting measures be initiated to instil confidence in the staff to enable them to face the future with fortitude.

8. May I also take this opportunity to thank the officers and staff of the Group HQ for all the help, support and cooperation extended to me and the unit during my tenure as OC JD Indep Coy NCC.

(A Sudharsanan)
Wg Cdr
Officer Commanding

Copy to :- Dy DG NCC
J&K Directorate
Jammu

NOO: Maj Gen BS Jaswal VSM | (Through Col Edn
COS HQ 16 Corps & Chairman LBA | HQ 16 Corps)

CONFIDENTIAL

Sainik School Nagrota
Jammu-181221

SSN/20098/pers 30 May 05

Registrar
Sainik School Nagrota

CREDIT BILL : SILENCE ON IMPROPER FINANCIAL TRANSACTIONS : REPLY AWAITED

1. Refer credit bill of Apr 05.

2. With reference to SSN/20098/pers dated 26 Apr 05, 17 Mar 05 and 28 Feb 05, no replies have been received so far. In addition, areas, where clear grounds for recovery of improper and unethical expenditure exist, were brought out through a note attached with the previous telephone bill of phone number 2673023. It's learnt that this bill, with a note addressed to you, has also joined the long list of financial documents that have vanished/disappeared from their original files/folders into cupboards (as skeletons?).

3. When the Accounts Section is not interested (or instructed?) to recover tens of thousands of rupees of school money misappropriated through unethical means as brought out in one of the letters mentioned above, its misplaced priorities need to be checked before it goes off the rails. Such disinterest on the part of the Accounts Section in forgoing school money should've been conveyed to the LBA during its recent meeting for its 'approval' so that the 'benefits' of living off public resources could be extended to others as well like parents not paying fees, not refunding scholarships after withdrawal, etc.

4. Further please refer SSN/913/Accts dated 07 May 05 regarding missing financial documents in the Accounts section that were essential for taking over the duties of the Registrar. When auditable documents are not kept in the Accounts section, it's clear that the staff have strayed from their basic duties in the maintenance and safe custody of books of accounts.

5. When collusion of the lower level staff in despicable deeds inimical to the interests of the school cannot be ruled out considering the type of probes initiated by the Army and the Air Force, the attention of your accounts and QM staff may once again be drawn specifically to paragraphs 9.01 (f), (n), (o), (p) & 9.03 (v) of SSS Rules & Regulations.

6. A cheque for Rs.482/- (No.477270) dated 20 Jun 05 is enclosed as full and complete payment of the May 05 credit bill. Please acknowledge receipt.

(A Sudharsanan)
Wg Cdr
Headmaster

Encl:- Cheque No.477270 dt 20 Jun 05

Sainik School Nagrota
Jammu-181221

SSN/32/MO 24 Jun 05

Principal
Sainik School Nagrota

RETURN OF ASTB PROCEEDINGS DUE TO INSTIGATED NON-INVOLVEMENT OF STAFF IN COMPLETION

1. Reference is made to SSN/32/MO dated 14 May 05 and 07 Jun 05 with copy to Registrar for which no reply's been received so far.

2. The nonchalance of an ordinary QM, obviously briefed not to reply to an officer's letters in spite of written reminders for a period of about two months, is indicative of the moral rot that has seeped in. Since the Board cannot be completed under such disorderly and demeaning conditions, when the lower level staff are instigated to disregard an officer, the ASTB is returned as replies to queries haven't been forwarded by the QM clearly under unethical instructions.

3. While the formality of this yearly exercise may be gone through with someone else signing on the dotted line, it's once again brought out that dues to the school on account of misuse of school resources be recovered from the individual/s concerned to maintain some semblance of respect for the rule.

(A Sudharsanan)
Wg Cdr
Presiding Officer

Copy to : Maj Gen BS Jaswal VSM |
COS HQ 16 Corps & Chairman LBA |

(Through Col Edn | The Army Enquiry team was also informed
HQ 16 Corps) | of these irregularities

Save the Sainik School

It serves an important national cause and should be given every possible support

INTERVENTION

M. P. ANIL KUMAR

POST-INDEPENDENCE, the officer cadre of the Indian Armed Forces lacked a grassroots ethos and needed to be 'Indianised'. Since public schools were beyond most, then defence minister, V.K. Krishna Menon, envisioned Sainik Schools in 1960. The idea was to set up at least one school in each state to select boys from across the spectrum through an open entrance examination and train them for leadership in the forces.

Sainik Schools were modelled on public schools minus the vainglory. The syllabus-examination approach was also cast aside. They aimed at all-round development to enhance competitive and survival skills, and foster personality development. To ensure that promising boys from economically backward strata joined the school, states were mandated to provide scholarships. Given their background, these students were also expected to identify themselves with the men they command — the sine qua non of military leadership. Sainik Schools would thus serve as feeders to the National Defence Academy and the three Service Academies.

Did it work? You bet. Remember how the young officers led their troops upfront, uphill, undauntedly through the cannonade to recapture the Kargil massifs? But even as Sainik Schools were rejoicing at the elevation of one of its students, General Deepak Kapoor, as army chief, they had been fighting a grim battle for survival. The state governments handed out scholarships to indigent students, depending on parents' income. Twenty years ago, the total charges of a student were approximately Rs 11,000, of which the fee component was Rs 5,500. By 1997, this rose to Rs 27,000, roughly half of it being the fee. This year the parents had to fork out Rs 60,000, with the fee touching 40 grand. The academic year 2000-01 delivered a double whammy: one, the board decided to jack up the fee by 10 per cent every year; two, the majority of states resolved not to underwrite the hike in the fees of those earning scholarships.

Unlike other government schools, the salary and pension of teachers and staff are not borne by the government; it is met from consolidated fees and bursaries. Given the steep rise in the fees, Sainik Schools, once extolled as the Poor Man's Public Schools, have become unaffordable for the poor man!

True, good education comes at a price. But Sainik Schools were devised to serve a national cause. So is there a way out? There are 22 Sainik Schools, and the average bill for each school is approximately Rs 1 crore. The defence budget for the year 2007-08 is Rs 96,000 crore — 22 crore is a mere 0.023 per cent of this. If the Centre picks up this tab, it would lift the burden from the shoulders of the parents by about a third.

The defence minister himself must take the call. Letting national assets like the Sainik Schools go to seed will be unpardonable self-destruction.

City Diary

Corruption galores in Sainik School Nagrota, Authorities are stalling the Probe

Controversy and corruption charges ranging from favourtism in appointment, misuse of official vehicles, receiving kickbacks from contractors and involvement of its staff with outsiders in getting their wards admitted in school through backdoor means cloud Sainik School Nagrota in the touble torn state.

According to reliable sources, Sainik School Nagrota, figures in a few last position in the national tally, when it comes to rating its performance despite receiving best of the support from the state as well as from the centre. "Our school has been keeping the last position in the national level competition as if it were a monopoly of Sainik School Nagrota," said the sources.

The sources further said that it was due to the independent command and lackadaisical attitude of the Principal (a naval officer) posted in the school in addition to supply of substandard materials to the students. Some of its officials in the last and present are alleged to be on the pay roll of the contractors supplying food materials, equipments including uniforms and kits for the students.

It is also alleged that officials who are involved in this racket enjoy the patronage of the higher officials in the Sainik Schools Society, New Delhi. It is further alleged that some officials in the school give undue favour to their kith and kin and siphon off the fund allotted for the welfare of the students.

The officials of the Sainik School Nagrota are also indulging in pick and choose method in appointments. To quote, a glaring example, in August last year, one driver of the school(who is a matriculate) was appointed as Hostel Superintendent while other highly educated candidates who were rejected. One of the candidates (M.A., BE.d) who too was rejected said, "for Sainik School authorities qualification don't matter. However money and links are the most effective measures."

Similarly, violations of rules in promotions is also common. The seniors employees are superceded by those who are close to the Principal Registrar. Employees are compelled to put their cases before the court of law for justice. It is pertinent to mention here that four cases against the school authorities are subjudice in the Hon'ble High Court of J&K Jammu. Numerous of the cases has already been decided in favour of the employees. But in order to harass the employees, authorities are again putting the cases before double bench of the Hon'ble High Court. Large scale of the money is wasted on the litigations cases from the school exchequer.

The vehicles allotted to the school are also misused on a large scale. The vehicles are pressed into service unofficially for long tours of the officer and their families. Even the staff car is used to get the principal's dog to the Dog unit for getting him trained. Last year, the vehicle (Balero car) of the school was seen at Lakhnow in Uttar Pradesh added sources.

During the course of investigation by the 'STRET VOICE' it was found that the Headmaster of the school is a dedicated and honest. He wants to bring a change in school from the academic side, bu the Principal and Registrar are drying to get him transferred from the school being a stumbling block in their way.

Another startling fact that come to light is that students of the school are involved in sodomy. Seniors students are exploiting physically new comers. In the month of January 2005, a student of 9th class was expelled from the school on the charges of sodomity. It is also alleged that the year 2003, a teacher of the school was forced to get premature retirement as the same charges were proved against him. Principal and Registrar hushed up the case and asked him for premature retirement. Numerous students were warned and there was written on their note sheet.

It is pertinent to mention here that some officials are involved in getting week students admitted in the school at the time of admission through back door means, the modus operandi used by them is leakage of papers to the outsiders and helping the candidates during admission test. These week students cannot bear the burden of the study and fail an finally leave the school after one year.

This is only the tip of iceberg. There are other hidden activities in the Sainik School Nagrota. The need of the hour is streamline and revamp the whole administration of the school in order to restore the glory and name of the institution. ■

STREET VOICE -42- MAY, 2005

Corruption rules roost in Sainik School Nagrota

Principal refuses to comply with transfer orders

BY RAVINDER SINGH

JAMMU, APR 25— *Sainik School Nagrota once considered as number one school in J&K has become a den of corruption due to the mendacious tendencies of none other than but the school principal. The school is receiving considerable aid both from the centre and state governments but to the utter surprise of many, the principal, Capt (TS) Salil Baron Ray and his henchmen have been swindling the grants with both hands.*

Following hue and cry made over large-scale bungling and dictatorship of school principal, the Commodore Principal Director of Personnel, RM Purandare transferred the school principal on March 29, 2006 to Indian Naval Ship Shivaji as SEDO and directed him to report to the unit at Lonavla before Apr 6, 2006 but the principal Capt Ray throwing all norms to winds did not comply with the transfer orders. Ironically the chairman of the school, Maj Gen B.S. Jaswal has also not taken cognizance of the matter, which leaves a question mark even on his integrity.

It may be recalled that the former Headmaster, while handing over the charge to Balwinder Singh, had levelled serious allegations of corruption against the principal, Capt (TS) Salil Baron Ray.

He had said that the principal after receiving considerable amount appointed one Harbajan Singh, driver as Hostel Superintendent, even though he could not even speak English, while the school takes pride in calling itself an English medium residential school.

Similarly violation of rules in promotions is also common. The senior employees are superceded by those, who are close to the heart of Principal Registrar.

Employees are compelled to put their cases before the court of law for justice. It is pertinent to mention here that four cases against the school authorities are subjudice in Hon'ble High Court of J&K Jammu.

The vehicles allotted to the school are also misused on a large-scale.

The vehicles are pressed into service unofficially for long hours of the officers and their families. Even the staff car is used to get the principal's dog to the Dog Unit for getting him trained.

The principal is also involved in getting weak students admitted in the school at the time of admission through backdoor means.

This is only the tip of iceberg. There are other hidden activities in the Sainik School Nagrota.

The need of the hour is to streamline and revamp the whole administration in order to restore the pristine glory of the institution.

Huge misappropriation of funds: CBI raids Sainik School Nagrota, seizes records

■ STATE TIMES NEWS

JAMMU: A team of CBI raided Sainik School, Nagrota on Wednesday in connection with alleged misappropriation of huge funds amounting to lakhs. The team, after seizing all relevant records, interrogated the staff including clerks and Vice Principal was for about 10 hours. According to sources, the records scrutinized so far revealed that in years 2019 and 2020, the school management bought goods worth more than Rs 1 crore from open market at expensive prices.

During investigation, it was found that the purchases took place during the tenure of acting Principal Lt Col Pawan Kumar and Administrative Officer Major Angat, who has been transferred.

CBI team also found that an article, worth Rs 2 lakh in market, was bought for Rs 4 lakh from the market. "School management has issued tenders for it and shopkeepers gave three quotations. It was found that despite quoting high price, the goods were bought from the same shopkeeper at expensive prices from the market rate", CBI sources said adding that back-dated signatures of officers were also found on some of the quotations, due to which scam in the purchase of school items came to fore.

Sources further said that during last financial year, some clerks were appointed in school from backdoor and even caretaker Principal wasted Government money, for selfish reasons, by installing 22 plastic speed breakers within a distance of 1 kilometer. CBI sources further said that the electronic barrier installed at the gate of the school, which costs around Rs 80,000 in market, was bought for Rs 2.50 lakh, there causing huge appropriation of funds by the school management amounting to lakhs of rupees. The CBI

■ CONTD ON PAGE 9

Reminder

(By Registered Post / Ackknowledgement Due)

From :- RAM GOPAL SHARMA
LASKAR
J.D. INDEP. COY
N.C.C. SAINIK SCHOOL
NAGROTA , DISTT.JAMMU,
J&K SATE.

30th July,2002

To

~~The Central Vigilance Commissioner,
Government of India,
New Delhi.~~

The Hon'ble Chief Minister
J&K Govt.
JAMMU.

Subject :- INQUIRY INTO THE NEWS PUBLISHED IN A DAILY ENGLISH ' STATE TIMES' AT JAMMU ON 10TH FEBRUARY 2002 TITLED " CORRUPTION GALORES IN J&K NCC " (COPY OF NEWS PAPER ENCLOSED).

Sir,

In the above mentioned News item under the heading " Corruption galores in J&K NCC " published in the daily News paper (STATE TIMES) AT JAMMU on 10th day of Feb,2002, (Copy enclosed), in this connection I would like to submit as under with the hope that your goodself will look into this matter personally in the interest of the Administration of the Central/ State Government in particular and in the interest of the poor employees in general.

That when the news came in open before the eyes of all concerned, it hasbeen observed that no action is being taken in the matter. If the News is found genuine then necessary action should be taken in the matter against the concerned officers of the J&K N.C.C, and if the News is found wrong, then Necessary action should be taken against the publisher of the News.

For your kind information, I am a poor class IV employee working in N.C.C at Jammu for the last about sixteen years, with my hard work, honesty and dedication.

(Contd.. .. P/ 2)

C.T.C

Annexure - D.

(16)

CONVENING ORDER

A Board of Officers composed as under will assemble in 2 J&K Girls BN NCC Jammu on the date and time to be fixed by the Presiding Officer for the following purposes:-

(a) to establish the impropriety of action on the part of Sh. Ram Gopal Sharma (Lascar) of JD Indep Coy NCC Sainik School, Nagrota District Jammu for directly approaching Central Vigilance Commissioner, Govt of India, New Delhi vide his reginst-ered application dated 30 Jul'2002 with a copy endorsed to DG NCC New Delhi and Defence Secretary New Delhi.

(b) The court will also seek verification of antecedents of Sh. Ram Gopal Sharma from State agencies.

(a) Presiding Officer: Lt Col R S JAMWAL
OC
2 J&K Girls Bn NCC Jammu

(b) Members : Lt Col S S Sambyal
Adm Officer
NCC GP HQ Jammu

: Major Anil Bakshi
Trg Officer
NCC Group HQ Jammu

2. The Board proceeding duly completed in all re-spects will be submitted to this HQ by 16 Sep'2002.

No.001/A/NCC-
NCC Group Headquarters,
82 A/D Gandhi Nagar,
Jammu

31 Aug'2002

Sd/-
(A K Madhok)
Col
Group Commander

Copy to:-

NCC Directorate J&K	- For inf
2 J&K Girls BN NCC	- -do-
JD Indep Coy NCC	- -do-

C.T.C

Date receipt of application - 10-9-2002
Date of issue C.T.C - 10-9-2002

certified True Copy has been issued to Sh. Ram Gopal Sharma on 10-9-2002

Major
Officer Commanding
JD Indep Coy NCC
Sainik School Nagrota
(Jammu)
10/9/2002

Page - 2

I have appeared before the Departmental Promotion committee for my due promotion, but I was not given my due promotion, whereas some official working in the department under Probation period has been promoted namely Sh. Shashi Chargotra who was working as a LASKAR in N.C.C and has been promoted as Jr. Assistant, thus causing a great injustice to me.

So, I had no other alternative to seek the justice in the Hon'ble Court at Jammu and have filed my Writ Petition, against the undue promotion given to an employee who has only fourteen month's service on his back and is still under probationary period.

Since the News against the J&K N.C C has come out in the leading news papers at Jammu, it is quite clear as crystal that there is corruption in the J&K N.C.C. the reason of which I have been ignored for my due promotion having 16 years of service on my back, and having my academic Qualifications Twelth pass, thus causing me great injustice.

If the apprpriate action is taken against the corrupt officers of J&K N.C.C, my problems can be solved to enable me to get my due promotion and can with-draw my Writ petition from the Courts. If the News published in the local News papers against J&K N.C.C, then action should be taken against the Publishers of the News Papers and in that case, I will follow up the court case to seek the justice.

Keeping in view of the above facts, I request your goodself to kindly do the needful in this matter and I may kindly be informed about the action taken by your goodself in the above titled case, for this act of kindness I shall remain highly obliged.

Thanking you.

Yours faithfully

(RAM GOPAL SHARMA)

Sainik School Nagrota
(Jammu)
10/9/2002

(6)

RGPJ—8/2002 of 10,000 Form

IN THE HIGH COURT OF JAMMU & KASHMIR
JAMMU

Petition No. SWP No: 2372/2002
Petition No.

Revision Petition No.
Civil Suit No.

Date of decision 27/9/2002

Ram Gopal Sharma Versus State of J&K and others
(PETITIONER) (RESPONDENTS')

Coram :
The Hon'ble Mr. Justice T.S.Doabia
The Hon'ble Mr. Justice
The Hon'ble Mr. Justice
Whether approved by reporting ?
For the Appellant(s)/Petitioner(s) : Shri B.S.Slathia
For the Respondent(s) :Shri S.S.Nanda, Sr.CGSC

The short submission made by the learned counsel for the petitioner is that he is a Civilian and a State Government employee cannot be tried under the Army Act.

Shri S.S.Nanda, Sr.CGSC appearing for the respondents submits that petitioner has neither been tried under the Army Act nor is being tried under the Army Act.

In view of the above stand taken by the respondents, no further direction is required to be given.

Disposed of accordingly.

JAMMU
DATED:27/9/2002
Nagri

(T . S . DOABIA-J.)

Juniors in NCC throw rules to wind, sell jobs to unemployed

BY RAVINDER SINGH

JAMMU, SEPT 3-At one hand the top brass in chairs at NCC Group HQ are promising for more discipline and dedication among NCC cadets in state, but ironically the lower cadre has made the same place a perching ground for mal-practices. The black sheep and their henchmen are busy in taking people on ride by offering jobs at lower level, sources said.

Sources in the said department informed that one Romesh Chander Sharma had spread a well knit nexus within the Group HQ so as to meet his materialistic and worldly gains. They mentioned that above mentioned Section Officer who way back in 1986 was apprehended by the Gandhinagar Police has entered into a nexus with one Fagghu Chowdary of Rani Talab.

"Feeling obliged to the Fagghu Chowdary who had got his bail and got Sharma released, he could not deny the proposal of getting his relative employed in the same department as Chowkidar (the guard)", sources added.

"Then masterminding the plot Sharma asked Chowdary to produce a school leaving cum date of birth certificate, then Chowdary using his all tools in his bag managed a fake certificate for his relative from a Middle School Rattian," sources said.

Somewhere in October 1986 Romesh Sharma managed to get Des Raj s/o Bhagmal of Dhindey Kalan R S Pura appointed as Chowkidar," they maintained.

However, to evade any controversy over the said fake document Sharma suggested another 'million dollar idea' to appoint Des Raj and asked him to submit an affidavit about his permanent citizenship and date of birth. Following mentor's instructions Des Raj managed the affidavit dated 7th September 2000. Sharma who is kingpin of the plot pinned out the fake birth/qualification document and replaced that with the said affidavit, which is still in the office files. Interestingly the old certificate has been destroyed and the affidavit issued by one Notary Narinder Kour is now serving the purpose in office files, sources revealed.

Sources also mentioned as this experiment of adjustment of a person in the department has clandestinely encouraged the kingpin Sharma who set up a good employment nexus within the department by joining hands with some other counterparts. Knowing the inside stories and appointing norms, the nexus managed to get fake stamps of Distt Employment Exchange and during the need they use these stamps on the documents of their clients and produce them as the registered candidates from the Distt Employment Exchange in front of the senior authorities, sources added.

"The senior ranks without sensing anything wrong take the candidates genuine called by the Distt Employment Exchange Jammu for interview and select any one of them especially who had given the best bid to the nexus for the advertised job, giving a benefit of doubt to top rank", sources said.

NCC service rules being flouted; employees working in private sector simultaneously

BY: RAVINDER SINGH
JAMMU, SEPT 29

Service rules and regulations have been kept on the shelves in the NCC Divisional Hqrs making the some influential enjoying not only the privileged positions but are making dollars by serving at government and the private sector simultaneously, sources in the department said.

Sources said that while many may be indulged in breaking of service rules but an odd trio of Ved Prakash a head assistant, Romesh Chander and another clerk who were working at the other private establishments is a blatant and a known fact to all within the headquarters. Ironically none can speak against their double jobs i.e. mal practices because of their access in the higher circles. If sources are to be believed then their influence has let their subordinates to remain tight-lipped in this regard and keeping their eyes closed to actions of the trio fearing transfers or other disciplinary action against the informer, sources said.

On promised anonymity one ministerial staff member informed that Ved Prakash Sharma head assistant at NCC Hqrs has been associated with last over a decade as an accountant with one Jain Industries (M/s Sudershan Jain Industries). As he has been following an appeasement policy to keep the higher up pleased no senior has bothered about his working with the private sector, he said.

While Romesh Chander Sharma is associated with a private financier namely M/s Monica Finance Company Jammu with another clerk working as a Munshi cum typist with a local advocate. All this is a known fact to all seniors and juniors in the head quarters but every one has adopted a aloof attitude in this context.

Surprisingly the J&K Employee Government Rules 1971 Rules-10 depicts totally contrary to this practice as it says no government employee can't work in any other concern/organization without the prior sanction of the government or ***(Cont. on P 2)***

SUNDAY, OCTOBER 1, 2006 P 2

KNOW YOUR STARS

ARIES (March 21-April 19): Make hay while the sun shines. Today and tomorrow you can gain the cooperation of others to get your projects launched. Romantic partners will be willing to accept an apology.

TAURUS (April 20-May 20): Butter your bread on the right side. Your generosity and sincerity will bring positive results. People will be delighted to lend you the assistance you need and are willing to compromise.

GEMINI (May 21-June 20): One good turn deserves another. Believe in the sincerity of others and your trust won't be misplaced. This is a good time to straighten out a rocky romance or misunderstanding.

CANCER (June 21-July 22): Be a busy business bee. Get agreements or contracts signed that have been sitting on the back burner. Don't spend too much time or money on hobbies when there is work to be done.

LEO (July 23-Aug. 22): Take steps to guarantee your future success. Put your plans into motion. It is a good day to ask for favors or to ask for advice. Don't fritter your money away on tasteless, overpriced items.

VIRGO (Aug. 23-Sept. 22): Accept opportunities that fall in your lap. This is a good day to make important phone calls or ask others to fulfill past promises. You may need to use sweet, syrupy phrases to achieve compliance.

LIBRA (Sept. 23-Oct. 22): Heart-to-heart chats and quiet meetings lead to success. With a little effort you can come to an agreement and mend some very important fences. You may receive an unexpected blessing.

SCORPIO (Oct. 23-Nov. 21): Social functions can open up wider horizons. The celestial traffic light is turning green for love or money, but it might not be the best time to buy items that require taste and discrimination.

SAGITTARIUS (Nov. 22-Dec. 21): Make every effort to clear up misunderstandings or mix-ups. Call in a few favors and pull a few strings. Restrain the tendency to spend too much time hanging around the water cooler.

CAPRICORN (Dec. 22-Jan. 19): Concentrate on tightening bonds with people whose trust and cooperation are needed. It is a good time to correct misunderstandings and restore faith by completing promised tasks.

AQUARIUS (Jan. 20-Feb. 18): The piggy bank's condition can improve if you put pennies to good use. Your honesty and sincerity shines like a guiding light. Hold a frank discussion and clear the air with a special someone.

PISCES (Feb. 19-March 20): The scales are tipping in your favor, so count your lucky stars. A few generous gestures will guarantee a spirit of good will and cooperation. Take steps to improve your future.

NORTHERN RAILWAY TIINGS

S/Train No.	No	Arrival	Departure

Police clueless even...

servant Sonu and driver Jagan were murdered on late night of the September 17. The gruesome murder reportedly was surfaced on the next morning when nephew of the unfortunate person called the police and relatives when he visited the silent Shanti Kutir on September 18.

While police in an effort to take a lead has also grilled some relatives of the deceased family which was criticized by the close relatives of Chopras and the Chopra biradhari which had staged a protest dharna on the other day. The protestors were demanding justice and arrest of culprits at the earliest. However, they expressed their deep concern over the slow pace of investigation and at the same time relatives of the deceased family have also accused the police of harassing them. Amidst this criticism lobbed on police, Raju's son Punit too is surprised on the case investigation and also demanded early arrest of the accused.

NCC service rules...

the concerned employer agency. While Rule 10(4) underlines that no government employee can accept any fee or favour/token from any organization/concerns while working in a government set up.

Ministerial staff at NCC head quarters is unrestive on this issue as many of the feel it resulting in indiscipline and a provocative action that is also luring the others to look for another job while working with NCC Hqrs. It is also believed that the trio had kept the things well under their control in their respective offices and the seniors are not in a position to take any action against these three whose name had been time and again remained in the news in the corridors of the NCC Hqrs. It is also pertinent to mention that following the complaints of the locals the crime branch has sought records from the NCC about some persons of the NCC Hqrs, sources added.

CBI asked to submit...

Shah and Syed Altaf Hussain. The bench said the status report did not indicate what action had been initiated against other persons whose names surfaced during the investigation to which, the CBI sought more time to file a complete report.

The court on Wednesday adjourned proceedings as lawyers struck work against the death sentence on Mohammaed Afzal Guru in the Parliament attack case.

The CBI has so far arrested 18 people, including two former state ministers, an IAS officer, two police officers, a DIG of the BSF, an ex-additional advocate general, a hotel manager and the alleged kingpin of the racket. It has filed two chargesheets in the case against 14 accused. The trial of the case has been shifted to

FLIGHT TIMINGS

INDIAN AIRLINES (FLIGHT TIMINGS)

FLIGHT SCHEDULE EX JAMMU (w.e.f 15 May, 2004)

IC 821 ALL DAYS			IC 825 ALL DAYS		
A 320 (AIRCRAFT)			A 320 (AIRCRAFT)		
DELHI	DEP	1045	DELHI	DEP	1140
JAMMU	ARR	1155	SRINAGAR	ARR	1255
JAMMU	DEP	1235	SRINAGAR	DEP	1335
SRINAGAR	ARR	1310	JAMMU	ARR	1410
SRINAGAR	DEP	1400	JAMMU	DEP	1445
DELHI	ARR	1515	DELHI	ARR	1555
IC 742/IC 7425 (TUE/SAT)					
B 737 (AIRCRAFT)				B 737	
LEH	DEP	0730	JAMMU	DEP	0900
JAMMU	ARR	0830	LEH	ARR	1000

Un-Warranted comments on Fourth Estate

Crime Branch's axe likely to fall on Col Bajwa

BY RAVINDER SINGH

JAMMU, NOV 20- *In keeping with its reputation as the pioneer of investigative Journalism in the state, the Daily 'The Latest' had carried out exclusive series of investigative stories pertaining to the mal-practices in appointments and promotions in NCC Gp HQ Jammu. The states premier investigative agency Crime Branch, J&K, Jammu took serious note of the alleged corrupt activities going on in the Gp HQ, NCC, Jammu with great curiosity.*

The state Crime Branch was already in possession of valuable informations about the blatant corruption going on in this HQ for quite sometime. After taking cognizance of serious nature of reports carried out in this News Paper, the Crime Branch initiated indepth inquiries into the matter and after it was felt that there something fishy was going on in NCC GP HQ Jammu, decided to summon the record of dividends carried out by Mr. R.C. Sharma, Ved Parkash Sharma Munshi (Majoo) and others in the office from time to time.

After the summoning for scrutization of the details, the corrupt officials of NCC Gp HQ, Jammu who were enjoying power and glory with impunity have suddenly became perturbed for fear of serious nature of action which would likely to be initiated by the crime branch at any time. To cover their misdeeds and other corrupt activities the above stated officials involved misbriefed Col. K.S. Bajwa, Gp Cdr, NCC Gp HQ, Jammu the factual ground reality and anyhow by share manipulation succeeded in getting a letter No. 001/A/NCC/15 of 14 Oct. 2006 issued to Dy. DG, NCC Dte J&K, Jammu, IGP, Crime & Railways and SSP Crime & Railways, Jammu which bears the signature of Col. K.S. Bajwa, Gp Cdr, NCC Gp HQ, Jammu.

The contents of the said letter written to IGP, Crime & Railways, Dy DG, NCC J&K and SSP Crime & Railways, Jammu are being carried out in today's edition of the News Paper.

The contents of the very letter revealed the unholy nexus and manipulation tactics of the lower officials who are allegedly involved in various corrupt activities with the Gp Cdr Col K.S. Bajwa. It is very astonishing that an officer of the rank of Colonel is playing into the hands of these unscrupulous elements.

It is pertinent to add here that the said Col. K.S. Bajwa who is also the provincial head of NCC has not taken the contents of the stories published in this Newspaper seriously. On the contrary without verifying the hard facts seriously and also authenticating the information and taking serious action against officials involved in his office, the said Col. started rating of the News Paper which had dared to expose corruption in the office headed by him. From the contents of the letter it appears that the said officer has forgotten his duties towards the office where he is supposed to work in an efficient manner rather it appears that he has been tasked by the government to give rating to the News Papers being published in the state which is highly objectionable and uncalled for.

If NCC Gp HQ is clean for all the reports and is sure that nothing unusual of the sort took place then why Col. Kuljit Singh Bajwa is writing to various investigative authorities to safeguard the interest of the few black sheep in the department.

A senior officer from NCC, GP HQ, Jammu on the condition of anonimity told the 'The Latest' that Col. Bajwa is himself facing a court of enquiry at BRO, TamilNadu from where he had been transferred to this HQ.

'The Latest' Newspaper is not against anybody and therefore, there is no question of casting any slur on the leadership of the army officers.

It is high time that senior officers at the helm of affairs should take the matter seriously and render all possible co-operation to the state Crime Branch in order to get the black-sheep trapped and clear the image of the working of the office in the eyes of public.

BEFORE THE HON'BLE HIGH COURT OF JAMMU AND KASHMIR AT JAMMU.

Naresh Dutt Sharma

Vs

State of J&K and Ors.

000011

BREIF FACTS

The petitioner is a Photo Journalist & Social activist and is also associated with NGO Manav Ekta Sangathan. The petitioner was shocked to read the item in the Newspaper 'THE LATEST' which carried the story of illegal appointment of one Shri Des Raj on the basis of forged and fictitious certificates. The story has been published in the Newspaper 'THE LATEST' in its issue-dated 04.09.2006. Petitioner went to Respondent No: 2 and lodged a complaint and apprised him of the malpractice going in the NCC. Though the Respondent No: 2 started preliminary inquiry, but the Respondent No: 3 instead of co-operating with the investigating agency, openly said that the enquiry be stopped and he will not furnish any document for investigation. Petitioner again approached to the officers of the Crime Branch, but no action upto this time has been taken, then the petitioner served the legal notice also. The action of the Respondent No: 2 for not conducting any investigation against the accused persons is against law, particularly when the Respondent No: 2 has been apprised of the offence committed by them, in the NCC Directorate. Hence the present writ petition

Dated: 6/3/ 2007.
Place: Jammu.

Petitioners
Through Counsel

(NITIN BHASIN)
ADVOCATE.

HIGH COURT OF JAMMU AND KASHMIR
AT JAMMU

OWP No. 182/2007, MP No. 279/2007.

Date of order: 21.11.2017

Naresh Dutt Sharma
Vs
State of J&K and others

000009

Coram:

Hon'ble Mr. Justice Sanjay Kumar Gupta, Judge

Appearance:

For the petitioner (s) : None.
For the respondent(s) : Mr. W. S. Nargal, Sr. AAG.

The matter pertains to the year 2007. No application has been filed by the petitioner for listing of this case. Even today, one appeared on behalf of the petitioner, which shows that the petitioner has lost interest in prosecuting the instant writ petition. Accordingly, the writ petition is **dismissed** for non-prosecution along with connected MP.

Interim direction, if any, shall also stand vacated.

(Sanjay Kumar Gupta)
Judge

Jammu
21.11.2017
(Muneesh)

CHAPTER – 5

On May 12, 2008, when the High Court judgement was ruled in my favor, a gathering took place at the officers' mess of NCC Group Headquarters Jammu. This assembly included all the officers including Colonel JS Salathia, who was a local officer.Some lawyers had been consulted to strategize how to counter my efforts. Ultimately, they decided that I would not be granted a promotion. Around that time, the 2nd Jammu Kashmir Boys Battalion's Training Camp was also in progress, with JS Salathia serving as its camp commandant. He openly expressed his intent in the camp to discredit me, even suggesting that he could manipulate the outcome of an army board to change my status from living to deceased or vice versa.

I becamc aware of this through a close friend in the Camp and was advised to be more cautious in future. Given my ongoing stance against corruption, I saw this as another opportunity to stand firm. These officers were resolute in denying me a promotion.So they devised a scheme. They decided to form their own board, conduct a test and interview, and later produce a report stating that I had failed to pass the promotion examination. My written exam had already been completed, followed by a computer typing test. After completing both papers, I proceeded to attend the interview where three officers were present including Colonel Salathia. It seemed that Colonel Saladhia was somewhat uneasy in my presence, which could explain why he refrained from questioning me. However, the other officers asked me various questions, to which I replied accurate answers.

All of them were aware of my anti-corruption stance, and they had already decided to withhold my promotion. After the interview concluded, I candidly informed Colonel Malook Singh who was among those present that I was not concerned about securing a government job or coveting a promotion. I further conveyed my determination to expose the corruption allegations against him in the media. In addition to my prior work and book on corruption, I also shared interviews with prominent IAS/IPS officers to illustrate my commitment to this cause.

Observing these developments, the anxiety among these officers intensified, and they began pondering ways to prevent me from contributing to the media. To achieve this, they issued an order from Group Headquarters Jammu stating that disciplinary action would be taken against any employee who was found engaged in private employment. While this directive was ostensibly aimed at me, our office promptly responded, asserting that no employee aside from their official duties shall pursue any private work. Subsequently, I submitted an RTI request to ascertain if any such actions had been taken against individuals like Susheel Kumar, Ramesh Chandra, Ved Prakash, Bal Krishna, Sangram Singh, YN Sahni, Sham Lal, RR Sharma, and Rajmal Sharma, who in addition to their government positions,were also engaged in private work, such as private accounting or typing services for a lawyer.

Upon receiving my RTI request,the Group Commander,Colonel Malook Singh visibly grew uneasy. Nevertheless, other officers encouraged the notion that not only should my promotion be halted, but also that I should face disciplinary action for my media contributions that could lead to my suspension.

However, as I mentioned earlier, I held no attachment to my job and faced no financial constraints. By the grace of God, I was content with my life. My sole objective was to expose corruption and unveil how officers in NCC were engaging in fraudulent activities while wearing their uniforms.

During that era, NCC was engulfed in corruption from Jammu and Kashmir to Delhi. The officers found themselves in a dilemma regarding how to thwart my promotion. Nevertheless, I remained resolute in my fight against corruption. Going a step further, I ensured to affiliate myself with institutions such as CAG and CBI, and established contact with national media outlets. Approximately two months later, the promotion orders were released, and just as these officers had anticipated, my name was conspicuously absent from the promotion list. This marked a direct confrontation leading me to once again initiate legal proceedings against this decision.

During that period, a massive scam worth crores had unfolded within the NCC Directorate. I was determined to expose it. In the magazine for which I served as the editor, the author's photo was featured alongside their articles. Deliberately, I sent copies of one such magazine, in which my photo was prominently displayed, to these officers. My plan unfolded just as I had envisioned. Colonel Malook Singh believed that he had an opportunity to prove my involvement with the private media and, based on this, he could secure my suspension,unaware of my strategy. Eventually, he penned a letter to the Officer Commanding, informing him that I held the role of a magazine editor.

When our Officer Commanding, Lieutenant Colonel Krishna Yadav contacted me and required an explanation, I clarified that I did not receive any salary from the magazine. In response, he asked me to obtain a written statement from the magazine's owner affirming that I did not receive any compensation and that I was engaged in writing solely for skill improvement as a matter of my interest. That very evening, I secured a written certificate from the magazine owner stating that I did not receive any remuneration and that my writing endeavors were solely for self-improvement. I provided this certificate along with a comprehensive letter to the Officer Commanding, who appended it with the covering letter and sent it to his superiors.

Meanwhile, Colonel Malook Singh and Lieutenant Colonel Sukhbir Singh began posing unnecessary questions and harassing the magazine's owner without careful consideration. They even resorted to threats of potential legal action against him.

I had been anticipating this moment when these officers would engage in a direct confrontation with the media. Upon reading the letter sent by Lieutenant Colonel Sukhbir Singh, the magazine's editor-in-chief was incensed. He urged me to openly write against Colonel Sukhbir so that he could be taught a lesson. Simultaneously, we reached out to the Deputy Director of the NCC Directorate, Brigadier Anil Gupta, seeking clarification regarding the authority under which he had written that letter to the magazine. In response, he assured us that he would inquire into the matter and provide us with an explanation. However, after three days had elapsed, we did not receive any response.

The magazine then filed an RTI request, seeking information about all the bills approved by the NCC Directorate, including copies of those vouchers. Upon seeing this RTI request, Brigadier Anil Gupta contacted the magazine's chief editor and requested the withdrawal of the RTI in exchange for apologies from Colonel Malook Singh and Lieutenant Colonel Sukhbir Singh. Subsequently, the chief editor of the magazine received apologies from these two officers, the contents of which will be further elaborated for the readers' reference.

This incident occurred in the month of June 2010, and in the following month,the owner of the magazine entrusted me with all the responsibilities as he himself went abroad to be with his children. During this period, Colonel Malook Singh began avoiding any interaction with me. At the same time, other officers who had faced mistreatment from Colonel Malook Singh and Brigadier Anil Gupta joined my cause. Consequently, these officers who supported me began providing evidence.

One of these officers, Lieutenant Colonel K Battacharya, who held the role of a training officer, would visit my magazine's office and assist in preparing RTIs. I, in turn, composed RTIs aimed at Brigadier Anil Gupta. Each day saw the submission of a new RTI against Colonel Malook Singh and Lieutenant Colonel Sukhbir Singh, which left these officers baffled. They were puzzled as to how I was obtaining information about their wrongdoings. Fearing exposure, Colonel Malook Singh would frequently hold meetings in his office and at the officer's mess.

As someone wisely stated, only those with narrow-minded thinking engage in unethical actions. A displaced woman who had been working as a clerk at NCC Group Headquarters was transferred to NCC in Sainik School, Nagrota. She lacked proficiency in her duties and frequently had unauthorized absence. She had been with our office for only about 70 days, during which she was absent for 56 days. To compensate for her absence, I had to shoulder the additional workload. Consequently, our officer commanding, Lieutenant Colonel Krishna Yadav instructed the woman to work under my supervision.

The woman knew that she could not be transferred back to Jammu before completing her two-year tenure. Seeking advice from two other clerks, Ashok Chopra and Amar Kumar, she plotted a way to secure her transfer back to Jammu. Illustrating the poor judgment, one of the clerks advised her to falsely accuse me of harassment in the office as it would potentially lead to her transfer and also I would be in thick soup as well.

Following this advice, the woman went to the group headquarters and made a false complaint against me to Colonel Malook and Lieutenant Colonel Sukhbir. These two officers had been eagerly waiting for someone to lodge a complaint against me that could provide them with an opportunity to take action against me. As the woman had desired, she was indeed transferred back to Jammu and an inquiry was initiated against me. However, none of my colleagues in the office had any knowledge of this incident. Since the woman had not submitted her complaint in writing, the Group Headquarters instructed a female officer, Lieutenant Yasha Moudgil, who was associated with the 2nd Jammu and Kashmir Girls Battalion, to obtain a written complaint from the woman. Additionally, the three clerks - Amar Kumar, Ayaz Ahmed, and Ashok Chopra - were also asked to provide written statements. Realizing that they were being implicated in a false complaint, these clerks refused to testify falsely. Furthermore, the woman declined to submit a written complaint because she had already achieved her goal of getting transferred to Jammu.

The following day, when the woman returned to Nagrota,the news of her actions quickly spread throughout the area. When Officer Commanding Krishna Yadav inquired about this scenerio, the woman placed the blame squarely on Colonel Malook Singh and Lieutenant Colonel Sukhbir Singh. She divulged all the details, explaining how she had been coerced into making false allegations against me in an attempt to stifle the anti-corruption campaign I had initiated.

In all my years, I have never encountered an officer as troublesome as Lieutenant Colonel Sukhbir Singh. Despite facing humiliation repeatedly, this individual persisted in trying to discredit me. At our Nagrota base, there was a Subedar named Antar Singh. When Subedar Antar Singh went for a review with the ACR Group Commander and Colonel Sukhbir sought information about my weaknesses from him. In response, Subedar Antar Singh candidly told him that I was an honest person. When they couldn't find any grounds to take action against me from him, they subjected Subedar Antar Singh to numerous office visits. Subedar Antar Singh personally informed me of the turn of events that was unfolding..

Meanwhile, Brigadier Anil Gupta retired from the active service, and a new Deputy Director-General took over. During this time, Lieutenant Colonel Battacharya and I met CBI SSP MK Bhatt and handed over all the evidence of corruption within the NCC to him. Our aim was to prompt an investigation into the NCC Directorate in Jammu and Kashmir. For this purpose, Inspector SS Sodhi was appointed as the investigating officer and accordingly he sought records from the NCC to initiate the investigation. This investigation continued for two months. But despite these efforts, no FIR (First Information Report) was filed.

On another note, I published the entire story in the magazine. Once the magazine reached the general public, the editor of Dainik Bhaskar contacted me, requesting evidence to corroborate the news so that they could also publish it. Given the significant nature of the news, Dainik Bhaskar featured the fraud on its front page, making it a national headline. This widespread coverage led to the news spreading across the entire country, and JK channel also aired the story on its channel. With the news garnering such widespread attention, the NCC Directorate J&K faced criticism and embarrassment from all directions.

Subsequently, I gathered copies of the news articles published in magazines and newspapers, attached these with an application, and promptly forwarded a detailed account to the Union Defense Ministry. The CAG then relayed this information to the CBI and other relevant departments. As a result of these actions, Colonel Malook Singh was relocated to Bareilly (UP), Colonel Sukhbir was transferred to Haryana,

Colonel Devkaran was reassigned to Station Headquarters, and Colonel Victor found himself in Maharashtra. While this entire matter was subject to investigation, as it had occurred previously, high-ranking officials shielded these corrupt officers from facing significant repercussions.

With the arrival of the new Group Commander, Colonel A S Chandhok at the NCC Group Headquarters, the team began to take shape. Lieutenant Colonel K Battacharya and Lieutenant Colonel Jaweed Mir, who were already performing commendable work, were part of this cohesive unit. Overall, a competent team had assembled that was delivering commendable results with transparency.

Three months later, NCC Group Headquarters in Jammu conducted a DPC (Departmental Promotion Committee) in which 15 employees participated. On Lieutenant Colonel Jaweed Mir's insistence, I also took the test. And through diligent effort, I achieved the highest score. Since there was only one available promotion slot, and I had secured the top position, I was duly promoted,much against the wishes of few. Although there were still some clerks in the office who were not in favor of my promotion, they found themselves powerless in the face of Colonel Jaweed Mir's professional conduct.

I had served at NCC in Sainik School Nagrota for duration of 11 years, and I was due for my transfer. Although my next assignment was supposed to be in Jammu, no one from Jammu was willing to serve in Nagrota. Our Officer Commanding, Col MP Singh, was reluctant to see me go because he was highly satisfied with my work, and I too didn't wish to leave after dedicating so many years to this institution. However, the final decision regarding the transfer lay with the Group Headquarters. Fortunately, luck was on my side once again. Group Commander Colonel Chandhok presented me with the choice of transfer to Jammu or continue in Nagrota. When I opted to stay in Nagrota, he readily approved my decision. The displaced woman was subsequently transferred to Jammu, and I assumed responsibility for the office here.

At this point, Sainik School Nagrota boasted an exceptionally honest and dedicated team of the Principal, Group Captain Ajay Kumar, Vice Principal Lieutenant Colonel MP Singh, and Registrar Wing Commander Domenic Rathan, which improved the work atmosphere.

Everything was progressing smoothly. I efficiently managed office tasks, and continued my role as a magazine editor. However, due to my promotion, some senior officers manipulated the ACR (Annual Confidential Report) of Colonel Javed Mir. The reason for this was evident: I had previously exposed all the corrupt officers who had been present in the region. A few days later, Lieutenant Colonel Sukhbir Singh visited Jammu from Haryana during his leave. I unexpectedly ran into him while shopping at the NCC canteen. During our conversation, I mentioned my recent promotion, and the expression on his face was quite strange. I didn't engage in an extended conversation with him, but upon returning inside, he remarked to Colonel Javed Mir that today a Lieutenant General had bowed down before an ordinary man because of him.

While things appeared to be running smoothly within the Jammu and Kashmir NCC, a nationwide audit by the CAG was underway, scrutinizing NCC records from 2008 to 2010. This investigation revealed a scam amounting to Rs. 20 crore, primarily related to mosquito nets. The moment this scam was exposed in the media, chaos ensued across the board. It marked the first instance in history when NCC underwent an audit by the CAG, and all of this had been triggered by a complaint from an ordinary individual like me. Consequently, corrupt officers spanning from Jammu and Kashmir to Delhi, had turned against me.

In 2013 upon assuming office from the female employee, I discovered several glaring deficiencies. Cash books had gone unattended for numerous years. Cadet certificate papers had not been prepared, and the ACR of ANOs (Associate NCC Officer) remained un-updated for a staggering 15 years. Moreover, the lady clerk was unfamiliar with regimental funds as to how to manage the unit's share. One of the most significant issues I uncovered was that from 1999 until that point in 2013, there had been an annual shortage of arms and ammunition but no inspection had been carried out. Prior clerks had shown no regard for this matter, and even the Officer Commanding remained unaware. The responsibility for conducting annual inspections rested with the EME (Electrical and Mechanical Engineers), but the Group Commander had consistently overlooked this requirement, making annual visits in the name of inspection, partaking in tea and breakfast, and then departing. Within 15 days of taking charge, I rectified all recordkeeping deficiencies. Observing the improvement in the office's efficiency under my supervision, ANO BBR Chhibber initiated the preparation of A certificate papers from the same year. However, non-conduct of annual arms and ammunition inspection was a grave concern, as we possessed 8 rifles and 1500 bullets, none of which had undergone annual scrutiny for years. I was convinced that if I didn't address these shortcomings, it could lead to future troubles, including potential job loss. Consequently, I drafted a letter on this matter and submitted it to the Officer Commanding, who subsequently informed the NCC Group Headquarters. It was communicated that an annual arms and ammunition inspection must be carried out without further delay. Simultaneously, an inquiry was to be initiated from the Army Headquarters to determine why these weapons had gone uninspected for so long and who bore responsibility for this lapse.

This development alarmed our Officer Commanding, but I assured him that I would scrutinize the past records to identify the source of this problem, fearing that my job might be at risk if I didn't act. Within two days, I discovered that it was the Group Headquarters Jammu that was to blame. Over the past 15 years, JD(i) Coy NCC, SSN had never been included in the inspection list, and each year the clerks at the Group Headquarters simply filled out the previous year's inspection report. Astonishingly, none of the Group Headquarters officers had ever paid any attention to this discrepancy. Nevertheless, our Officer Commanding found some relief, and I was content knowing that the Group Headquarters would be implicated in the upcoming inquiry by the Army Headquarters, that will force them to find a resolution. Additionally, we recovered seven thousand rupees that had been held by the lady clerk and deposited it into the regimental fund account. With all the files in order, office work began to progress smoothly and in the right direction.

Our Officer Commanding at NCC, Lieutenant Colonel MP Singh, was due for promotion. During the same year my son was born, bringing joy to our household. Previously, I had access to a press office car with a driver from their side, but due to my daughter's insistence, I had purchased a new car of my own. Nevertheless, the driver remained from the press. Babu Ram Laskar had recently joined our office, and within six months, I had trained him in all the clerical tasks. Now, Babu Ram handled all the office responsibilities, while I sat in the staff room and oversaw the entire workflow from there.

During that period, the Centres for the annual exams of class 12th were set up within the Sainik School premises. This allowed the school's teachers to facilitate cheating among students to help them achieve high marks in their subjects, while the Principal turned a blind eye to this practice. In response, I tried to establish examination Centres for the students outside the school.

My next initiative was to have the entrance exams for classes 6th and 9th at Sainik School conducted by the National Testing Agency (NTA). This decision stemmed from the widespread confusion regarding student admissions to Sainik Schools across India. Teachers were extorting significant sums of money from students under the guise of admissions. These same teachers put in less effort and engaged in sycophancy towards officers to secure the President's Award. This was the driving force behind my decision to remain in my role even after completing 20 years of service. I believed that if I could eradicate corruption and irregularities in NCC and Sainik Schools, it would represent the most significant achievement of my journalism career. Although I had already exposed numerous corrupt officers and clerks, resulting in many of them facing consequences, the challenge of reforming the system remained a daunting task I was determined to tackle.

At NCC Group Headquarters Jammu, before departing, Colonel Malook had canceled the fourth category selection list out of fear. Now, only eligible candidates were employed, but many of them still secured employment based on the recommendations of BL Raina, the administrative officer in the NCC Directorate. Raina had accepted Rs 1.5 lakh in exchange for helping someone secure a job.

HIGH COURT OF JAMMU AND KASHMIR AT JAMMU.

Present : Hon'ble Mr. Justice Sunil Hali - Judge

SWP No. 220/2001.

The Seal of The High Court J&K Jammu

Ram Gopal Sharma, age 37 years
S/o Shri Mangat Ram Sharma
R/o 254 Sector-G Sainik Colony
Jammu

CANCELLED

................Petitioner

V/s

1. State of J&K
   Through its Chief Secretary,
   Govt of Jammu & Kashmir
   Civil Sectt, Jammu.

2. The Commissioner/Secretary
   General Administration Department
   J&K Govt, Civil Secretariat
   Jammu.

3. The Commissioner/Secretary
   Education Department,
   J&K Govt, Civil Secretariat
   Jammu.

4. Union of India
   Through Secretary,
   Ministry of Defence,
   South Block
   New Delhi-110001

5. Deputy Director General,
   NCC-Dte Camp Office
   Near Indira Theatre, Jammu.

Respondents no. 1 & 3 stands deleted vide Hon'ble Court order dt. 24.8.

True Copy Attested

Asstt. Registrar
High Court of J&K
JAMMU.

(2)

(2)

6. Lt Col V K Khullar,
Adm Officer
NCC Group Headquarter
A/D Gandhi Nagar, Jammu

7. Lt Col PK Yadav,
Training Officer,
NCC Group Headquarters
82 A/D Gandhi Nagar,
Jammu.

8. Shri Shiv Ram
2nd J&K Bn NCC
Shastri Nagar, Jammu

9. Shri Shashi Chargotra
NCC Group Headquarter
82 A/D Gandhi Nagar, Jammu.

……………Respondents

True Copy Attested

Asstt. Registrar
High Court of J&K
JAMMU.

4/9

(3)

SWP No. 220/2001 Date of Order: 12.5.2009

Ram Gopal Sharma Vs. State & Ors.

Mr. B.S. Salathia, Advocate for petitioner.
Mr. P.S. Chandel, Advocate for respondents.

Petitioner has questioned the appointments of respondent Nos. 8 & 9 as Junior Assistants in the NCC. His grievance is that he has better merit than respondent Nos. 8 & 9 but despite that he was not considered.

On the other hand, respondents state that the petitioner could not make the grade, as a result of which he was not promoted. It is specifically stated in the reply that the petitioner was called for the written as well as typing test but could not meet the standards laid down by the DPC. The consequence of this was the petitioner was placed under consideration for a period of five months time so that he could improve his skills.

I have heard learned counsel for the parties and perused the record.

The petitioner is still working in a lower category and no decision has been taken by the respondents to promote him as Junior Assistant. The decision of the respondents to place the petitioner under consideration for a period of five months was with the intent that he could improve his skills to be fit for the post.

True Copy Attested

Asstt. Registrar
High Court of J&K
JAMMU.

(4)

The respondents have not rejected claim of the petitioner as yet, but have given him time to improve his skills to suit for the said post.

In these circumstances, I deem it proper to direct the respondents to evaluate the merit of the petitioner. After evaluation, if the petitioner is found suitable he shall be given promotion from that the date the period of five months had elapsed. This exercise shall be completed by the respondents within a period of three months from the date a copy of this order is received by them. In such a situation the petitioner shall also be allowed to all consequential benefits.

Disposed of alongwith connected CMP(s).

Jammu
12.5.2009
Ajit

Sd/- Hon'ble
(SUNIL HALI)
Judge

Registration No. 12024
Date of Application for the Copy 24/8/18
Name of the ... Mr. Raghu ...
the Charges ... Extra Fee for
Urgency 10/-
Date on which the Copy was Ready for
Delivery 4/9/18
Date of ... the copy to the
Applicant 4/9/18
Stamp ... 10/-
Name of the ...
... of Copy ...
Compared by Ganesh

Certified to be True Copy
... Officer
4/9/2018
High Court of Jammu & Kashmir
Dated ... 4/9/18
Authorised By Section 76 ...
Evidence Act
4/9/18

BY HAND

Civ Tele-2430239

NCC Group Headquarters,
82 A/D Gandhi Nagar,
Jammu.

No. 001/A/NCC-

1[illegible] May 2010

Sh. Santokh Singh,
Editor,Printer,Publisher & Owner,
"Street Voice"
English Newsmagazine,
Editorial and Administrative Office,
Sainik Colony, Jammu Tawi.

PRIVATE EMPLOYMENT BY GOVT EMPLOYEE

1. Reference your letter No. SV/Misc/X/2010 dated 28th Jan 2010 addressed to JD Indep Coy NCC, Sainik School, Nagrota under which a certificate No. SV/Misc/X/2010 dated 28th January 2010 has been issued.

2. In your above letter, you have mentioned that Sh. Ram Gopal Sharma, a State Govt. full time employee with NCC Group Jammu, is being imparted training in developing his skills by writing articles for your magazine. You have also mentioned that he is not being paid any remuneration for the above training.

3. In the copy of "Street Voice" magazine published by you, Sh. Ram Gopal Sharma has been clearly shown as "Editor-in-Chief". This office needs to confirm veracity of above issues as it involves discipline and conduct related issues of a serving Govt. employee. Before we approach police and other State Govt. authorities we seek your co-operation in obtaining following information about "Street Voice Magazine" and your organization:-

(a) Details of training, similar to the one being provided by you to Sh. Ram Gopal Sharma, to other persons, by your organization.

(b) Authority which has entitled/authorised you to conduct such training especially for Govt. employee.

(c) Details of registration of your "Street Voice" whose editor-in-charge is said to be Sh. Ram Gopal Sharma, a serving Govt. employee, working with NCC Group Jammu.

(d) Exact details of training so far imparted to Sh. Ram Gopal Sharma and his performance .on the same.

(e) Details of office bearers of your organization and policy regarding imparting of training to State Govt. employees.

(f) Details of clarifications issued, if any, through the said magazine or other newspapers regarding the exact and specific appointment and duties or status of Sh. Ram Gopal Sharma, the said Editor-in-Chief of "Street Voice" magazine.

4. Your kind co-operation is sincerely solicited on the above issues. We would be grateful if your reply is forwarded to us within 15 days of receipt of this letter.

(Sukhvir Singh)
Lt Col
Adm Officer
For Gp Cdr

Copy to:-

JD Indep Coy NCC SS, Nagrota :

1. Ref your letter No. 004/A/NCC dt 22 Apr 2010
2. You are requested to forward details of permission given, if any, to Sh. Ram Gopal Sharma to undergo training at "StreetVoice" News magazine published from Sainik Colony, Jammu
3. Your reply is requeted by 30 May 2010.

STREET VOICE

ENGLISH NEWSMAGAZINE

Editorial and Administrative Office :
Sainik Colony, Jammu Tawi (J&K)
INDIA - 180 011
Ph : 0191-2468943, 2468060(Resi.)
Fax : 91 - 0191 - 2468943
Cell: 94191-16366, 97960-36203
email: streetvoicejk@yahoo.com

No.: SV/2010/
Dated: 14 May, 2010

To

The Controller of Defence (Accounts)
Narwal Pane, Satwari,
Jammu

Subject: Requisition of Information under Right to Information Act about the National Cadets Crops (NCC) Directorate, J&K and units under its commands for the year 2008-10.

Sir,

The following information is required under RTI Act in respect of NCC Directorate J&K, Jammu. It is requested that the information may kindly be furnished to the undersigned at the earliest..

1. CTC copy of Vouchers of MT repairing, CHT, Motor Vehicle Maintenance and Fuel.
2. Details of Transport Allowance claimed by the Officers.
3. CTC copy of bills of Information Technology funds.
4. CTC copy of the vouchers of Generator repairing.
5. CTC copy of vouchers of Clothing purchased from a Lucknow based firm.
6. CTC copy of vouchers of Office expenditures and other items.

A Postal order of Rs 20/- as required is enclosed herewith.

If I am denied the information about the matter related to seeking information regarding the above stated points, I shall have the right to apply for action for delay/ lapse on your part, overtly/ covertly. to shield the department.

Thanking you.

Yours faithfully,

14/5

(SANTOKH SINGH)
Editor, Printer & Publisher

Confidential
No.SC/III/2385/LNR/10-11
O/ o the PCDA (NC)
Narwal pain, Satwari
Jammu
Dated: 21-05-2010

To,

NCC Directorate J&K
Canal Road
Jammu-180001

Subject:- **Requisition of Information under Right to Information Act.**

An application dated14-05-2010, from Sh.Santokh Singh, Editor, Printer and Publisher "Street Voice" Sainic Colony, Jammu, received in this office for seeking information under RTI Act,2005, is forwarded herewith in terms of Para 6(3)(ii) of the Act, as the matter is closely related with your Directorate. You are therefore advised to furnish the desired information / CTCs of the documents to the applicant immediately within the stipulated time under intimation to this office, for the records are held in your Directorate in terms of Rule 42 of FR Pt-II.

The Indian Postal Order bearing no. 81F 428384 for Rs 20/- has been retained in this office for further necessary action.

Please acknowledge receipt.

Encl: As above.

Kartar Ram,IDAS
Asstt CDA

S

Copy to:-

Sh.Santokh Singh
Editor, Printer and Publisher "Street Voice"
Sainic Colony, Jammu-180011

Civ Tele-2430239

NCC Group Headquarters,
82 A/D Gandhi Nagar,
Jammu.

No. 001/A/NCC-117

21 May 2010

Sh. Santokh Singh,
Editor,Printer,Publisher & Owner,
"Street Voice"
English Newsmagazine,
Editorial and Administrative Office,
Sainik Colony, Jammu Tawi.

PRIVATE EMPLOYMENT BY GOVT EMPLOYEE

1. The case mentioned in our letter No. 001/A/NCC-111 dated 10 May 2010 is hereby being treated as closed.

(Sukhvir Singh)
Lt Col
Adm Officer
For Group Commander

Copy to:-

JD Indep Coy NCC : For info wet our letter under reference.

NCC Dte J&K : For info please.

To.

The Hon'ble Prime Minister of India
Prime Minister Office
Govt. of India, New Delhi

(Through proper channel)

Sub: **REQUEST FOR INQUIRY AND ACTION AGAINST IRREGULARITIES AND CORRUPTION IN J&K NCC**

1. May I have the honour to bring to your kind notice the rampant malpractices, irregular accounting procedures, deliberate misdeeds of authorities so as to defraud public money by the NCC Directorate J&K and its subordinate offices.

2. I have repeatedly tried to bring to the notice of concerned, the corrupt practices, misuse of official position and power coupled with misuse of govt. property entrusted to their care like vehicles, generator sets and other official equipment. Misuse of army and civil manpower by Dy DG, Gp Cdt and COs. However, none of the concerned authorities seemed to have taken note and initiated action.

3. I am enclosing the clippings of the reports published in "STREET VOICE", a well known magazine and of "DAINIK BHASKAR", the leading newspaper of India. The investigation carried out by media is an eye opener and especially pin-points lapses and corrupt practices along with evidence.

4. I am also enclosing the copies of RTI applications filed by me and copy of legal notice pointing out the contempt of court which the organisation was willing to face to gain time so that they could hide their misdeeds towards reports, returns and records of my RTI application's information which I had asked pertained to only factual data which if they had provided, would have proved their malafide action in misusing govt. money/property including selling of canteen liquor and grocery items, at time also in bulk, to non- entitled civilians and general public by canteen located at 82 A/D Gandhi Nagar Jammu. This clearly shows the implicitly and complicity of all concerned of this organization including the senior officers especially those in command at every level.

5. My efforts to bring out corruption in NCC by approaching the local administration and Military authorities like GOC-IN-C, Northern Command and Commander 71 Sub Area has shaken the DGNCC office Delhi and a new policy that all such matter should be dealt itself by NCC Dte has been initiated. But it may not be out of place to mention that DGNCC, Lt General RK Karwal visited J&K Dte in the month of October 2010 on govt. expenses just to visit Vaishno Devi along with his wife and did not visit or inspected any office other than perfectionarily the J&K Dte office for 30-40 minutes. The entire state money and machinery was used to visit Jammu and Kashmir Dte. You may check from PCDA whether the officer claimed TA/DA, though he was provided free accommodation, transportation, boarding and lodging.

6. I have also brought to the notice of Hon'ble Defence Minister of India vide my application dated 10 Feb 2011 (copy attached). But nothing has been done so far.

7. The money allocated for the welfare of cadets is siphoned off by these officers who enjoy the patronage of NCC Dte Delhi.

Contd......2

BY HAND

Civ Tele-2430239

NCC Group Headquarters,
82 A/D Gandhi Nagar,
Jammu.

No. 001/A/NCC- 127

14 Jun 2010

Sh. Santokh Singh,
Editor,Printer,Publisher & Owner,
"Street Voice"
English Newsmagazine,
Editorial and Administrative Office,
Sainik Colony, Jammu Tawi.

PRIVATE EMPLOYMENT BY GOVT EMPLOYEE

1. Our letter No. 001/A/NCC-111 dated 10 May 2010 is hereby being treated as cancelled.

(G Victor)
Lt Col
Offg: Adm Officer
For Group Commander

was used to visit Jammu and Kashmir Dte. You may check from CDA whether the officer claimed TA/DA, though he was provided free accommodation, transportation, boarding and lodging.

6. Sir, what will be position of this organization if such types of officers are posted who are otherwise expected to impart training to our cadets - the future of our country.

7. Keeping in view the above mentioned facts with evidence, your good-self is requested to order an inquiry and bring the guilty to the book as the essential witnesses are either getting retired or transferred from this place.

Thanking you,

Yours faithfully,

RGSharma.

(Ram Gopal Sharma)
Laskar
JD(I) Coy NCC
Sainik School Nagrota
Jammu (J&K)
Mobile No. 94191-57741

Dated. 10.2.2011

Enclosure: - 19 pages duly numbered and signed

Advance Copy to: -

1. Hon'ble Defence Minister of India
2. Defence Secretary
3. Adj. Gen Discipline and Vigilance Wing, Army HQ, New Delhi
4. Chief of Army Staff

Copy to: -

1.	CVC	-	For needful inquiry
2.	CAG	-	For Test Audit for all purchases made by NCC Dte J&K (pl refer to as brought out by RTI applications)
3.	CDA/PCDA Northern Command	-	To confirm TA/DA claimed by Lt Gen RK Karwal during his visit to J&K during 22 Oct to 24 Oct 2010 and officers of J&K during camps.
4.	LAO/CDA	-	For comments on the evidence appeared in Magazine Street Voice clipping.
5.	Chief Minister-J&K		With the request to direct State Vigilance to initiate inquiry about the so-called Auditorium purportedly constructed at the cost of Rs. 4 crore.

BY HAND

Civ Tele-2430239

NCC Group Headquarters,
82 A/D Gandhi Nagar,
Jammu.

No. 001/A/NCC-

25 Jun 2010

Sh. Santokh Singh,
Editor,Printer,Publisher & Owrr,
"Street Voice"
English Newsmagazine,
Editorial and Administrative Oice,
Sainik Colony, Jammu Tawi.

PRIVATE EMPLOYMNT BY GOVT EMPLOYEE

Our letter No. 001/A/NC-111 dated 10 May 2010 is hereby withdrawn.

(G Victor)
Lt Col
Offg: Adm Officer
For Group Commander

SPECIAL REPORT

TAINT AT THE TOP IN J&K NCC, CBI SUMMONS THE RECORD

With scams rocking our country like earthquakes every now and then , STREET VOICE in keeping with its reputation as a pioneer of investigative journalism, decided to carry out some investigation as to how safe our future generation are in the hands of persons they spend a lot of time with, at schools, colleges etc , every second day we read in the newspapers about the national cadet corps or NCC as they are popularly called in short, though the photographs and published matter tell us a lot of what the DDG of NCC does or did, something struck us that we must look into this organization primarily staffed by armed forces officers, we were sure that we would be able to bring out that 'yes' this should be the role model, and so we set out ,speaking to cadets, staff and people to know ,checking out facilities created, equipment, conduct of the officers staff from the armed forces and others, and as we progressed instead of the feeling of greatness and pride that we should be getting , we found that all is not what appears on the surface, and so we thought and planned to delve deep in the case and what we found was shocking. So where all are the scams.......

CLOTHING SCAM

As we went in for investigation we noticed that nearly 60-70% of the cadets were not wearing their full uniform. In most of the cases we saw that the shoe was missing, other items of uniform too were not worn. Asking the cadets we were shocked to learn that most o[f] the cadets don't get thei[r] uniform and generally only one set of khaki trouser o[r]

Ctv Tele: 01965-220274

1 J&K Arty Bty NCC
PIN: 934881
C/O HQ 93 Inf Bde
C/O 56 APO

0003/BV/NCC

13 Aug 2010

Office of the ALAO 25 Inf Div
C/O 56 APO

FORWARDING OF SUPPLEMENTARY OBJECTION STATEMENT FOR THE PERIOD FROM 04/09 TO 03/10

1. Please refer to your letter No.L/Raj/Obj Statt/04/09 to 03/10/NCC Pnch dated 30 Jul 2010.

2. It is intimated that as per the records the stores mentioned in the subject voucher have not been received by this unit or collected by the rep of this unit. The voucher is neither authenticated by any official of this unit nor signed for the collection of the same by any rep of this unit.

3. In view of the above you are requested to verify about the cosignee from the cosigner and drop the objection against this unit.

(Arun Kumar)
Lt Col
Officer Commanding

Copy to :-

- It is requested that the necessary consignee unit may be checked and accordingly be corrected at your end.
- For info please along with copy of the Voucher.

Photocopy of ARTY BTY Poonch letter to audit authority and the questionable voucher. Please note that the vouchers has official stamp and seal of Col. Deva Karan and his signature too.

STREET VOICE 41 OCTOBER, 2010

To be completed by the Issuing officer

Issue voucher No : IV/c.2-/SHDC/NCC/
Dated : 03 Feb 2009
Unit : NCC Directorate J&K
Station : Jammu

To be completed by the Receiving officer

RV No :
Dated :
Unit : 1 J&K Arty Bty NCC
Station : Poonch

The articles enumerated blow have been (a) issued to received by/ manufactured by(b) .... in (a) part/full in compliance with (c) ....

Auth :

The articles enumerated below hve been expended under the authority of ©

S.No	Name of the item	Qty	Ledger page
(a)	Shirt PWPC Khaki (S11-50, S9-50, S5-100)	200 Nos	
(b)	Short PWPC Khaki (S6-10, S9-30, S4-40, S5-20, S8-100)	200 Nos	
(c)	Socks NTP Black (S27-100, S29-100, S20-100)	300 Prs	
(d)	Hackle Red	2000 Nos	
(e)	Bag Kit Universal	200 Nos	
(f)	Boot DMS	200 Prs	
(g)	Arms Title Army	1000 Prs	
(h)	Trouser PWPC Khaki	200 Nos	
(i)	Belt Waist Web	150 Nos	
(k)	Misc Stores and equipment	06 Box	

(Please sign and return one copy duly receipted)

Certified that the a/m item have been issued alongwith packing material and checked 100% at the time of collection.

ISSUED BY **COLLECTED BY** **RECEIVED BY**

shirt is issued and some other item is issued, what is more shocking was that at times uniform from cadets are taken away to give to other cadets during VIP visits , we enquired and we found that 20(approx) items are authorized to be issued to cadets, consisting broadly of two sets of uniform , belt , black shoes , pt shoe, vest, socks etc, however to date hardly any cadet has been issued his/her complete kit.

We enquired and were made to understand by sources from the directorate office and group headquarter staff at Jammu and Srinagar that though money is released by the DG NCC office at New Delhi, hardly any purchase is made in reality, paper purchases are made, false issue vouchers are made, one such voucher which was obtained by our investigative team is as shown in the picture above .

in this a unit of NCC ,was asked by the local audit authority , to verify stock issued, and the unit informed the local audit authority that these stores were not issued, incidentally the cost of these items is nearly Rs one lakh ,but this is only the tip of the iceberg........., we tried to contact the officer who had signed the issue voucher , however Col Deva Karan, (Ad. Adm) refused to comment, we contacted the Brig Anil Gupta, he raised his voice and told us to mind our own business and that any such interference in army work will get us arrested by the police. In fact this question was raised by an officer, during a training conference at Patnitop this year. Resulting he was also asked to keep silence and allegedly being harassed. More so, as he is the son of the soil and feels for poor cadets of his state.

Any way such threats don't scare us and we dug a little deeper and then we came to know that:

* NCC Directorate Jammu and Kashmir had been allotted Rs 1.3 crores in 2008-09 for purchasing of clothing, by DG NCC, New Delhi and the amount fully spent for purchase of clothing by the office of the Jammu and Kashmir, Directorate Canal Road, Jammu.
* NCC Directorate Jammu and Kashmir had been allotted Rs 1.5 cores in 2009-10 for purchase of clothing by DG NCC, New Delhi and the amount fully spent for purchase of clothing by the office of Jammu and Kashmir Directorate.
* NCC Directorate Jammu and Kashmir has been allotted for this financial year till going to press a sum of Rs. 33 Lakh already, and

(Next page, please)

SPECIAL REPORT

Col. Victor House surrounded by CGI sheets

total enrolment for this eyar not even completed.

Form this we deduced that there was no dearth of funds yet why were our children who we wanted to wear the uniform of the Nation with pride not getting them since all the money alloted was also being spent, after assuring our sources in the Directorate procurement branch and other offices of NCC in the city and Srinagar. We came to know that one officer from one of the unit there was helping the DDG is Col G. Victor, we wanted to talk to him but could not reach him. Some one told us his residential address in Satwari Cantt and our team went to meet him as we neared his house we were shocked the house was surrounded with new iron sheets nearly 200 hundreds of them from all sides, the contractor who supplies to the NCC in Jammu was supervising some labourers and one or two army men on various work being done, we asked a man who appeared to be some sort of supervisor working there whether the MES was repairing or putting up the fence of CGI sheets, he laughed and said that now everything was being done by the contractor as he (the contractor) and some of his other colleagues had been cleared by *saab* for lot of contract worth crores for the next one or two years, as we persisted he also told us th as it is this contractor loo after camps , now he w also supply clothin through his friends and al for RDC ,TSC and m even be given contract f NIC,(all these are speci camps for which hug budgets are allotted eg f TSC Rs 18 lakhs, for RD Republic Day Camp, near Rs 20 Lakhs), suddenly th army man working there sa us , and asked our business we said we wanted to meet Col Victor, he told us " *bha jayo saab yahan nahi hain*", and so we went awa and asked our source in th directorate as to why he ha sent us there as prima faci there appeared to b something wrong ... he sai that had he told us we ma not have believed him so h sent us there , he asked us is i not very strange that a office who has been tasked wit procurement and for othe "works" related(works i army means getting sanctio for construction /repair etc suddenly gets a fence of CG sheet , which even senio officers in Satwari Cantt d not have, he said it wa primarily to ensure that n one saw the contractor visiting his house, w decided to go back and fin out some more, however w saw that the fence had bee created and the officer ha been provided with two

(Next page, please)

SPECIAL REPORT

PRE-FABRICATED SHELTERS

PHASE-1	2 x Girls's Living	Rs. 27, 99,390/-
PHASE-2	- Auditorium - Camp Comdt. Office - Offrs Living - Offrs Mess - 1 x Boy's Living - Dispensary	Rs. 96,74,071/-
PHASE-3	- 3 x Boy's Living Shelter - Parents Waiting Room	Rs. 90,46,567/-
PHASE-4	- SM Living Room - TRG Store - NCO Living - ANO Living - PMT Staff Living - 1x Boy's Living	Rs. 88,59, 498/-
	Total	**Rs. 303,79,556/-**

Photocopy of a presentation given to VIP by Gp Cdr of Jammu group showing break down of shelters note the pricing of two girls shelter in phase,-i and compare with phase-iii,three boys shelter and parents waiting room which is 1/3rd the size is costing more than what 4 girls shelte' will cost ,(2799390x2=5598780/-) size of boys and girls shelter is same in fact girls shelters have privacy partitions and cost slightly more.

army soldiers for working in the house(kitchen and other menial work) and also for protection, by some senior officers who are his friends in some regular army units, in Udhampur, Nagrota and Jammu .We will investigate this angle of misuse of jawans in our subsequent issue, however we did ask why does this officer require protection. The two jawans told us to go away , we did but also took, photographs of the fortified house, we wonder why the senior officers do not question this. Does anyone sincerely believe that any officer will spend nearly Rs 35-40 thousand(nearly 80% of this officer monthly pay) from his own pocket.

A few days back all the newspapers were filled with photographs of DDG of NCC inaugurating a AUDITORIUM !! for NCC at the NCC camping Ground, Nagrota, though most of the photographs showed the DDG only we decide to go to the camping ground to see the AUDITORIUM, we were not allowed to take our cameras inside, but what we saw left us totally shocked, what was being touted as a AUDITORIUM, was a hall made of pre-fabricated structure as is commonly used by the Army for making temporary shelter for troops , very commonly seen in J & K more so in Kashmir valley used by troops of RR , We traced the builders who are working through a local contractor. They are from Hyderabad, Andhra Pradesh, and asper them each such building costs only 7-8 lakhs to make.

Deeper investigations by our team and inputs from our sources in Directorate, Group Head Quarter and Joint Director Planning, State Government revealed that the DDG heavily lobbied to ensure that PWD or any other Govt. Agency (CPWD, MES etc) did not get the contract for building the project by falsely enhancing the cost projection of Govt. Agencies and stating urgency and inability of the NCC to hand over ground for long period and resultantly splitting the entire project so that cost could be brought within his financial powers.

Once this was achieved, the contract was handed over without any issuance of notice for tender or seeking bids at national level but handing over the project arbitrarily Ad. Adm. and other officers to a non supplier of NCC. A very low grade construction of temporary nature is in progressing since 2009with hardly 30% of the project having been completed. Therefore proving his URGENCY, very unurgent cost today is nearly the same what the PWD projected for permanent brick and concrete structure which should have been complete.

* PWD has projected Rs 4 crore approx.
* DDG lobied for his supplier with project cost at 2.5 crore but temporary structure.
* Present status cost of temporary structure stands at 3.3 crores.

You must have a look at this AUDITORIUM, plastic chairs are placed inside, the floor is BAD made of thin cement, no dedicated sound system is available , there is no cooling system, and no exhaust fans , we attended a programme and had to leave midway as we all felt suffocated, and only 250-275 persons can sit there, it is therefore not an auditorium but just a hall of poor quality named as auditorium to hoodwink sanctioning authorities , one must see the auditorium being built by Sainik School, Nagrota just opposite to the camping ground. We also cannot fathom the reason for making temporary structure , where a permanent structure would have been more comfortable for living and cheaper too, these livings etc created cannot be occupied in Summer and rainy season, One cannot stay there during July/August, now who were the officers who were involved. well! The group commanders of J&K GROUPS more of the Jammu group, under whose jurisdiction this falls.

(Next page

STREET VOICE 44 OCTOBER, 2010

SPECIAL REPORT

Misuse of government manpower and vehicles

Well we thought so far the persons involved in all these nefarious activities may not be influencing our children directly , so we decided to look at the other officers and their conduct and look what we found:-

➢ all officers other then two use official vehicles to come to office and **also claim transportation allowance, all officers other than two park their official vehicles at their residence and use them for personal work after office hours.**

➢ Instructors meant for schools and colleges are not sent to any institute instead they work in the houses of the officers, thus our children suffer and do not get NCC training.

➢ Official vehicles are pressed into long tours by the officers for their personal work. In the last week of March, 2010, Col. Malook Singh took his official vehicle to Hoisharpur in Punjab, where the vehicle met with an accident and Havaldar Gar Din who was driving the vehicle got injured and Col. Malook Singh was also injured on the face and he did not attend the office for few days unofficially. Later on the vehicle was repaired by corrupt means. If a vehicle crosses the state to other state it has to get the permission from DG NCC Delhi and that too for official work only. Again Col Malook Singh went to Hoisharpur and vehicle was taken to Pathankot at 4 to 4.30 p.m. in the month of Sept., 2010. But who cares for norms. These officers are enjoying power and glory with impunity.

➢ The numbers of cadets in each camp is reported wrongly by nearly 100-150 cadets and their money for food , petrol and other is misappropriated, only one officer has honestly reported and returned nearly Rs 3 lakhs, so the same amount by others is misused, no sudden check or other form is utilised to keep track by group head quarters

➢ Srinagar group claims full amount as equal to Jammu, however it is a known fact that camps are not run there and specially now for last six months when you cannot even come out of house how can you go to camp and which parent will permit an independent sheck as per our sources reveal the depth of irregularities, each camp costs the state Rs 6 lakh , and only Rs 4 lakh utilised, Rs two lakh made spare by commanding officer of NCC unit , each year there are 16 camps each in Jammu and kashmir divisions

➢ Conferences are held at tourist places and officers go with their wives free of cost and are even provided with bills to claim, where as poor staff members like lascars and drivers were made to pay by Gp. Cdr., Jammu.

➢ Canteen is run openly with all items being sold to civilians otherwise with limited number of serviceman and ex serviceman dependent on them how are they making so much profit, also anyone in Jammu knows that canteen items are easily available at 82 AD Gandhinagar. Army instructors used as sale persons which are against the order of army headquarter.

➢ An amount of **nearly Rs 3 lakh was surrendered by Jammu group** on the last week of march 2009, the same allotted to srinagar group **and completely utilised by Srinagar group in two days, surprising fast work where even a letter takes ten days to reach** surprisingly there were no camps there and you cannot find so much stores to take this suddenly. This amoun was meant for hiring o transport from civil which i known as CHT fund.

Well, this is the beginnin we are yet to decide hov honest are these persons i whom we trust and send ou children to be fair to dat they have not been ill treated, but seeing what th Govt provides surely a lo can be done, a big complain of the cadets is that they d not get any exposure.

A senior staff member o NCC Directorate J&K on th condition of anonymity said the India's Premie Investigative Agency CB (Central Bureau o Investigation) took seriou note of the alleged corrup activities going on in the NCC Directorate J&K with great curiosity as it was in possession of valuable information about the blatant corruption going on in this Directorate for quite some time. After taking cognisance of the serious nature of the case, CBI initiated secret investigation into the matter and after it was felt that there is something fishy was going on in the Directorate, decided to summon the record of misdeads carried out by these officers. Hope Street Voice investigative story would help as a ready reckoner for those who want to eradicate the corruption in this organization. ■

STREET VOICE 45 OCTOBER, 2010

एनसीसी में वर्दी घोटाला

सीबीआई ने रिकार्ड जब्त कर जांच शुरू की

भास्कर न्यूज | जम्मू

नेशनल कैडेट्स कोर (एनसीसी) में वर्दी की खरीद का करोड़ों का घोटाला सामने आया है। सीबीआई ने एनसीसी निदेशालय कार्यालय जाकर पिछले तीन साल की खरीद का रिकार्ड जब्त कर जांच शुरू कर दी है। घोटाले में ब्रिगेडियर रैंक के एक अधिकारी समेत दर्जनों अन्य अधिकारियों के खिलाफ जांच चल रही है। इसमें दिल्ली में बैठे कुछ अधिकारियों के अलावा एनसीसी को सामान की सप्लाई करने वाले ठेकेदार भी शामिल हैं।

जेएंडके एनसीसी निदेशालय ने वर्ष 2008 से लेकर अब तक तीन करोड़ से ज्यादा रुपया कैडेटों की वर्दी खरीदने में खर्च दिखाया है। इतना खर्च होने के बाद भी 60 से 70 प्रतिशत कैडेटों के पास अच्छी वर्दी नहीं है। पिछले तीन सालों से उन्हें पुरानी वर्दी दिया जा रहा है। कैडेट को मिलने वाली किट में दो जोड़ी वर्दी, बेल्ट, बूट, पीटी शू समेत 20 अन्य चीजें शामिल होती है। दस्तावेजों के अनुसार दिल्ली मुख्यालय ने वर्दी की खरीद के लिए निदेशालय को वर्ष 2008-09 के लिए 1.3 करोड रुपये जारी किए थे, जबकि 2009-10 के लिए यह रकम 1.5 करोड रुपये थी। चालू वित्त वर्ष अब तक 33 लाख रुपये जारी हो चुके है। ये रकम सिर्फ वर्दी खरीदने के लिए जारी हुए है। अधिकारियों ने वर्दी की खरीद भी दिखा थी और सप्लाई की भुगतान भी। असल में न तो ऐसी कोई वर्दी खरीदी गई और न हीं कैडेटों को दी गई है।

कैसे हुआ खुलासा

फर्स्ट जेएंडके आरटी बैटरी के कमांडिंग आफिसर ने 13 अगस्त 2010 को निदेशालय को एक पत्र लिखकर जानकारी दी थी कि अप्रैल 2009 से लेकर मार्च 2010 के बीच में उनकी बटालियन को वर्दी जारी नहीं की गई है, जबकि रिकार्ड में खरीद दिखाई गई। उक्त अधिकारी ने ऐसा ही पत्र दिल्ली मुख्यालय को भी लिखा था। इसके बाद शुरू हुई जांच में निदेशालय के अधिकारियों के शामिल होने की बात सामने आई थी।

जांच चल रही है

मैं कुछ दिनों से छुट्टी पर हूं। एनसीसी वर्दी की खरीद के मामले की जांच चल रही है। जांच के बाद ही सही बताया जा सकता है। अन्य घोटालों की भी जांच चल र ही है।"

एमके भट्ट, एसएसपी-सीबीआई

भारत का सबसे बड़ा समाचार पत्र समूह

भास्कर

सोमवार
18 अक्तूबर, 2010

11 आलोचकों को दिया करारा ज

एनसीसी में और भी हुए घोटाले

अधिकारियों की मिलीभगत ने लगाया करोड़ों का चूना

भास्कर न्यूज | जम्मू

एनसीसी में वर्दी घोटाला उजागर होने के बाद तीन सालों में और भी घोटाले होने का खुलासा हुआ है। इसमें एक बड़ा घोटाला नगरोटा स्थित कैंप स्थान पर निर्माणधीन सभागार का है। इसके अलावा अधिकारी वाहनों तथा कर्मचरारियों का भी दुरुपयोग हुआ है। इसकी भी जांच चल रही है। जांच में सामने आया है कि इस घोटाले में संलिस क बड़ा अधिकारी इसी साल रिटायर्ड हो गया है।

वर्ष 2009 में एनसीसी नगरोटा कैंप में एक सभागार बनवाना चाहती थी। इसके लिए एनसीसी ने राज्य सरकार की एजेंसी पीडब्लयूडी से संपर्क साधा। पीडब्लयूडी ने इसकी अनुमानिम लागत 4 करोड़ रुपए बताई थी लेकिन निदेशालय के अधिकारियों ने दिल्ली मुख्यालय को बताया कि वह कम समय में सिर्फ 2.5 करोड़ की लागत से सभागार का निर्माण प्राइवेट एजेंसी से करवा सकते हैं। इसके बाद निदेशालय ने दिल्ली मुख्यालय से किसी तरह सभागार का निर्माण स्वयं करवाने की अनुमति ले ली।

चार चरणों में बंटवाया काम : अधिकारियों ने मिलीभगत से काम को चार चरणों में बंटवाया था जोकि आज तक पूरा नहीं हुआ है। पहले चरण में 27 लाख 99 हजार 390 रुपए से ज्यादा खर्च किया, दूसरे में 96 लाख 74 हजार 71 रुपए, तीसरे चरण में 90 लाख 46 हजार 567 तथा चौथे चरण में अब तक 88 लाख 59 हजार 498 रुपए खर्च हो चुके हैं। कुल मिलाकर इस पूरे काम में अब तक 3 करोड़ रुपए खर्च किए जा चुके हैं। सभागार को तैयार करने में अभी इतना ही खर्च और होने की आशंका है।

सिविल हायर्ड ट्रांसपोर्ट में भी धांधली : तीन सालों की समय सीमा में बड़े पैमाने पर सिविल हायर्ड ट्रांसपोर्ट स्कीम के तहत भी धांधली की गई। इसमें सरकारी वाहनों को भी इसतेमाल किया गया और उसके बदले में सालों से ट्रांसपोटेशन अलाउंस भी लिया जा रहा है। दिल्ली मुख्यालय का आदेश है कि सिर्फ राज्य में ही एनसीसी के वाहनों का इस्तेमाल किया जा सकता है। अगर किसी काम के लिए राज्य से बाहर जाना हो तो उसके लिए प्राइवेट वाहनों को लिया जाए। उन वाहनों को सिविल हायर्ड ट्रांसपोर्ट के तहत लिया जाता है। लेकिन उसके बदले सरकारी वाहनों का इस्तेमाल किया गया और पैसे भी लिए गए। इसी तरह से सरकारी वाहन को राज्य से बाहर लेकर गया एक आलाधिकारी दुर्घटना का शिकार भी हुआ था। लेकिन मामले को दबा दिया गया था। अधिकारी वाहनों का इस्तेमाल करते रहे और कागजों में दिखाया कुछ और गया। इस तरह से वह सरकारी कागजों में हेराफेरी करके प्रति वर्ष सरकार को लाखों रुपए का चूना लगाते रहे।

अधिकारियों ने मचाई लूट खसूट: जांच के दौरान एक खुलासा हुआ कि अधिकारियों की मिलीभगत से एनसीसी कैंटीन के सामान का भी दुरुपयोग हो रहा है। इसमें एक तो प्राइवेट लोगों को सामान दिया जा रहा है। इसके बदले अधिकारी हर माह मोटी कमीशन ले रहे हैं। केडट्स को ट्रेनिंग देने वाले प्रशिक्षक भी सिर्फ कागजों में ही आ रहे हैं। उन्हें ओर ही जगहों पर लगाया गया है। इसमें से कुछ तो कैंटीन में काम कर रहे हैं। जबकि कुछ से अधिकारी अपने निजी काम करवा रहे हैं।

5 दिनों में कहां खर्च किए 3 लाख : हैरानी की बात है कि अधिकारियों ने पांच दिनों में तीन लाख रुपए खर्च कर दिए। पैसा कहां गया कोई नहीं जानता। जम्मू स्थित एक बटालियन ने इसी साल 26 मार्च को डायरेक्टरेट को तीन लाख रुपए वापस दिए थे। बटालियन ने कहा था कि खर्च में उसके पास पैसे बच गए हैं। लेकिन उसी दिन उन पैसों को श्रीनगर की एक बटालियन को जारी कर दिया गया। 31 मार्च से पहले श्रीनगर की बटालियन ने 28 मार्च को उन पैसों को निकाल लिया। उसके बदले में ट्रांसपोर्ट का खर्च दिखाया गया और उसके बिल भी दिए गए। सवाल यह उठता है कि दो दिनों मे श्रीनगर की बटालियन ने किन गाड़ियों पर तीन लाख रुपए खर्च कर दिए।

जांच जारी है : इस संदर्भ में सीबीआई के एसएसपी एमके भट्ट से पूछा गया तो उन्होंने कुछ भी बताने से मना कर दिया। उनका कहना है कि अभी कुछ नहीं बताया जा सकता। सीबीआई जांच में लगी हुई है। ऐसे मामले का पहले खुलासा नहीं किया जा सकता।

दो आरटीआई एक्ट के बीच धक्के खा रही एप्लीकेशन

पहले लटकाया अब टरकाया

भास्कर न्यूज. जम्मू

केंद्रीय सूचना एक्ट (आरटीआई) और राज्य सूचना एक्ट के अलग-अलग होने का लाभ कई सरकारी संस्थान उठा रहे हैं। ये संस्थान आवेदकों को केंद्रीय सूचना एक्ट के बजाये राज्य सूचना एक्ट के तहत आवेदन करने को कह रहे हैं।

ऐसा ही एक मामला सामने आया है। राज्य के एनसीसी निदेशालय से मांगी गई सूचना के लिए आवेदन को पहले काफी देर लटकाया जाता रहा। उसके बाद जब एपेलेट अथारिटी को आवदेन किया गया तो आवेदनकर्ता को जम्मू-कश्मीर सूचना एक्ट के तहत आवेदन करने को कहा गया। गौरतलब है कि एनसीसी पर पूरी तरह से नियत्रंण रक्षा मंत्रालय का है और सेना के अधिकारी ही निदेशालय को चलाते हैं। बेशक प्रशासनिक कार्यों के लिए कुछ स्थानीय लोगों को नियुक्त किया जाता है। एनसीसी के बजट का अधिकतर हिस्सा केंद्र द्वारा ही जारी किया जाता है।

आरटीआई एक्टिविस्ट ने मांगी है जानकारियां: आरटीआई एक्टिविस्ट राम गोपाल शर्मा ने एनसीसी निदेशालय से आरटीआई एक्ट, 2005 के तहत तीन अलग-अलग आवदेनों के जरिए 22, 28 तथा 29 मई को जानकारी मांगी थी। उन्होंने एनसीसी निदेशालय द्वारा वर्ष 2008-09, 2009-10 तथा 2010-11 में कैडेट्स के लिए खरीदी गई वर्दी तथा अन्य सामान, इन पर हुआ खर्चा व खरीद, किराए पर ली गई गाड़ियों एवं उन पर हुए खर्च तथा जम्मू ग्रुप और कश्मीर ग्रुप को सिविल हायर्ड व्हीकल के लिए जारी फंड संबंधित जानकारियां मांगी थी। इन तीनों आवेदनों को एनसीसी निदेशालय ने एक महीने बाद वापस भेज दिया। यह तर्क दिया गया कि आवदेन तय फार्मेट अनुसार नहीं है और न ही तय फीस भरी गई है। इसके बाद दोबारा आवेदन करने पर आधी अधूरी जानकारी दी गई। इस जानकारी से असंतुष्ट राम गोपाल शर्मा ने 5 अक्तूबर को एपेलेट अथारिटी में अपील की। फिर एपेलेट अथारिटी ने अपील को जेएंडके निदेशालय भेजते हुए आरटीआई एक्ट के रूल 6(3) के तहत आवश्यक कार्रवाई करते हुए 27 अक्तूबर 2010 तक जवाब देने को कहा। इसके बाद 11 नवंबर को एपेलेट अथारिटी ने आवेदक को पत्र लिख कर कहा कि उसने आवेदन के लिए आवश्यक बातें ही पूरी नहीं की है। इसलिए आवेदक को जम्मू-कश्मीर आरटीआई एक्ट 2009 के तहत दोबारा निदेशालय को आवेदन करें।

22

एनसीसी के डीजी जांच के लिए जम्मू आ रहे

भास्कर न्यूज़ | जम्मू

एनसीसी में हुए घोटाले की जांच के लिए खुद डीजी जम्मू आ रहे है। वह तीन दिनों के दौरे पर आ रहे है। उनके दौरे को लेकर पूरी तैयारी कर ली गई है। दौरे के दौरान वह घोटाले के बारे में पूरी जांच करेंगे ताकि पूरा पता चल सके कि हुआ क्या है। जानकारी के अनुसार रियासत की एनसीसी यूनिट को दिल्ली से एक पत्र आया, जिसमें कहा गया कि डीजी 22 अक्तूबर से लेकर 24 तक दौरे पर रहेंगे। आदेश में साफ कहा गया है कि इस दौरान तीन साल की खरीद का पूरा रिकार्ड रखा जाए। ताकि उसे गौर किया जा सके। सूत्रों का कहना है कि रिकार्ड को लेकर कड़े आदेश दिए गए हैं ताकि उनके आने के बाद कोई बहाना न चल सके। स्थानीय अधिकारियों ने उनके दौरे को लेकर अपनी तरफ से तैयारी पूरी कर ली है। वह हवाई मार्ग से जम्मू आएंगे। उनके आने के बाद कड़ी कार्रवाई हो सकती है। ज्ञात रहे कि भास्कर ने लगातार दो दिन एनसीसी में हुए घपले का भंडाफोड़ किया था। जिसमें वर्दी से लेकर सभागार तथा अन्य मामलों को उजागर किया गया था। उसके बाद दिल्ली ने इन मामलों का कड़ा नोटिस लिया था। उसी के बाद डीजी का रियासत दौरा बना है।

भास्कर इम्पैक्ट

एनसीसी में वर्दी घोटाला

सीबीआई ने रिकार्ड जब्त कर जांच शुरू की

Procurement irregularities cost NCC ₹20 cr: CAG

VIJAY MOHAN
TRIBUNE NEWS SERVICE

CHANDIGARH, DECEMBER 24
Adopting incorrect practices in the procurement of various items for use by cadets, the Directorate General National Cadet Corps (DGNCC) bought items like tents, mosquito nets at exorbitant prices, thereby incurring an extra expenditure of about Rs 21 crore over the past five years.

Scrutiny by the Comptroller and Auditor General (CAG) has revealed that the DGNCC violated provisions of the Defence Procurement Manual in the procurement of mosquito nets by buying 80 per cent of the total quantity of 97,762 from secondary sources. This resulted in a higher expenditure of over Rs 2 crore.

Similar violations were found in procurement of 34 other items procured through 349 supply orders, entailing an extra expenditure of Rs 17.87 crore, CAG has said in its latest report.

Based on Annual Provisioning Review for 2007-08, the DGNCC made an open tender enquiry in August 2007 for procurement of 97,762 mosquito nets for which 37 tenders were received. One firm offered the nets at the rate of Rs 180 plus taxes, which received only 20 per cent of the order, while the remaining 78,210 nets were bought at the rate of Rs 429 plus taxes.

The Ministry of Defence stated in February 2011 that the practice being followed in the DGNCC was as per Director General of Supplies and Disposals (DGS&D) Manual whereby 80 per cent of order quantity is given to past suppliers with a proven track record and 20 per cent is ordered on new suppliers.

The Ministry added that unlike the Army, the NCC had no reserve stock and to ensure timely availability of stock, supply orders were issued to different suppliers.

In another case, 4088 Tents Extended Frame Supported (TEFS) were procured by the DGNCC between February 2010 and May 2010 from commercial firms while the same item was available on rate contract at lower rates. This was also in violation of provisions. Thus despite the availability of above item on rate contract at cheaper rate, an extra expenditure of Rs 1.09 crore was incurred.

The DGNCC has maintained that the tents procured were mentioned with specification number and schedule number, whereas the tents available under the rate contract were mentioned only with the specification number, which meant that the specification of the tents procured by the DGNCC are different from those available on rate contract.

> "The purchase of the common user items at exorbitant rates from the past suppliers in preference to the lower rates offered by other suppliers defied all procurement norms and was in gross disregard of the accepted standards of financial propriety. These resulted in an extra expenditure of about Rs 21 crore."
>
> — CAG

CAG slams Def Min for Rs 21 cr excess expense on mosquito nets

New Delhi, December 20

OBSERVING that "incorrect practice" was adopted in procuring items such as mosquito nets by National Cadet Corps (NCC), CAG today slammed the Defence Ministry for incurring additional expenditure of Rs 21 crore in this regard.

The mosquito nets were procured by the Director General of National Cadet Corps (DGNCC), which is manned by personnel of three services and headed by an Army Lieutenant General.

"DG, NCC violated provisions of financial rule and Defence Procurement Manual (DPM) while procuring mosquito nets for its cadets," the Comptroller and Auditor General(CAG) report tabled in Parliament said.

"By adopting incorrect practice of purchasing 80 per cent quantity from past suppliers at higher rates than that of the lowest bidder firm, extra expenditure of Rs 21 crore had been incurred," it said.

The Government auditor said "audit of procurements made by the DG,NCC from 2006-07 to 2008-09 in respect of 34 more items revealed that 349 supply orders were placed on firms other than the lowest bidder resulting in an extra expenditure of Rs 17.87 crore."

In its report, the CAG also pointed out to the case of "irregular dehiring" a house constructed on leased land by the Chief of Staff of Army's Southern Command in Pune. The officer is also of the rank of Lt Gen.

"Chief of Staff, Southern Command in January 2006 accorded sanction for de-hiring of a house hired prior to March 1976 although the powers for dehiring in such cases is vested with the

Contd on page 2

CAG slams...

Defence Ministry," it said. This move by the Southern Command enabled the lessee to transfer the leasehold rights of 1.14 acres of defence land valuing Rs 2.77 crore to a private party for possible commercial exploitation of the land without any cost to the private party, it said. PTI

कल सूर्योदय	7:19
आज सूर्यास्त	6:10

शहर में खास

प्रदर्शन

कहां : बच्चन डिपो

समय : सुबह 11.00 बजे

खबरों में खास

झूमी छात्राएं

बसंत पंचमी के अवसर पर कई शिक्षण संस्थानों में कार्यक्रमों के आयोजन किए गए.... • 2

बजरंगियों का प्रदर्शन

बजरंग दल के कार्यकर्ताओं ने धार्मिकस्थल के निर्माण को लेकर फिर प्रदर्शन किया... • 3

कैंप से लापता हुई कैडेट अपहरण का मामला दर्ज

» दिल्ली में गणतंत्र दिवस की परेड में भाग लेकर लौटी थी

» आक्रोशित परिजनों ने बनाया एनसीसी अधिकारियों पर दबाब

भास्कर न्यूज़ | जम्मू

दिल्ली में गणतंत्र दिवस के परेड मे भाग लेकर जम्मू वापस लौटी एनसीसी की एक कैडेट के संदिग्ध परिस्थिति में लापता होने का मामला प्रकाश में आया है। श्रीनगर की तिसमा रफीक बट नाम की कैडेट नगरोटा कैंप से शनिवार को अचानक लापता हो गई। उसके परिजनों के काफी दबाव पर मंगलवार को नगरोटा पुलिस ने भद्रवाह के एक युवक के खिलाफ अपहरण का मामला दर्ज कर मामले की जांच शुरू कर दी है। इधर, इस मामले को लेकर एनसीसी के अधिकारी काफी परेशान हैं। तिसमा के परिजन जम्मू में ही डेरा डाल रखा है। वे एनसीसी अधिकारियों पर लगातार उसे तलाशने के लिए दबाव बनाए हुए हैं।

जानकारी के अनुसार दिल्ली में गणतंत्र दिवस की परेड में भाग लेने के लिए राज्य से 107 कैडेट का ग्रुप गया था। इसमें 22 युवतियां भी शामिल थी। दिल्ली में कैंप पूरा होने के बाद 2 फरवरी को ग्रुप वापिस जम्मू लौटा। परंपरा के अनुसार लौटने के बाद ग्रुप की मुलाकात मुख्यमंत्री से करवाई गई। उसके बाद ग्रुप को वापिस नगरोटा ले जाया गया। तयशुदा कार्यक्रम के अनुसार ग्रुप में शामिल सभी कैडेट को रविवार अपने-अपने घरों के लिए भेजा जाना था। लेकिन तिसमा रफीक बट शनिवार को ही अचानक लापता हो गई।

लापता होने की जानकारी मिलने से कैंप में हड़कंप मच गया। तिसमा के लापता होने की जानकारी तुरंत अधिकारियों को दी गई। अधिकारियों ने भी उसकी तलाश शुरू कर दी, लेकिन उसका कोई पता नहीं चला। उधर, तिसमा के घर नहीं पहुंचने पर परिजनों ने एनसीसी अधिकारियों से संपर्क किया, जिससे पता चला कि वह कैंप से गायब है। उसके बाद तिसमा के परिजन उसकी तलाश में जम्मू आ गए। जम्मू में परिजनों ने एनसीसी के आला अधिकारियों से जानकरी मांगी। लेकिन किसी के पास कोई जवाब नहीं था। उसके परिजनों का कहना था कि कैडेट के घर पहुंचने तक एनसीसी की ही जिम्मेवारी रहती है। इसलिए उसकी तलाश जल्दी से जल्दी करवाई जाए। तीन दिन तक जब उसका कुछ पता नहीं चला तो सोमवार को इस घटना की जानकारी नगरोटा पुलिस को दी गई। थाना प्रभारी परवेज सज्जाद ने कहा कि परिजनों की शिकायत पर भद्रवाह के एक युवक के खिलाफ अपहरण का मामला दर्ज कर डोडा पुलिस को भी सूचित कर दिया गया है।

Dated: 12-7-2010
Place: Jammu
ID. No.

To

The Central Public Information Officer
/ Asstt. Public Information Officer
NCC Directorate J&K Jammu
Rashid Villa, Canal Road, Jammu

From:

Ram Gopal Sharma
H.No. 254, Sector-G,
Sainik Colony, Jammu

Sub: Information under RTI Act, 2005.

Sir,

The undersigned hereby require the following particulars of information.

(i)

a) Please inform the allotment of funds thru various sources for purchase of clothing items and equipment for the NCC cadet of J&K Directorate and also allotments for kitting for TSC and RDC for the financial years 2008-09, 2009-10, 2010-11. Whether these funds were sub-allotted to the groups or units or were expended centrally. Please also intimate date of receipt, date by which funds expended, and if any surrendered or still held with you.

b) Please intimate the expenditure of the above funds separately for each financial year, item wise and separately for TSC and RDC, and if sub allotted then separately for each group/ unit.

c) The names and dates of news paper where the tender/ bids/ quotations were asked for, of each financial year, were bids asked for each individual item separately or otherwise, kindly provide details, as well as TSC and RDC. A photocopy of the advertisements may kindly be provided.

d) In case no advertisements were placed how was the supplier chosen, and on whose recommendation, please also intimate the relevant government order/ regulation/ authority, which permits on adherence to established procurement rules.

e) The details of the bids received, and prices quoted by various dealers, for all the items, please provide similar details of TSC and RDC also. (for each financial year separately).

f) Was the order placed on a single agency or on separate agencies, kindly provide details also for TSC and RDC (for each financial year)

g) Was inception of the manufacturing/ supplying/ facility of the chosen dealer carried out to ascertain the competency of the dealer/ manufacturer to supply the order, if it was carried out, by whom and on which dates, please provide copy of the office order so deputing the official.

h) Please give details of purchase made (separately for each financial year, and items) if supplier was different for each item, including for the purchase made for TSC and RDC and whether all item order and placed or supplies has been received.

Contd...P/2

-2-

(7)

i) Had any/committee/ board comprising of competent officials been formed to assess the requirement, prior to projecting demand for funds or prior to placing advertisement/call for quotation, if so when, please provide copy of office order, and the recommendations of the said committee along with names of the officials, also the TSC and RDC. Was any board/ committee consisting of competent officials formed to effect the purchase, open the tenders and all other formalities associated the government purchases, the details of the said board and a copy of the office order so detailing the board, kindly provided.

j) Was any specific officer detailed to co-ordinate the purchase/procurement/ provisioning/ accounting directly by name by your directorate was a detailment given to a Group or unit to detail a officer. Copies of relevant office order/ letters be kindly provided. Were the committees if detailed as asked in the above queries (F.G.H) detailed by name directly by your directorate or was any group /unit directed to detail any official, copy of letter from your offices/ order may kindly be provided, please also provide similar details for TSC and RDC.

k) Did a independent committee or board not involved in the purchase carry out a check of the purchased items to ensure that quality and quantity were of the highest order. If it was done a copy of the order detailing such board/ committee and its findings/ proceedings be kindly enclosed.

l) How were the items so procured distributed, was any officer in charge of the distribution, have all the items purchased been distributed, are any items left in the inventory. Please provide details separately for each financial year, and also TSC and RDC.

m) Was any government manufacturing agencies/ co-operative approached for the supply of uniforms/ clothing items/ equipment, is the supplier chosen by your organisation supplying any of the clothing/ other equipment to armed forces / police/ fire brigade etc. If yes kindly give client list along with total amount in rupees of items supplied, and dates on which supplied.

n) Were officials of CDA/ central audit organisation/ state audit organization involved in the process of the purchase, or was their advice taken/ documents send to them for scrutiny, verification or approval, including purchases made for TSC and RDC.

o) Whether store, clothing/ equipments have been received by the Directorate/ Gp/ Unit from any govt. agency/ DGNCC, if so when how much break to every year items were as above.

From 2008-09, 2009-10, 2010- onwards

Relevant Documents.

Preferred language of the said information is: English

It is submitted that information will be collected in person upon intimation.

Encl: Postal Oder of Rs. 10/-

Signature/ Thumb impression of the applicant
(Name): Ram Gopal Sharma

Dated: 12-7-2010
Place: Jammu
ID. No. ....
To be allotted by PIO

To

The Designated Central Public Information Officer
Dy. Director General NCC, Jammu & Kashmir
NCC Directorate J&K,
Rashid Villa, Canal Road, Jammu- 180 001

From:

Ram Gopal Sharma
H.No. 254, Sector-G,
Sainik Colony, Jammu
Mobile: 94191-57741

Sub: Information under RTI Act, 2005.

Sir,

A. The undersigned hereby require the following particulars of information.
B. The Period to which the information is requested is 2008-09, 2009-10, 2010-11.

1. Please inform the allotment of funds for hiring CHT (Civil Hired Transportation) from all sources to the Directorate, for the financial years (a) 2008-09 and (b) 2009-10 (c) 2010-2011. **PLEASE NOTE INFORMATION OF JAMMU AND SRINAGAR GROUP IS ALSO REQUIRED FOR ALL QUERIES.**

FY	SOURCE/ DEPTT	FROM WHOM RECEIVED	AMOUNT
2008-09			
2009-10			
TOTAL AS ON 31 MARCH 2010			
ALLOTMENT AFTER 31 MARCH 2010			

2. Please intimate the DETAILED disposal of the funds allotted as mentioned above (CHT FUND), separately for each financial year as required in para 1 above, as follows:-
   - Amounts sub allotted to Jammu group (and directly to any of its units)
   - Amounts sub allotted to Srinagar groups (and directly to any of its units)
   - Amount retained in Directorate
   - The amount of funds surrendered by Jammu Group in 2008-09, 2009-10 and 2010 -11 (to include all units under it) and to whom surrendered, a copy of the letter surrendering the same, is also requested.
   - The amount of funds surrendered by Srinagar Group in 2008-09, 2009-10 and 2010 -11 (to include all units under it) and to whom surrendered, a copy of the letter surrendering the same, is also requested .

(9)

- The amount of funds surrendered by Directorate in 2008-09, 2009-10 and 2010 -11 (to include all units under it) and to whom surrendered, a copy of the letter surrendering the same, is also requested.
- The amount surrendered by any unit, group to directorate, the further disposal of the amount be kindly informed along with copy of the letter authorizing the same.
- Please intimate the amount surrendered by Jammu Group which has been reallocated to Srinagar Group and its utilization by the Srinagar Group along with the detailed correspondence on the subject.
  * Please intimate the detailed expenditure* date wise of the funds surrender by Jammu Group to Srinagar Group and reallocated by your Directorate
  * (details of CHT hired, dates, distance covered, by whom used, date of travel, duration, distance covered, type of vehicle.)
- Please intimate details audit by various authorities for the CHT funds a copy of the audit proceeding be kindly attached.
- Please intimate details of CHT hired by your organization for the financial years 2008-09, 2009-10, 2010-todate, by the Directorate and by the group, as follows.

S.no	Date	Type of Vehicle	Hired by whom	User name and rank	From	To	Distance	Time utilized	Amount paid

* Note please intimate type of load carrier, stroke, luxury cars for Officers, JCO/Ors.

3. Please intimate the name/designation of the competent authority to sanction use of CHT.
4. A copy of newspaper in which tender/ notice was given for hiring of CHT.
5. The details of firms supplying the vehicles along with copy of registration for doing business in supply of vehicles and vehicle registration numbers of the vehicle used for military duty for the entire period.

C. Preferred language of the said information is: English

D. In case the subject matter/ any of the information is held by/ related to another public authority, you are requested to transfer the application or such part of it as may be appropriate to that other public authority with an intimation to the undersigned (section 6(3) of RTI Act).

E. Information will be collected in person upon intimation.

F. Postal order bearing No. 77E 417854 Dated: 07.07.2010

(10)

It is submitted that information will be collected in person upon intimation.

Encl: Postal Oder of Rs. 10/- and proof of identity (copy of voter I-card)

Signature/ Thumb impression of the applicant
(Name): Ram Gopal Sharma

Sharma (11)

Dated: 12-7-2010
Place: JAMMU
ID. No. ....
(To be allotted by PIO)

To

The Designate Central Public Information Officer
Dy. Director General,
NCC Directorate J&K Jammu
Rashid Villa, Canal Road, Jammu

From:

Ram Gopal Sharma
H.No. 254, Sector-G,
Sainik Colony, Jammu
Mobile: 94191-57741

Sub: Information under RTI Act, 2005.

Sir,

A. The undersigned hereby require the following particulars of information.

B. The Period to which the information is requested is 2008-09, 2009-10, 2010-11.

1. Please intimate the list of all officers posted, their appointment and the funds being held on their charge, if any, the countersigning authority for each, please provide details separately for Group Headquarter and for the units, for the financial years 2009-09, 2009-10, 2010-11. Kindly also indicate temporary charge where applicable in case of holding officer proceeded on leave/duty etc., please also confirm against each whether drawing transportation allowance.
2. Please intimate the following information in respect of the vehicles held with your Head quarters and the Units under you separately.
   a. Details of passenger car vehicles (Gypsy, Van, Indigo etc) held on your charge, and since when (and to date).
   b. Details of load carriers (canter, eicher, 1ton, 3ton etc) held on your charge and since when.
   c. The source of procurement of these vehicles have they been procured from army or from the state government/ central.
   d. The registration number of all the vehicle held on your charge category wise.
   e. The list of Civilian Drivers posted currently to the Directorate along with their license detail.
   f. The list of army drivers posted for driving of vehicles along with their license details.
   g. Please provide list of civilian employee, other then civilian driver (lascar/chowkidar etc) driving any vehicle.

(12)

h. Please intimate the source of funds for purchase of petrol/diesel, for the following financial year along with amount, 2008-09, 2009010, 2010-11. Please also intimate vehicle wise consumption monthly, for each financial year, and also intimate whether any amount surrendered if so how much and to whom a copy of letter surrendering may kindly be enclosed.

i. Give details of these vehicles used for any personal work like conveyance for children/ other family member, to school or place of work, for persons not drawing any transportation allowances.

j. Please provide details of vehicles being parked each vehicle wise. List of vehicles taken by the officers of the directorate (DDG., AD. Adm. , and AD. Trg.) to their residence, after office hours for parking/ garaging. Please provide the copy of the rules and govt. orders permitting the same along with copy of sanctions of competent authority.

k. Please provide list of vehicles and type (passenger car or load carrier) which are attached, from other units/Groups to your HQ along with dates of attachment. Please intimate the purpose of these attachments, please intimate alternate arrangements made by the units for the functions, in the units to which these vehicles originally belonged, being carried out.

3. Please intimate the amount released from various sources for fuel for vehicles for 2008-09, 2009-10, 2010-11. Kindly provide complete details separately for each year, Please provide details of advertisement of newspaper or otherwise for purchase of bulk fuel for the vehicles held with you, from IOC/ HP/ any other agency, at competitive rates, details of purchase of fuel carried out, (monthly or fortnightly or weekly or daily or on required basis), persons responsible and carrying out purchase.

4. Details of amount released for repair of vehicle, is it held and expended centrally by the directorate, please give details of allotment including source, the distribution if any to units under you for the following financial years 2008-09, 2009-10, 2010-11. Please also give details of expenditure under this head for the financial years 2008-09, 2009-10, 2010-11. Kindly provide details vehicle wise (giving engine/ chassis number and army registration number) along with date of said repair.

5. Please intimate whether repairs to vehicles carried out by authorized service center or thru contractor, whether contractor appointed thru advertisement and with consultation with PCDA/ STATE AUDIT AUTHORITY, please give details of procedure adopted.

6. Please intimate the total amount of funds demanded and released for camps and courses to heads like catering, petrol/ diesel, misc etc. please give its state of utilization.

7. Please intimate amount directly paid by your HQ to any contractor, for any items of camps and courses.

(13)

8. Please provide details of office equipment fund for the 2008-09, 2009-10, 2010-11. Please give details of purchases and the names of the officials of the committee/ board with carried out these purchases.

C. Preferred language of the said information is: English

D. In case the subject matter/ any of the information is held by/ related to another public authority, you are requested to transfer the application or such part of it as may be appropriate to that other public authority with an intimation to the undersigned (section 6(3) of RTI Act).

E. Information will be collected in person upon intimation.

F. Postal order bearing No. 77E 417856 Dated: 07.07.2010

Encl: Postal Oder of Rs. 10/- and proof of identity (copy of voter I-card)

Signature/ ~~Thumb~~ impression of the applicant
(Name): Ram Gopal Sharma

Khatri
(14)

Dated; 12-7-2010
Place: Jammu.
ID. No. ....
(To be allotted by PIO)

To

The Central Asstt. Public Information Officer
Group Commander, Jammu Group
NCC Group HQ Jammu
82 A/D Gandhi Nagar,
Jammu

From:

Ram Gopal Sharma
H.No. 254, Sector-G,
Sainik Colony, Jammu
Mobile: 94191-57741

Sub: **Information under RTI Act, 2005.**

Sir,

A. The undersigned hereby require the following particulars of information.
B. The Period to which the information is requested is 2008-09, 2009-10, 2010-11.

1. Please intimate the officers posted, their appointment and the funds being held on their charge, if any, the countersigning authority for each, please provide details separately for Group Headquarter and for the units, for the financial years 2008-09, 2009-10, 2010-11. Kindly also indicate temporary charge where applicable in case of holding officer proceeded on leave/duty etc.
2. Please intimate the rate of transportation allowance being paid to each of the above officers.
3. Please intimate the following information in respect of the vehicle held with your Head quarters and the Units under you separately:-
    a. How many passenger car vehicles (Gypsy, Van, Indigo etc) are held on your charge, and since hen (and TO DATE), and present location.
    b. How many load carriers, (canter, eicher, 1 ton, 3 ton etc) are held on your charge and since when, and their present location.
    c. The source of procurement of these vehicles have been procured from army or from State government.
    d. Please intimate the registration number of vehicles held.
    e. Please intimate the rules and regulation of their operation in your organization and copy of the said rules may kindly be enclosed.
    f. Please intimate list of civilian drivers with their valid driving license detail.
    g. Kindly intimate list of army drivers along with valid license no.

(15)

h. Please intimate the no of persons, civilians and army who have been reallocated fresh duty other than for those appointed and posted. The copy of office order/ govt. order/ army order duly signed by competent authority may kindly be enclosed.

i. Please intimate the amount and source of funds for purchase of petrol/ diesel, for the following financial year along with amount, 2008-09, 2009-10, 2010-11. Please also intimate vehicle wise consumption, monthly, for each financial year and also intimate whether any amount surrendered if so how much and to whom a copy of letter surrendering may kindly be enclosed.

j. Are any of these vehicles used for any personal work like conveyance for children/ other family member, to school or place of work.

k. Please give details as to where all vehicles are parked, each vehicle wise, is any vehicle taken by any officer to his residence, after office hours for parking/ garaging, if yes why, and under which government rule, whose permission has been taken and who will be responsible for making good any loss which may occur due to this.

l. How many vehicles and type (passenger car or load carrier) are attached, from other units to your HQ and since when, when for what purpose are these attached, how are the functions in the unit to which these vehicles originally belong being carried out, whether any vehicle is also attached from one unit to another if so for what purpose, are the vehicles if attached or attached with drivers. If no drivers are attached who are driving them.

m. Are any vehicles from your Group Headquarter or any unit under your Group been attached out to NCC Directorate, Jammu & Kashmir or to any other Headquarter/Organistion, if yes please provide details o attachment and dates since then attached, please also intimate whether any vehicles permanently transferred if so to whom and when, whether due to attachment / transfer of vehicle any staff rendered surplus, also how are the duties for which these vehicles released being performed, or is that duty redundant as on date.

4. What amount has been released from various sources for fuel for vehicles for 2008-09, 2009-10, 2010-11. Please give details separately for each year along with breakdown of amount for Headquarter and Units under you, was any advertisement placed on any newspaper or otherwise for purchase of bulk fuel for the vehicles held with you and your units directly, from IOC/ HP/ any other agency, at competitive rates, how is purchase of fuel carried out, is it monthly or fortnightly or weekly or daily or on required basis, who decides and authorizes the purchase, is it purchased from any single outlet or multiple outlets.

5. Please intimate the amount released for repair of vehicle, is it held and expended centrally by the Group Head Quarter, please give details of allotment including source, the distribution if any to units under your for the following financial years 2008-09, 2009-10, 2010-11. Please also give details of expenditure under this head for the financial years 2008-09, 2009-10, 2010-11, Kindly provide details separately for headquarters and for units

(16)

under you, vehicle wise (giving engine/ chassis number and army registration number) along with date of said repair.

6. Please provide details of repairs to vehicles carried out by authorized service center or thru contractor, whether contractor appointed thru advertisement and with PCDA/STATE AUDIT AUTHORITY/ CENTRAL AUDIT AUTHORITY, please give details separately for HQ and units.
7. Please intimate the total amount of funds demanded and relased for camps and courses to various units under your HQ for 2008-09, 2009-10, 2010-11, please give breakdown under separate heads like catering, petrol/diesel, misc etc. please give its state of utilization.
8. Please provide details of office equipment fund for the FY 2008-09, 2009-10, 2010-11, please give details of purchases and the names of the officials of the committee/ board which carried out these purchases, whether any amount surrendered.
9. Is CSD being operated by your Group Headquarter, if so under whose permission. Kindly attach copy of letter authorizing running of CSD canteen, from competent authority and the rules hereon.
10. Please provide detail of staff for running of canteen.
11. Is any PI staff utilized for running of canteen, if yes kindly provide details.
12. Please provide detail of PI staff is running canteen, who is carrying out the authorized work of the PI staff.
13. What is the basis of distribution of canteen profit. When unit is given the maximum.
14. Is any extra pay given to PI staff involved in the canteen.
15. Is canteen items sold to any un-authorized civilian, if yes to whom all, if no how the same is ensured.
16. Who is the officer in charge of CSD and since when is he holding charge.

C. Preferred language of the said information is: English

D. In case the subject matter/ any of the information is held by/ related to another public authority, you are requested to transfer the application or such part of it as may be appropriate to that other public authority with an intimation to the undersigned (section 6(3) of RTI Act).

Information will be collected in person upon intimation.

Postal order bearing No. 77E 417853 Dated: 7.07.2010

It is submitted that information will be collected in person upon intimation.

Encl: Postal Oder of Rs. 10/- and proof of identity (copy of voter I-card)

Signature/ Thumb impression of the applicant
(Name): Ram Gopal Sharma

(17)

NITIN BHASIN

ADVOCATE
J&K HIGH COURT, JAMMU

CHAMBER:-
H.NO. 102-A, GOLE MARKET
GANDHI NAGAR, JAMMU

Ref No. ....

Dated: 19.11.2010

The Addl. Director General (A)
Appellate Authority for DG NCC,
NCC Directorate, West Block-4,
R.K. Puram New Delhi.

Subject :- LEGAL NOTICE.

Sir,

Under the instructions of Sh. Ram Gopal Sharma R/o H. No. 254 Sec- G Sainik Colony, Jammu (herein after referred to as My client), I serve upon you the following notice:-

1) That my client filed applications before the Asstt. Public Information Officer Group Commander, Jammu Group, NCC HQ Jammu and the Deputy Director General and CPIO NCC Directorate J&K, Camp Office, Jammu for providing him certain information regarding utilization of funds for purchase of clothing, engagement of man power and for use of official vehicles in the NCC Directorate and units under its command in the state of Jammu & Kashmir, under the Right to Information Act 2005.

2) That the said information was not furnished to my client and after one month, he was asked to file the applications on the prescribed format accompanied with the requisite fee provided under the RTI Act.

(18)

NITIN BHASIN
ADVOCATE
J&K HIGH COURT, JAMMU

CHAMBER:-
H.NO. 102-A, GOLE MARKET
GANDHI NAGAR, JAMMU

2.

Ref No. .... Dated: 19.11.2010

3) That my client accordingly filed fresh applications on the specified format along with the requisite fee prescribed under the Rules before the Authorities concerned but despite that the information was not furnished to my client on one pretext or the other.

4) That my client after the expiry of the statuary period provided under the Act for furnishing the information, filed an appeal before your goodself on 5th of Oct. 2010.

5) That on 18th of Nov. 2010, my client has received letter No. 15312/RTIA/NCC HQ/Coord dated 11.11.2010, wherein it is mentioned that my client has not fulfilled the pre-requisites while applying the RTI and he has been advised to make fresh RTI application addressed to DDG, J&K in the prescribed format as per the Jammu and Kashmir RTI Act 2009 alongwith RTI Fee as applicable in J&K. Copy of the letter is enclosed.

6) That the information sought by my client pertains to the utilization of funds allocated by the NCC Director, New Delhi which is a Central Govt. Organization and comes under the Ministry of Defence, Govt. of India, so it is not understood that how my client has been informed that the application is not proper and the same has to be filed under the J&K RTI Act.

7) That the letter dated 11.11.2010 issued by you is a deliberate attempt to mislead my client and tantamount to denial of the

19

NITIN BHASIN
ADVOCATE
J&K HIGH COURT, JAMMU

CHAMBER:-
H.NO. 102-A, GOLE MARKET
GANDHI NAGAR, JAMMU

3

Ref No. ....

Dated: 19.11.2010

information sought by my client, which call for legal action under law and also attract penalty under the Act.

8) That is also relevant to mention here that Delhi High Court in its ruling has held that RTI Applies to Central Govt. bodies in J&K and the authorities are obligated to disclose the information. As such, the authorities concerned are under an obligation to disclose the information sought by my client.

You are, therefore, called upon through the medium of this notice to direct the authorities concerned to furnish the information to my client on the applications already filed by him, within a period of 15 days from the date of receipt of this notice, failing which my client will have no option but to take the legal recourse permissible under law, which will be entirely at your own risk and cost.

A copy of this notice has been retained in my office for further necessary action as and when required.

Yours Sincerely,

Nitin Bhasin
(Advocate)

Copy to:

1. Commander 71 Sub Area C/o 56 APO.
2. G.O.C in C Northern Command C/o 56 APO.

OPINION

Former Union Minister & BJP Leader
Prof. Chaman Lal Gupta

' Omar Abdullah is Hijacking The Agenda of Geelani in Kashmir '

What is the inside story of the demise of Dr. Shyama Prasad Mukerjee?

Dr. Shyama Prasad Mukherjee was an eminent person of national and international repute who after quitting Nehru's Cabinet became founder president of the Bhartiya Jan Sangh in 1952. The government had imposed ban on entry into the state of Jammu and Kashmir. Being a Member of Parliament and leader of opposition party, Dr. Mukerjee declared at Delhi that he would enter J&K State of his country without any permit. On his arrival at Lakhanpur he was stopped and arrested at 4 pm (Date could not recollect) But I can still recollect his last words spoken to Atalji at Lakhanpur as I was also present there to welcome him. "Mr Atal, go and tell the country that I have entered Kashmir though as a prisoner". Alas! He came as a prisoner but never returned.

He was taken to Kud and next day shifted to Srinagar where detained in a private house at Nishat. He was then suffering from pleurisy and his condition deteriorated. It is said that Dr. Ali Jaan was called for his medical check up but the doctor did not reffered him to hospital. When his condition became critical, he was shifted to hospital where he died on June 23, 1953.

He died under mysterious circumstances and yet to ascertained whether he died his natural death or due to heart attack. But one thing is certain, it was sheer negligence of the then government.

Bakshi Ghulam Mohd, the Home Minister, in-charge Law and order; and Sham Lal Saraf in-charge Health & Prison were the people at helm of affairs and did not allow his other companions to see him. Even Uma Shanker Trivedi who was pleading for his release was not allowed to meet the client. His parents were not informed about his illness. We did not get his health report. One morning the news of his sad demise was, however, broken to us and his body was airlifted to Kolkatta without conducting the autopsy.

Then how to establish the real cause of his death?

It is unfortunate that a member of parliament died in custody and till date no inquiry has been conducted. Let the Right to information Act (RTI) be made applicable in J&K State, we shall move an application under this act for information about the real cause of his death.

Only BJP is the political party which is opposing the Pakistan inclusion for talks for finding solution of the Kashmir problem. What exactly is the BJP's political stand on Kashmir?

When Maharaja Hari Singh signed the Instrument of Accession, with India we became part and parcel of India. Not only Jammu & Kashmir but other 562 Princely States signed the same Instrument of Accession with the is exception we have been granted special status in the Indian Constitution . We have accepted Indian Constitution before we were granted special status. Section 1 of the Indian Constitution states, there are 26 states in India and Jammu & Kashmir stands at number 15. Section 3 of Jammu & Kashmir Constitution states that Jammu & Kashmir shall be on integral part of India. These sections can't be amended as the constitution does not allow amendment. How we can say Pakistan is a party? Pakistan has illegally occupied a part of State called Pakistan Occupied Kashmir. However, for the disputed occupation it can be a party. We shall get our area back.

You are talking about abrogation of Article 370 while out of power. Why not when BJP was in power?

While in power we had a coalition government agenda of the NDA government. The NDA's priority was to run the government smoothly and didn't want to create hurdle. So,

(Next page, please)

STREET VOICE 43 DECEMBER, 2010

OPINION

BJP alone was not in majority itself.

Our agenda is very clear about the abrogation of Article 370 and Atal ji has also said "bring us in absolute power and we will abrogate article 370"

Should people wait for the day?

Yes. We certainly believe BJP will soon come in power and we shall come to the expectations of the people of our country.

What are your views about Chief Minister's controversial speech in the assembly?

Omar Abdullah has crossed his limits. The BJP, in the light of these utterances, firmly says that Jammu & Kashmir is an irrevocable and integral part of India and its future is not negotiable. Actually, he is hijacking the agenda of Geelani. He is challenging the Indian constitution after taking the oath.

Jammu and Kashmir government is unable to provide arrears of 6th pay commission's recommendations to its employees. Your comments please?

The performance of the government is surely dismal. No body is paying attention to the problems of the employees. I feel the administration had turned irresponsible. The present government may be making tall claims but the ground realities speak differently. When Abdul Rahim Rather was the leader of opposition, he used to raise this issue in the house. But now when he is the Finance Minister, he is taking the matter casually.

Being Ex-Minister of State for Defence, your comments on corruption in army, particularly Adarsh Society Land scam?

When corruption scams involve high personages in the armed forces we are outraged because army is one institution which people admire and proud of. That is the terrible aspect of Adarsh Land scam in Mumbai.

UPA government has lost its credibility. It has no moral right to continue. There is no check on corruption in our country at present. The government tries to cover up every scam.

"STREET VOICE" has dig out a scam of multi crores in NCC Directorate Jammu & Kashmir in which top officers are involved and authorities are stalling the probe. Your action please?

It is another blot on Army's image. I shall bring it to the notice of Sushma Swaraj, our leader of opposition in Parliament to ask Defence Minister about the action and myself shall raise the question before State government during Assembly session. It is the matter of 22,000 cadets of our State who are the future of the country.

What are your views about US President, Barak Obama's visit to India?

Obama visited India for business deals and American policies in South Asia. India can purchase some modern technologies from US.

But irony is that we need to worry much more about American policies in South Asia now than we ever did unless US President Obama can find some ways of making Pakistan stop supporting terrorism.

What are your future plans?

I started my journey from remote village Kaleeth and reached Indian Parliament House. So I am contented with my lot. Only I want to serve the people of my country. ■

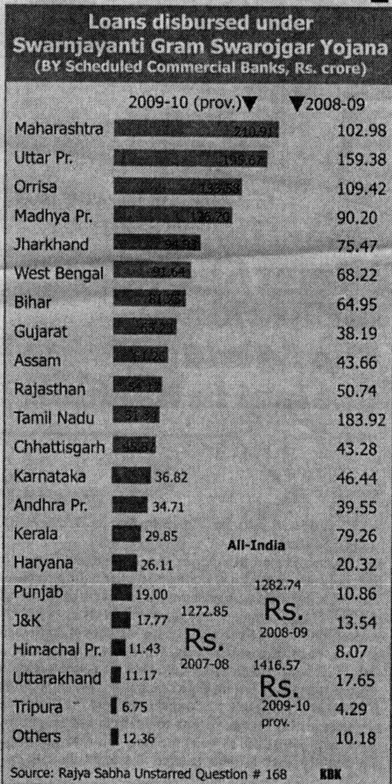

STREET VOICE March, 2010 32 STATE VOICE

Mr. C.M., Are You Serious To Eradicate Corruption ?

Inaugurating the 9th State Level Departmental Vigilance Officers Conference in Jammu on January 28, 2010. The Chief Minister, Omar Abdullah stated that the dishonour bestowed to the state of Jammu and Kashmir by declaring it as second most corrupt state of the country need to be erased as people of J&K have never liked this title. Therefore, state machinery particularly vigilance department has to gear up to bring the state out of the macabre clutches of corruption and corrupt elements.

The fact however, remains that the Jammu and Kashmir State has never been serious in fighting corruption against high-ups including bureaucrats and politicians. If we delve deep, we shall find State Vigilance Organisation (SVO) has always been dancing to the tunes of party in power. In rare cases only big fishes were booked just to settle personal/political scores. The stringent provisions of Prevention of Corruption Act have always been applied against lower class employees e.g. Patwaris, Girdawars, Work Supervisors and other clerical cadre employees or Children of lesser God. The performance of SVO in securing convictions is always before the public and successive governments. Except gaining cheap publicity of lodging FIRs in a trap case of few hundred rupees, then framing of charges and subsequent acquittal after couple of years is the hallmark of SVO. The SVOs credibility can be judged from their manner of investigation particularly when high-ups come in their net. How professionally the SVO gave clean chit to high profile IAS officers of the State Viz. I.S. Mali, Vijay Bakaya; and couple of others also involved in sex scandal need no explanation. The case diaries in such cases reveal rampant misuse of official position by the sleuths of SVO to shield such high profile bureaucrats. The expert opinion in such cases were summoned again and again from appropriate laboratories / agencies so as to ensure closure of cases against them. Even investigating officers were

replaced repeatedly to avoid the annoyance of such high ups. How biased and partial is the mode of working can be judged from a case when in a complaint of illegal appointment in SKICC (Sher-i-Kashmir Inter-nation Complex) against the then director Tanveen Jahan (IAS), the enquiry was ordered to be closed on the ground that such appointments which had been made without following codal formalities were made at the behest of the them Chief Minister Dr. Farooq Abdullah (the Chairman, Board of Governors of SKICC).

This is just a tip of the iceberg, numbers of FIRs are being lodged selectively by SVO against various Heads of the Departments, or competent authorities for making appointments in contravention of rules even Challans, in some prima facie cases, have also been filed in the court of law.

Recently, Special Judge Anti-Corruption, Jammu convicted former Director Health Services, Jammu Dr. M.P. Gupta for making illegal appointments but acquitted Pt. Govind Ram Sharma, the then minister of State for Health as SVO had not obtained sanction from the government to prosecute the former minister. The irony of fact is that SVO initially did not book the former minister although allegations in the complaint were mostly against the minister concerned. The Challan was presented in the court against former Director Health Services and it was only the then Special Judge Anti-Corruption, Jammu M.K. Hanjura who after prima facie being satisfied about the involvement of the then minister summoned and arrayed him as an accused.

The seriousness of the State Government in containing the menance of corruption can be well visualised from the fact that since June, 2008, the highest anti-corruption body i.e. State Accountability Commission (SAC) is headless and the complaints of corruption against several MLAs and sitting ministers and bureaucrats are gaining dust day-by-day. Even media/public pressure did not have any effect on young Chief Minister, for the reason best known to him only. Annals of history are full of evidence that J&K had witnessed sermons from Bakshi Ghulam Mohd., Sheikh Mohd. Abdulah, Dr. Farooq Abdullah, Mufti Mohd Sayed, Ghulam Nabi Azad and now Omar Abdullah to sternly deal with corruption. But it proved empty rhetoric and nothing concrete was done to control the cancer of corruption.

Omar Abdullah, after becoming the Chief Minister gave the slogans of corruption free states, accountability and work culture. But all these are missing on the ground and are proving only as hollow slogans because corruption rates rose to many fold which would prove costly to National Conference.

The chart showing prevailing rates of corruption in various departments concerned by survey conducted by Street Voice team under my supervision are as under.

(i) Earlier the amount received as corruption was returned if the particular work could not be done but now there is no return of money.

(ii) Transfer of Patwari used to cost less than rupees one lakh and rise to rupees five lakh.

(iii) Earlier the corruption act was restricted to one person but now it is group activity. More people joint collect huge amount.

(iv) It is also alleged that State Public Service Commission are charging rupees six lakh for the selection of a gazetted officer.

Government which is not only shielding some of the officers and politicians convicted of corruption charges but has also rewarded them with ministerial berths or high administrative posts.

Omar should set example, act against corrupt minister and but against corrupt ministers and bureaucrats. ■

CHAPTER – 6

Sham Sundar Anand Lahar and BS Salathia, both esteemed senior lawyers were my close friends and I often used to discuss judicial issues with them. In 2008, while I was seated in Sham Sundar's office, he informed me about an upcoming judicial swearing-in ceremony the following week. He encouraged me to attend the event along with my cameraman. I followed his guidance and on the specified date, went to the High Court of J&K, Jammu accompanied by my cameraman.

As we took our seats, a sub-judge arrived and inexplicably, exhibited rudeness towards my cameraman, instructing him to vacate his seat. Curiously, no one else in the room objected to my cameraman occupying the chair. In response, I advised my cameraman to remain seated and offered my chair to the sub-judge. During this period, I had already been writing about corruption within the judicial system and seeking counsel from Salathia Sahib. I had also amassed data on this issue from various regions of the country.

Fortunately, during a seminar, Chief Justice HS Kapadia made a statement suggesting that lower judiciary judges could be influenced by a simple peg of whiskey. This prompted me to delve deeper into the issue. With the guidance and support of individuals like Salathia Sahib, KS Jodal, Sham Sundar Lahar, Mandeep Kaur and numerous retired judges in India, I authored an article titled "Why Are People Losing Faith in Judiciary" for my column "Frankly Speaking." This article gained significant popularity and served as a testament to the power of truth. One day High Court Judge suspended the same Sub-Judge who mistreated my cameraman.

Upon hearing this news, I waited until the next morning for it to appear in the newspapers. Once it did, I paid a visit to the sub-judge's residence since he was a friend. Friends within the judicial system were well aware of who was at fault, and many believed that both individuals were quite similar. At this point, I felt that since the sub-judge had already been exposed, it was time to gather more information about the situation.

The situation had now escalated to the point where a High Court judge, with the influence of a retired DC, sought to remove the sub-judge from his position. Given the sub-judge's vulnerable position, I offered to assist him. I told him that if he could provide me with evidence of this undue influence, I would work towards having him transferred and safeguarding his career. Initially, he viewed this proposition with skepticism, but I had confidence in my ability to achieve it. Eventually, the sub-judge reached out to me and shared some crucial information.

Considering the delicate nature of the judiciary-related issue, I refrained from publishing it in the newspaper. Instead, I conveyed the matter to the Chief Justice of India and other relevant authorities. While Sham Sundar Lahar and BS Salathiya were aware of the facts, I also discussed it with the seasoned journalist Kuldeep Nayyar whom I had been introduced to by Balraj Puri Saheb. Given the significant implications involving a High Court judge, all parties involved exercised caution, and no one came forward openly. The Jammu Bar Association posited that it might be a conspiracy by individuals from Kashmir and voiced support for the judge's actions. However, when I discussed this with Sham Sunder, he disagreed asserting that such a scenario was unlikely. BS Salathiya also expressed his limitations, explaining that the issue involved formidable forces. At this juncture all I could do was offer my prayers and hope for the best.

Meanwhile, Kuldeep Nayyar remained in constant communication with me. Finally, he had the opportunity to meet with the Chief Justice of India. Although the meeting lasted only five minutes, it proved to be decisive. Four days later, I was informed that in consultation with Justice Altaf Alam and Justice Altamash Kabir, the Chief Justice of India had referred the case to the Intelligence Bureau (IB). After conducting an internal investigation, the IB reported to the Chief Justice that there was substance to the complaint. Given that the Law Ministry had also received complaints on this matter, the government found it challenging to intervene, prompting the transfer of the Judge from the Jammu and Kashmir High Court to the Allahabad High Court. It served as a testament to the potency of nature, strengthening my belief and propelling me to adhere even more closely to the principles imparted by Darvesh Saheb.

Sub-Judge Saheb was elated and grew closer to me. Representatives from the Jammu Bar Association, accompanied by BS Salathiya traveled to Delhi to meet the Law Minister. However, nature's course could not be defied and ultimately, the High Court judge was relocated to Allahabad. Subsequently, the sub-judge was reinstated and he wished to express his gratitude by extending a gesture of goodwill which I graciously declined. Recognizing my fondness for music, he arranged for the singer Fazal Faizi to perform at his residence, brightening my evening.

Upon initiating the CBI raid at Sainik School Nagrota on October 22, 2021, the news spread swiftly across the country through various media channels. Consequently, many teachers from Sainik Schools throughout India began inviting me to their institutions, eager to provide evidence of various improprieties occurring within their establishments. They were well aware of my steadfast commitment to combating corruption.

In 2008, the Sainik Schools Society in New Delhi allocated Rs 2 crore to each Sainik School across the country for the construction of auditoriums or swimming pools. While most schools opted to build auditoriums, Sainik School Sujanpur took a different approach by constructing an open water tank under the guise of a swimming pool. Remarkably, even the inspecting officer from the Sainik Schools Society failed to address this issue, and to this day, taps have not been installed for the so-called swimming pool.

Furthermore, six years ago, the Principal of Sainik School Kapurthala was involved in the theft of valuable French antiques dating back to the Maharaja's era, with an estimated worth of Rs 8-10 lakh at the time. When the new Principal arrived and attempted to continue listing these stolen items on the school's accounts, the quartermaster resigned in 2022 out of fear. Similarly, Quarter Master Rajinder Singh of Sainik School Chittorgarh, Rajasthan, was also expelled from the school after exposing the misappropriation by the Principal.

Additionally, the Principal of Sainik School Ambikapur made several controversial appointments within the school, which attracted widespread media coverage.

In my role as the Chief Editor of 'Street Voice', my responsibilities extended beyond reporting on NCC and Sainik School matters. I used the income generated from these articles to support cases involving disadvantaged girls and victims of domestic violence. This work provided me with a unique sense of fulfillment. In 2015, I came across a case where a father of a girl named Sapna sought my assistance. He informed me that the man his daughter had married was impotent, a fact known to the groom's parents before the marriage. However, they had concealed this crucial information from Sapna's family. In Hindu society there is a belief that if an unmarried man dies, his soul remains unsettled. To circumvent this superstition, the groom's parents deceitfully arranged the marriage.

Although the groom initially refused to consent to a divorce, I assisted Sapna's father in taking the case to court, and we successfully obtained a divorce within three months. Following the divorce, Sapna was able to marry a suitable partner. This incident underscored the importance of matching the medical profiles of both individuals before marriage, a practice common in foreign countries. In the interest of the public, I would submit a petition to the Jammu and Kashmir High Court on this matter.

In 2015, just a month after Sapna's second marriage, I had the privilege of meeting Joginder Singh, retired director of CBI, through the India International Friendship Society in New Delhi. On his recommendation, I was honored with the Rashtriya Gaurav Award. Fifteen days later, the Brahmin Sabha of Sainik Colony bestowed an honor upon me in the presence of MP Jugal Kishore and Industry & Commerce Minister Shri Ganga Prakash Sharma.

Furthermore, it came to my attention that none of the women IAS officers in Jammu and Kashmir were ever appointed as District Collectors or Deputy Commissioners.They were frequently subjected to premature transfers. I addressed this issue through my articles which led to women officers being entrusted with these responsibilities. I specifically mentioned the names of these officers in my articles, with a focus on individuals like Sonali Kumar and Sheetal Nanda.

In 2001, the Vice Chancellor of Agriculture University Jammu expelled Dr. Poonam Parihar for taking study leave. Surprisingly, this matter went unreported by any journalist or newspaper in Jammu due to the Vice Chancellor's influential connections, including ties to the Chief Minister of Jammu and Kashmir and the Chairman of JK Bank. However, I fearlessly wrote against the Vice Chancellor, shedding light on the unjust expulsion. When the new Vice Chancellor assumed office, I conducted an interview with him about the same issue. Six months later, Dr. Poonam Parihar was reinstated. Dr. Poonam now serves as an Assistant Professor/Scientist. Interestingly, Dr. Poonam's husband is a DSP in CBI.Our acquaintance deepened after they read my interview in the magazine.

My dedication to crime reporting led me to uncover a scandal involving the Chairman of the J&K Board of School Education and Jammu Municipal Corporation. It revealed how an officer, originally a Junior Engineer in the Jammu Municipal Corporation, managed to secure the position of Commissioner through political recommendations. In 2004, the then Chief Minister Mufti Mohammad Syed suspended this officer while he held the role of Superintendent Engineer. In 2016, when this officer regained the position of Commissioner, my magazine's report was fortunately republished in the 'Daily Latest' newspaper. Given that the Chief Minister at that time was Mufti Saheb, the Commissioner chose to retire early to avoid another suspension. This news garnered the support of many IAS officers because Engineers were holding the post of Commissioner in ERA and Jammu Municipal Corporation instead of IAS officers, who were the rightful holder of the position.

One of the most memorable achievements in my journalism career which I hold dear to this day, revolves around an incident that occurred on September 15, 2010 in my village, Mendhar. This incident Centreed on a phone call that potentially saved the life of the promising IPS officer, Vivek Gupta. During that time, Vivek Gupta was serving as an ASP at the SDPO office in village Mendhar. The region was plagued by terrorist attacks targeting police officers. One such attack left DSP Yugal Manhas injured, and he was getting treatment at AIIMS, Delhi.

I had the chance to meet Vivek Gupta during a visit to my village in Mendhar.Our brief ten-minute interaction left a lasting impression. We both admired each other's honesty and dedication, leading to regular phone conversations between us.

Two months later, while I was at my office in Sainik School, Nagrota, I received a call from a friend who informed me about violent clashes between anti-social elements and the police in Mendhar. Tragically, three civilians lost their lives in the ensuing gunfire, and tensions were escalating dangerously. Thousands of people were gathering, and there were reports of an impending attack on the police, primarily targeting IPS officer Vivek Gupta. The situation was dire as the number of policemen in the area was insufficient to handle the crowd.

Without hesitation, I immediately called Vivek Gupta, and fortunately, he answered. I relayed the critical information to him and urged him to seek refuge in the nearby military camp to which he agreed. By this time, thousands had assembled and some terrorists had infiltrated the crowd. However, Vivek Gupta managed to reach the military camp safely. He had risked his life to protect a Christian school within the area that was threatened by the angry mob.

Throughout the day,an enraged crowd set multiple government offices ablaze including the Tehsil office, Electricity Department office, BDO office, and Forest Department office, resulting in extensive damage to government assets worth billions of rupees. Faced with an uncontrollable mob, approximately 20-25 police officers sought refuge within the Mendhar police station. At 7 o'clock in the evening, the military conducted a Flag March. With the intervention of the Divisional Commissioner and IGP from Jammu, coupled with explanations provided to the populace, the situation eventually returned to normalcy. By

11 PM, Vivek Gupta was safely escorted to Jammu with the assistance of the army.

Vivek Gupta, originally from Kathua, hails from a family with a strong tradition of honesty. One of his uncles, Mr. PL Gupta held the position of ADG in the police at that time, while another uncle Jeet Lal Gupta, served as an IAS officer. Vivek Gupta, an IPS officer from the 2007 batch, presently holds the position of DIG in the Kashmir zone. He is renowned for his integrity and unwavering devotion to Mata Chandi. His family stands as a shining example of honesty and integrity in Jammu and Kashmir.

In 2006, corruption was rampant, affecting both the NCC and the police department. During police recruitment that year, six MLAs including two ministers exerted their influence and submitted lists of preferred candidates to the committee chairman, DIG NA Mir. They pressured him to secure positions for their favored individuals. One of the committee members was SP Mohan Lal Bhagat, who had only six years of service. Given that DIGs and SPs could not accommodate all the politically recommended candidates, they chose to disregard the recommendations and focus on recruiting qualified candidates. This decision angered the MLAs, leading them to unnecessarily assert their authority in recruitment proceedings.

Unfortunately, this incident coincided with the legislative session in Jammu and Kashmir, with Ghulam Nabi Azad serving as the Chief Minister at the time. All six of these MLAs were from the Congress Party and caused a commotion in the Assembly, accusing corruption in police recruitment. Without thorough consideration, the Chief Minister suspended DIG NA Mir. That evening, I came across this news on TV and promptly had it published in a newspaper through an editor I was acquainted with. Additionally, I began preparing a comprehensive report on the matter for my magazine. As DIG NA Mir was my neighbor, I informed him that I had published a brief news item and intended to publish an in-depth article in my monthly magazine 'Street Voice', following our publication schedule, which was set for 15 days later.

Nevertheless, the government promptly established an inquiry committee, with IGP Rajindra IPS serving as its chairman to investigate the police recruitment process. Concurrently, the six MLAs obtained a court-issued Stay Order to halt the recruitment proceedings. Over the next 15 days, I conducted extensive interviews with the six MLAs to gather their perspectives and comments. I also interviewed DIG NA Mir and the inquiry committee chairman. After a thorough analysis of all the facts, I sought legal counsel from Supreme Court lawyer S.S. Anand Lahar, and published the story in Street Voice magazine.

Upon the magazine's release, candidates who had participated in the recruitment process presented it in court. Consequently, the court exonerated DIG NA Mir of any wrongdoing and lifted the ban on the recruitment process. This outcome ensured justice for deserving candidates and held the errant MLAs accountable.

This news significantly raised my profile within the Jammu and Kashmir Police Department, and opposition party politicians began reaching out to me. I attribute all this to my honesty and the grace of my Guruji as I firmly believe that everything occurs according to God's will, and individuals are merely instruments.

In 2012, during a discussion on the political landscape with a former minister from my village, he suggested that legislative councils in states should be abolished. He revealed that in the past, an Imam from Delhi had got his people nominated in legislative councils directly from Sonia Gandhi in exchange for substantial sums of money. He encouraged me to write an article on this political issue. In that very month, I delved into this news, wrote a comprehensive article, and it's astonishing how after six years, Article 370 and 35A were repealed in Jammu and Kashmir, and the Legislative Council was permanently dissolved. I wish the individual who suggested this article were alive today to witness.

Sainik Colony was established in Jammu in 1980 as a tribute to the brave Indian soldiers who sacrificed their lives in the India-Pakistan war of 1971. It was managed by the "Sainik Cooperative House Building Society Limited, Jammu." The society's management committee, formed in accordance with cooperative laws, consisted entirely of retired soldiers and officers. This committee allocated approximately 5000 plots and shops to serving and retired officers, as well as other ranks at highly affordable prices. In no time, Sainik Colony became the largest and most prestigious residential colony in Jammu.

However, things took a different turn in Sainik Colony after 1990 when owners of plots and shops began selling their properties to civilians at inflated prices. The chairman and committee members started acquiring these properties from the sellers under the names of their relatives. With the exception of a few members, most of them anonymously acquired multiple plots and shops. Since committee elections occurred every four years, they had ample time to secure their positions, successfully retaining their seats during each election. As a result, a significant land scandal was unfolding, disguised as legitimate property transactions.Many chose to ignore it.

Furthermore, internal divisions within the committee led to the emergence of two factions, with the Padwal faction heavily involved in land transactions. Consequently, numerous legal cases were filed against this faction. What was once known as Sainik Colony now housed a diverse population, including doctors, engineers, IAS and IPS officers and numerous businessmen. The situation had evolved to the extent that almost every household had a property dealer.

Meanwhile, the management committee of Sainik Colony underwent a complete transformation, significantly altering the colony's landscape. The green belt, originally intended for lush trees, was encroached upon, leading to the creation and sale of plots. Even the parks were trimmed and reduced in size. The committee members were so deeply engaged in these illicit activities that they paid little attention to a massive shopping complex under construction within Sainik Colony. Consequently, this shopping complex remains unfinished to this day, attracting only migrant laborers in the morning and evening.

Frustrated by the manipulation and high-handedness of the first group, the second group approached me with concrete evidence. Consequently, in 2008, I published an extensive article titled 'Sainik Colony: A Pandora's Box' in a magazine ‘Street Voice’. This article featured comments from prominent individuals such as Revenue Minister Raman Bhalla, Councilor, and former Chairman Thakur Jai Singh, as well as Registrar of Cooperatives Society Jammu

Kashmir GM Kasba IAS. Following the publication of this article, retired Major BD Pangotra and retired Colonel KS Padhwal urged the state crime branch to launch an investigation against the management committee. Two months later, fresh elections were held, resulting in the victory of Colonel Padwal's group which had opposed the actions of the first group. Colonel Padwal was subsequently appointed as the chairman of the new management committee, bringing about a significant change in leadership.

However, as the saying goes, greed can often lead to one's downfall, and this truth became evident in Colonel Padwal's case. When he assumed the role of committee chairman, he exacerbated the existing issues. The first group, which had previously criticized the committee's members, returned to me with fresh evidence of misconduct. The Sainik Colony matter had evolved into a land scandal with an estimated worth of approximately Rs 750 crore, but no one in Jammu seemed willing to expose it. Even the Chief Editor of 'Street Voice' had declined to publish any news related to Sainik Colony due to his involvement in the real estate business and his friendships with several old committee members. This situation prompted me to collaborate with the BPN Publications Group from Delhi, which published the daily newspaper BPN Times and magazines like BPN Today. I assumed the role of Jammu Bureau Chief for BPN Today Magazine, and one of my initial actions was to publish a report on Sainik Colony.

Meanwhile, a parliamentary session was underway in Delhi, with Omar Abdullah serving as the Chief Minister of Jammu and Kashmir, and his father, Dr Farooq Abdullah holding the position of Union Minister. When Dr Farooq Abdullah came across the magazine's report, he promptly contacted Omar Abdullah and advised him to dissolve the management committee of Sainik Colony and appoint a government-appointed administrator. Without hesitation, the Chief Minister instructed the Chief Secretary to dissolve the committee, and Udham Das Sharma KAS was appointed as the administrator of Sainik Colony. Following this development, Colonel Padwal and others were removed from the committee's office by the police and an investigation was initiated.

Udham Das Sharma is renowned for his unwavering integrity. Prior to this appointment, he had also cleared the IPS exam, but he chose not to join the IPS.In 2008, he successfully passed the JKAS exam and joined the Jammu and Kashmir State Services.

From 2012 to the present day, the Sainik Cooperative House Buildings Society Limited in Jammu has been operating effectively under government supervision, and residents now find satisfaction with the current situation.

On the day the government disbanded the management committee of Sainik Colony in response to my magazine's report, a jubilant atmosphere enveloped the colony. Hundreds of residents celebrated by waving magazines, playing drums, and distributing sweets. Their actions clearly reflected their relief and joy at the removal of the corrupt individuals who had mismanaged Sainik Colony, with control now resting in the hands of the government.

All the media outlets in Jammu sought to publish a comprehensive account of this significant development.It was widely acknowledged that I was the most qualified individual to provide an in-depth and transparent analysis of the situation. Amidst these events, the Chief Editor of a newspaper called 'Daily The Latest' approached me to contribute to his publication, an offer I readily accepted. Given the staggering sum of approximately Rs 750 crore involved in this scandal and the menacing presence of the land mafia, my life was in serious jeopardy. Consequently, I held discussions with Chief Editor Sardar Gurjit Singh, accompanied by DGP Ashok Prasad IPS, ADG SP Vaid IPS, IGP Jammu Rajesh Yadav IPS and SSP Jammu Atul Goyal IPS, in which I explained the precariousness of my situation. All of them encouraged me to write fearlessly about such scams and assured me of my safety. I proceeded to write 30 consecutive articles on the Sainik Colony scandal over a span of 30 days. During this period, Sardar Gurjit Singh's security personnel and his vehicle were constantly at my disposal for protection.

Despite facing daunting and challenging circumstances, my resolve never wavered for a single moment. However, observing my involvement in such risky work under these conditions deeply impacted my daughter. She pleaded with me to cease crime reporting, reminding me that society could be improved not only by exposing wrongdoings but also by promoting virtuous actions. Her words filled me with immense pride, and based on her counselling,I bid farewell to crime reporting and transitioned into the field of social service.

National

Why are people losing faith in judiciary?

R. Gopal Sharma

FRANKLY SPEAKING

King Cambyses of Persia, who once after discovering that a judge took a bribe, had him executed, his skin stripped and stretched on the judgement seat. Then he appointed the ex-judge's son as the new judge and warned him to remember the way his seat had been "cushioned".

Judicial system in our country is in a mess. On the one hand Indian judiciary is known for its independent verdicts safeguarding the rights of citizens, on the other trials and hearings are delayed or speeded up because of pressures of various types. The fact is that the rich and the powerful that have one great advantage in this country of ours; access they have access to lawyers who are sharp; they have access to money which can at times delay the judicial process.

All of us know the adjournment story in courts and what is more they have access to those who control the system. The system is too costly and cumbersome for a common man. In some cases the decisions came after the death of a beneficiary. World of justice has the golden motto reminding advocates and judges that justice delayed is justice denied. But delaying tactics have become an inalienable part of the judicial procedure. New dates of hearing are given with or without a meaningful pretext. Courts adjourn hearing much to discomfort of the litigants. Many witnesses/witness avoid coming to courts because of long wait and delay/failure in recording his/the ir statements on the announced date and some litigants including advocates draw sadistic pleasure out of it without caring for the institutional failure.

If justice delayed in justice denied, then the high courts across the country are in deep waters. For the backlog of pending cases is now a flood that shows no sign of abating. At last count, in 2007, there were nearly 40 lakh cases of dispose of in 21 high courts. As many as 46,925 cases were yet to be adjudicated on by the Supreme Court.

The magnitude of the problem was highlighted in the 2007-08 annual report of the Delhi HC, which noted 3,32,141 cases in hand. Some 600 of these are over 20 years old. Lawyers and judicial officers say the situation demands an urgent revamp of the way courts functions. "It's a pathetic state of affairs," says former attorney general, Soli Sorabjee. "The only remedy is for the government to appoint

STREET VOICE -20- APRIL, 2009

National

COURTING TROUBLE

The first ever impeachment motion was sought against Justice V. Ramaswamy in 1993. He was found guilty of misuse of his office as the chief justice of the Punjab and Haryana High Court. But abstention by the Congress saved him.

Former CJI Y.K. Sabharwal faced allegations of delivering orders on sealing operations in Delhi against principles of natural justice. He was also accused of furthering his family's business interests. No charges, however, were proved.

The committee on judicial accountability had accused SC judge M.M. Punchhi of corruption. Before the requisite support of MPs for impeachment was gathered, he was appointed the CJI. Notice of the motion was not presented to the Speaker.

For over eight years since 1999, Ashutosh Asthana, former central treasurer of Ghaziabad court, had diverted about Rs 7 crore from treasury fund in collusion with judicial officers to buy expensive gifts for judges. He is now in police custody.

Justice Nirmal Yadav of the Punjab and Haryana Court has been recused from judicial work after her name surfaced during the interrogation of the accused in connection with cash-at-judge-door scam. She is now on leave.

Allegations of corruption were levelled against A.S. Anand pertaining to his term in the Jammu and Kashmir High Court. But the charges against him could not be proved.

(Source: frontline, weekly)

Punjab and Haryana High Court, Nirmaljit Kaur and Nirmal Yadav, in connection with the cash-for-judge scam. A law officer sent Rs 15 lakh to Justice Nirmaljit Kaur's official residence and later claimed that it was meant for Justice Nirmal Yadav and had been delivered to Justice Kaur by mistake.

Though intended to protect a Judge from frivolous prosecution and unnecessary harassment, the power also bestowed on the Chief Justice of India a great deal of discretion. In the Justice K. Veeraswami case, the Supreme Court laid down that no criminal case can be filed against a Judge or Chief Justice of the High Court or Judge of the Supreme Court without the consent of the Chief Justice of India.

In the Ghaziabad provident fund scam, involving 34 judges belonging to lower courts, High Court and the Supreme Court, a misappropriation of Rs 23 crore from the PF of Class III and IV employees was detected on the basis of confessional statement of Ashutosh Asthana, a Ghaziabad court official. He reportedly confessed that he used the PF funds to buy expensive gifts for judges and their families. Although the police had secured vouchers and delivery receipts as preliminary evidence, the Chief Justice of India permitted the police to interrogate the Judges only through questionnaires. However, with the Uttar Pradesh police pleading its helplessness to investigate further the case with all its ramifications, the Supreme Court conceded the State government's request to hand over the case to the CBI.

The outcome of these cases will be keenly watched as they have a bearing on the accountability of the higher judiciary. Shanti Bhushan, veteran lawyer and head of the Campaign for Judicial Accountability and Judicial Reform says that 40 percent of High Court and 80 percent of lower court judges are corrupt. The Supreme Court, may be about 20 percent, we cannot say that every judge in the Supreme Court is clean. We have known of various cases in which Judges of the Supreme Court are also corrupt. But most of the judges in the Supreme Court are honest, some are even crusaders against judicial corruption. He further says that most of the corrupt judges takes bribes secretly. Only an investigation can help.

Indians would seek to know how the guilty and the tainted judges would be traced out and punished under the law of the land.

(rgopalsharma11@yahoo.com)

STREET VOICE -22- APRIL, 2009

National

THE WORK LEFT...

Five minutes per case. That's what Delhi HC estimates it has in a day for its backlog. We apply the formula to all 21 Hcs.

Cases	High Court	Years, to give 5 min to each case.
808226	ALLAHABAD	60
426347	MADRAS	32
367409	BOMBAY	27
332141	DELHI	25
279318	CALCUTTA	21
255696	PUNJAB & HARYANA	19
227752	ORISSA	21
212451	RAJASTHAN	21
187677	MADHYA PRADESH	21
147537	ANDHRA PRADESH	11
115750	KERALA	9
110639	GUJARAT	8
104237	KARNATAKA	8
102165	PATNA	8
74701	CHHATTISGARH	6
59339	GUWAHATI	4
49276	JHARKHAND	4
45374	JAMMU & KASHMIR	3
26781	HIMACHAL PRADESH	2
22807	UTTARANCHAL	2
67	SIKKAM	2
3955690	TOTAL Years to give that 5 mins:	297

Source: law ministry GOI

senior advocates who have no connection with the respective courts as judges for six months up to a year".

The reason for the huge backlog of cases in the Supreme Court is the number and types of cases it accepts rather than the number of judges.

The major embarrassment to the peoples faith is the mounting allegations of corruption against judges across the country stress the need for an institutional mechanism to ensure judicial accountability.

In the case of Justice Soumitra Sen of the Calcutta High Court, the in house committee constituted by the removal of Justice Soumitra Sen, Judge Calcutta High Court.

SOLI SORABJEE
Ex-Attorney General

The Chief Justice of India's letter to the Prime Minister indicates his keenness to strengthen the people's confidence in Judges at a time when serious cases of judicial corruption have cast their shadow on the credibility of the higher judiciary.

Chief Justice Balakrishnan also happens to be the first Chief Justice of India to grant permission to an investigating agency to register a criminal case

Supreme Court admission and disposal statistics for 2007

Type of matter	Disposal of admission matters	Institution of regular hearing matters	Disposal of regular hearing matters
Criminal	14387	1641	974
Ordinary civil	8191	710	603
Service	7324	1177	737
Indirect tax	3503	520	651
Land acquisition	3000	417	351
Direct tax	2690	556	312
Labour	2406	376	212
Rent Act	2245	176	159
Letter petition/PIL	909	68	43
Five judge Bench	27	15	13
All other categories	12,109	1,244	999
Total	56,791	6,900	5,054

Source: Supreme Court of India

Chief Justice of India has accused him of breach of trust and misappropriation of receivers funds for personal gain.

In an unprecedented move, the Chief Justice of India, Justice K.G. Balakrishnan, wrote to the Prime Minister, Manmohan Singh, recommending that the proceedings contemplated by Article 217(1) read with Article 124(4) of the Constitution be initiated for against Judges of a High Court. This power, conferred on the Chief Justice of India in 1991 in the Justice KI. Veeraswami case, remained unused all these years even though several cases of corruption within the higher judiciary had come to light.

Chief Justice Balakrishnan allowed the Central Bureau of Investigation to interrogate two judges of

(Next page, please)

STREET VOICE -21- APRIL, 2009

INTERVIEW
JUSTICE
V.N. KHARE

'Corruption is rampant in the lower courts'

Yet another case of judicial corruption was exposed last month when the Andhra Pradesh High Court suspended additional special judge for CBI cases T. Pattabhi Rama Rao following allegations of corruption. Charged on the basis of a complaint filed by the CBI, the special judge had allegedly taken a bribe of ₹5 crore to grant bail to former Karnataka minister Gali Janardhana Reddy in the illegal mining case. The vigilance wing of the high court found the allegation to hold merit. Former chief justice of India **V.N. Khare** *told* **Chandrani Banerjee** *that such incidents are now rampant. Excerpts:*

Are bribes for bail endemic now?
There is no doubt about it. It is rampant. Corruption in the lower courts is no secret. Sometimes, in the high court as well, cases of corruption have surfaced, but in my experience while I was in the Supreme Court, I have not witnessed anything similar.

In the lower courts, it's alleged that everything comes for a price. Rates are fixed for quick divorce, bail and other favourable verdicts.
Cases in the media glare, constantly scrutinised, are different. Otherwise it is very difficult for the common man. There are huge time gaps between hearings. Years are spent to get an order from the lower courts. So, it is difficult.

Subordinate courts function under the supervision of high courts. Should the higher courts be accountable?
The respective high courts have so much of work that monitoring district courts is just part of the routine. High courts have inspecting judges who are responsible for monitoring district courts. They go with a lot of band baaja and have lunch while on inspection. Inspecting judges are presented with a rosy picture and then they file a report. Now, the greater problem is that they are overburdened with work. Cases are in addition to administrative work, besides other mandatory official work. As a result, the inspecting judges of the high courts have no time to follow up. We need dedicated staff to monitor the district courts.

SANJAY RAWAT

"Judges are only human, like us. They come from the same society. Our society is all about quick successes. Short cuts are taken. Even by the judges."

What kind of monitoring is needed?
A team of three serving judges should be formed. These judges should dedicatedly monitor the district judges. Their judgements should be analysed and questioned. Their attendance and work should be scrutinised. Someone should question them about their performance. I feel doing that will put in some checks.

You mean to say work overload and pendency of cases have themselves become a factor in corruption?
Yes, to a large extent. The high court judges are overburdened and they have no time. They always inform the district court authorities before the visits. It causes a situation where the real problem never comes to the surface. A dedicated committee of judges will help, but we are short of people. To my knowledge, we have 13.2 judges for 10 lakh people. If required to, we use excess strength in a particular situation, but there is no permanent arrangement. We work on an ad-hoc basis and so there are problems.

Would a few suspensions control corruption in the lower courts?
They will certainly convey a message. When I was serving, I did take certain measures which sent the message across the country that any charge of corruption will be probed. Fast actions and decisions on charges levelled against judges always work as deterrent.

What is the role of the inspecting judges in controlling corruption?
They should conduct sudden checks, always unannounced, and also follow up on any complaint registered in the district courts. However, to actualise this, we have to have a sufficient number of good judges. The monitoring will then be effective and result-oriented.

What is the mechanism to keep the lower courts free from corruption?
A dedicated committee of judges that will only monitor lower courts. Punctuality, integrity and court orders—everything should be under the lens. Such accountability will ensure the right kind of order is delivered in every petition.

Is consumerism responsible for fostering corruption in lower courts?
Judges are only people, like us. They come from the same society. Society is all about taking short cuts. Society is about quick successes. So, short cuts are taken and the judges are no different. ◘

16 9 July 2012 OUTLOOK

Should SAHAYAK system in Indian Army be abolished?

The Parliamentary Standing Committee on Defence asked the army last year to abolish the colonial practice of employing brave soldiers (Jawans) as *'Sahayaks'* of officers as it felt that this system was 'demeaning and humiliating'.

In reply to the Committee's suggestion, the Ministry of Defence (MoD) has said that a Sahayak is "a comrade-in-arms" to an officer. The army has reacted to this suggestion by issuing instructions to its units to ensure that combatant soldiers are not employed on jobs that are not in conformity with the dignity and self-respect of a soldier.

'Sahayak' is a Hindi version of Batman or Security Aide. The Ministry of Defence has rightly said that a Sahayak (batman) is a comrade-in-arms to an officer. His duties are to ensure that an officer's dress is kept ready and laid out for all appropriate occasions for instance, PT dress, Uniform, Mess dress etc.

In war, he carries the wireless set of the officer, JCO to whom he is employed with apart from being with him in the thick and thin of war.

In other words, he is a buddy of the officer/JCO with whom he is working. This relationship is life-long and does not end with the retirement of both the officer and his Sahayak.

During his visit to India in February 1968, Lieut-Gen Sir Regimald Savory recorded about his relationship with his old batman: "I joined the 14 Sikh 54 years ago in 1914 when I was just 20 years old. Only this morning (8th February) Lance Naik Bhola Singh of the 14th Sikh, who had been wounded to Gallipoli in 1915, took the trouble to come all the way from his home to call upon me, and after 52 years we saw each other again. Now he is Chitti Dahri Walla and I am old and bald; but although we both have grown so much older, yet our affection for each other and our mutual pride in our Regiment stays as young as ever. Long may this continue".

Presently, in the Indian Army, some officers are taking liberty to employ Sahayaks on the below dignity jobs. According to a Colonel (Retd) of Sainik Colony, Jammu "Sahayaks are used as watchmen, washermen and domestic helps by the officers in army, they are ill-treated by the wives of the officers." He further added that so many jawans are seen in Sainik Colony to perform the duty of labourers where private constructions of bunglows of officer's are going on. Such officers should be taken to task to stop this unethical practice.

True, there is hardly a system or rule which is not being misused or abused in the post independence era. Eye brows are raised when we witness the misuse on the rise in the armed forces. In the month of January, 2010, a driver of army gypsy was slapped by the wife of a Commanding Officer of his unit at a public place in Jammu city. The Jawan happens to be a Gorkha who could not bear such an insult and retaliated back to that lady. The matter was however hushed up by the army authorities.

There have been many such incidents earlier also, but then, wise commanding officers contained and controlled emotions at a manageable level.

Now, the group clash between officers and jawans in the highly sensitive border Ladakh area with China is unheard of and indeed shocking. The incident points towards certain deep-rooted aberrations in the man management aspects of the Army. The incident sent ripples down the 1.13 million strong military, justifiably proud of its disciplined ethos and esprit de corps, and the entire defence establishment in South Block.

(Next page, please)

This shameful breach of discipline in the Army, whereby officers and jawans of an artillery regiment deployed in the Nyoma sector of eastern Ladakh only 45 km away from the Chinese Actual Line of Control (ALoC) violently clashed with each other on 10 May. The ugly brawl ended with the commanding officer of the 226 Field Regiment deployed in Durbuk, Colonel Prasad kadam, Major SK Sharma and two jawans being admitted to the military hospital at Leh with multiple injuries.

According to reports, it began when an orderly (sahayak) was thrashed by a group of five-six young officers for misbehaving with a Major's wife. The jawans started agitating after the Sahayak was not allowed to be taken to hospital for medical treatment by the officers. The crisis deepened when the officers ganged up to thrash the unit CO who tried to intervene on behalf of jawans. Pertinently, raising another issue of how the officers were allowed to have wives and families present during a training firing camp, that too, at highly sensitive operational areas.

It has been observed that the inexperienced, vain, ill-bred and inadequately briefed officers wives are generally bloated with wrong notions about 'officer jawan' relationship. this exacerbates an odd strain in the working relationship of officers and his men, especially when soldiers perform orderly duties.

Gone are the days when the jawans realm of activities and thinking were just limited to their 'soldierly professional' and welfare because of poor education. Presently, with educational standards rising, their awareness of socio-economic and political matters has also attained new heights. While enforcing discipline and managing the affairs of such a comparatively enlightened lot, the officers need to modify and upgrade their handling methods and managerial skills.

Clearly, the Ladakh incident shows the Army in poor light. There has been a complete leadership failure due to poor man management in the Artillery Regiment, which should not be taken lightly. The officers behaved like ruffians with their subordinate soldiers, which is highly condemnable. This the process tarnished the Army's good name and image.

Incidentally, the Sahayak system is not prevalent in the army only but is also in vogue in the paramilitary and police forces. In the police forces, its misuse need no explanation. A lot of man-power of the police is used even by the retired officers in the name of security (33% strength of the J&K police is deployed on security duty).

While asking the army to shed the batman system, the Parliamentary Committee, perhaps, seems to had forgotten that army is mean to fight war, insurgency and internal security duty. All its establishments are therefore designed after careful deliberation, and long time well rehearsals to cater war-like situations and the seige within.

It is high time to abolish the 'Sahayaks' system than to disband the Unit. ■

FLASH BACK

In 1964, a battalion of the Assam Regiment was disbanded because of acts of collective indiscipline. Whereby, subsequent investigations showed this indiscipline was the direct outcome of poorest leadership and management.

9 Sikh unit was disbanded following Operation Bluestar at the Golden Temple Amritsar when some recruits posted at Ramgarh mutinied

In 2003, a Sahayak stabbed himself after molesting major's wife at Satwari Cantt in Jammu.

WHAT THEY SAID

There is no 'sahayaks' system in Indian Air Force and Indian Navy. Then, why in Indian Army?

- An Air Force Officer, on the condition of anonymity

"Good Officers, Good Army, Bad Officers, Bad Army."

- Field Marshal Cariappa

Mohammad Aijaz puts Poonch on Civil services map; ranks 268

26 year old Mohammad Aijaz has realized his dream. Ranked 268 in the merit list of the UPSC exam, Aijaz, son of Ch Ghulam Nabi, belongs to a tribal family.

He is the first ever candidate to clear the exam from Poonch district.

An ITI-Delhi pass out, he scored 95% marks in his B-Tech Mechanical. Last year, he was appointed as an Indian Revenue Service officer and is working as assistant income tax commissioner in Nagpur, maharashtra.

He has also been selected for the state services, KAS. "I had an aim to be an IAS officer since my childhood. I want to work for the empowerment of people of remote areas, told the Street Voice over phone.

Aijaz said that he had to walk 6 km to reach his school, and there was no guidance from his family or friends.

I have struggled a lot. I had passion to achieve my goal, and I have don it.

The topper did his schooling from a government school in Mendhar, Poonch and +2 from Jain School, Jammu. He did he B-Tech from IIT Delhi, and then selected for Indian revenue Services (IRS) before results.

Aijaz wants to work, for the empowerment of the people of the Jammu and Kashmir, especially people from backward areas like Poonch, Rajouri, doda, Kishtwar, where the resources are very limited.

"My first priority will be my own state, especially my own district Poonch," said Aijaz.

JUNE, 2012 STREET VOICE 30

Cleavage in Corridors of Power in J&K

FEMALES ARE WORST AFFECTED

IN his address on Civil Services Day, the Prime Minister advised civil servants "to fight the tendency of not taking decisions because of the fear that things might go wrong and they might be penalised for that." He went on to say that the bureaucracy should not be "100 percent risk averse" and concluded, rightly, that "a civil servant who does not take decisions might always be safe, but at the end of the day he or she would have contributed nothing to our society."

These views cannot be faulted. Indeed, over the past several months, while we have debated many issues, we have forgotten that, at the grassroots level, service delivery is in the hands of civil servants. If they fail to take decisions in time, governance will be seriously damaged. We need to ask why civil servants are risk-averse and what needs to be done to give them confidence.

R. Gopal Sharma

FRANKLY SPEAKING

The root of the problem lies in the administrative system that we have inherited and which we have sustained through the years. Any system based on distrust will tend to build safeguards and hurdles that inhibit, rather than promote, decision-making. The tendency of a middle-class, God-fearing bureaucrat who wants to survive without getting into serious controversy would be to avoid decision. Exhortations are unlikely to yield results. The only option is systemic change. Unfortunately, as most civil servants are lost in the routine of administration, very little time is devoted to reforms, as important in governance and in the economic sphere.

This is not that fear only paralyses all functionaries. Annals of civil services record are full of evidence that many young officers have significantly contributed to streamlining administration, starting innovative projects and reaching out to the people. Even today they are no less capable and more susceptible to temptation than former civil servants. Of course times have changed, what would be swept under the carpet earlier is now open to public scrutiny. This could create an illusion of lower ethical standards but it could not be a thumb rule that there has been a deterioration in the quality of administrative leadership.

What has changed is that decision making has become more complex and difficult. In most cases, when a civil servant takes a decision, he works in a zone of uncertainty. He does not have all the facts. He does not know all the possible outcomes. Yet he has to take a decision because he has no time. His decision, taken in good faith, may well prove wrong when judged in the future. Indeed, it could even look like an act of corruption or malfeasance. The court of law or an inquiry commission, the CAG or the CVC, looking into an administrative decision, has the benefit of hindsight. It has all the facts at its disposal, knows the outcome and, therefore, can pronounce with authority on what was right and what was wrong.

There have been many cases in the recent past when the sins of commission and, more often, of omission in the higher echelons of administration have been visited on junior functionaries. Perhaps the big difference between authority in the past and authority now is the reluctance on the part of the senior to take responsibility for the actions he has knowingly taken and to shift the blame as far down as possible. This is not an

(Next page, please)

GLARING EXAMPLES

Legislatures have been on war path with the Judiciary, Police and the Media. In J&K, they are always daggers drawn with the local administration thus setting crude examples of political interference in government functioning.

1. It is alleged that former Dy. CM & Senior Congress leader Mangat Ram Sharma always locked horns with senior IAS, Officer Smt. Sonali Kumar. In her 32 years of long career in J&K, she has not even been assigned the duty of Deputy Commissioner and Div. Com. Moreover, her next grade of Chief Secretary which is due, to her since 2000 is still pending. Sonali Kumar is now away on deputation.
2. In 2008, PDP Rajya Sabha Member T.S. Bajwa threatened the SDM R.S. Pura, Mandeep Kour of dire consequences over a land dispute and an FIR No. 19/2008 was registered against T.S. Bajwa and his supporters. Mandeep Kour also got deputation with Union Health Ministry.
3. In Dec 2011, government transferred Ms. Sheetal Nanda, IAS, Additional Deputy Commissioner Jammu to Deputy Commissioner Reasi, after four months she was attached with General Administrative Department and on 4th July 2012, the officer was adjusted as Additional Secretary to government Power Development Department.
4. In the same order by the cabinet meeting of December 2011, Ms. Yasha Mudgal,IAS, Project Director Sarv Shiksha Abhiyan, was transferred to district Kupwara as Deputy Commissioner but after two days only the order was amended and she was directed to continue at her previous place of posting.

environment conducive to decision-making.

The problem is compounded by political action, which can sometimes be arbitrary, capricious and manifestly unfair. In Jammu and Kashmir, average tenure of District Magistrate, and Superintendent of Police in each district was incredibly short sometimes even a month. Rediculous to note that when an officer reached a district HQ to assume the charge, he would find some one else occupying the chair and transfer orders awaiting him. Punishment need not necessarily be through a disciplinary proceeding or in response to a mistake, intended or otherwise. Punishment through transfers and humiliation can be inflicted for reasons of political inconvenience. In such circumstances, an honest officer would rather avoid taking decisions than inviting trouble.

In the present system, no effort is being made to link performance with reward. Seniority has precedence over merit. Non-action plus seniority is a sure-short combination for climbing up the hierarchical ladder. Of course, a bit of political savvy would help. Also a big slice of luck, as in any aspect of life.

Civil servants, particularly the honest among them, are highly vulnerable. The anti-establishment stance probably sells more, but restraint and balance are required while reporting. Also, giving some publicity to the good work they have done would play a big role in rebuilding our state and its administration. Unfortunate propaganda has also been given to unsubstantiated allegations against individual officers.

Strength of IAS Officers J&K State

1.	**Fixed Scale (80,000)**	02
	(i) Chief Secretary (fixed scale)	01
	(ii) Financial Commissioner, Revenue	01
2.	**Above Super Time Scale**	
	(HAG Scale-67,000-79,000 Annual Increment @ 3%)	10
	(i) Principal Secretary	06
	(ii) Chairman J&K Special Tribunal	01
	(iii) Principal Secretary to Hon'ble Chief Minister	01
	(iv) Principal Secretary to Governor	01
	(v) Principal Resident Commissioner	01
3.	**Super Time Scale**	18
	Pay Band (37,4000- 67,000 plus grade pay Rs. 10,000)	
	(i) Commissioner/ Secretary to Government	11
	(ii) Divisional Commissioners	02
	(iii) Transport Commissioner	01
	(iv) Chief Electoral Officer	01
	(v) Excise Commissioner	01
	(vi) Registrar Cooperative Society	01
	(vii) Commissioner Commercial Taxes	01
4.	**(I) Senior Time Scales**	45
	Selection Grade/Junior Administrative Grade/ Senior Scale 15,600- 39100 Grade pay-i. Rs 54,00 ii. Rs 6600, iii. Rs 7600	
	(ii) Deputy Commissioners	22
	(iii) Director Industries & Commerce	02
	(iv) Director Consumer Affairs & Public Distribution	02
	(v) Secretaries/ Special Secretaries/ Additional Secretaries to Government	06
	(vi) Labour Commissioner	01
	(vii) Settlement Commissioner	01
	(viii) Additional Deputy Commissioner	04
	(ix) Additional District Development Commissioners	07
	Total Authorized Strength	75
1.	Central Deputation Reserve not exceeding 40% of item 1 above	30
2.	State deputation reserve not exceeding 25% of item 1 above	18
3.	Training Reserve not exceeding 3.5% of item 1 above	02
4.	Leave Reserves and Junior Posts Reserve not exceeding 16.5% of item 1 above	12
5.	Posts to be filled up by promotion under rule 9 of Indian Administrative Service Recruitment Rules, 1954 not exceeding 50% of item 1, 2, 3 and 4	62
6.	Posts to be filled up by direct recruitment (items 1 + 2 + 3 + 4 + 5 - 6)	75
7.	Total Authorized Strength	137
	Existing strength as on 04.07.2012 (RR + SCS)	100
	On Deputation	19
	On Leave	01
	Probationer	09
	Inter-Cadre Transfer	01

To protect the rights of the individual, there should be a provision for legal remedy. Parliament needs to look at a possible privacy act, which exists in many other countries and at the provisions for defamation.

(rgopalsharma11@yahoo.com)

Should Legislative Council of Jammu & Kashmir be abolished?

The upper House of Assembly is a failed institution which needs terminal reform

The Constitution of Jammu and Kashmir was adopted on November 17, 1957 and given effect from January 26, 1957.

Part VI of the Constitution deals with the State Legislature, which shall consist of the Governor and two Houses to be known as the Legislative Assembly and Legislative Council. However, under the present Constitution the State Legislature is the highest law making body with the powers to legislate on all matters, except those with respect to which parliament has powers to make laws for the State under the provisions of the Constitution of India.

The Legislative Council is to consist of 36, indirectly, elected members giving representations to function groups, local bodies and other unorganised social interest. Of these, eleven members are elected by the members of the Legislative Assembly from amongst the residents of the Kashmir province who are not members of the Legislative Assembly and at least one each being elected to represent the districts of Ladakh and Kargil Tehsil. Eleven members are to be elected by legislative Assembly from amongst the residents of the Jammu province who are not members of the Legislative assembly, at least one each being elected to represent the districts of Doda and Poonch. One member, each from the two provinces is elected by the electorate constituted of the members of the Municipal Councils, of each of Councils, Town Area Committees and notified area committees of each of the two provinces. One member each from he two provinces is elected by the electorate constituted of the members who have been for at least three years, engaged in teaching in educational institutions recognized by the government. Two members by each of the two provinces are to be elected to the Council by the electorates constituted of the members of Panchayats and such other local bodies as the Governor may by order specify.

The Governor is empowered to nominate six members, not more than three of whom shall be persons belonging to any of the socially, or economically backward classes in the state, and the others shall be persons having special knowledge or practical experience in respect of matters such as literature, science, art, cooperative movement and social service. Both the Houses are to elect their presiding officers known as Speaker and Dy. Speaker and Chairman and Deputy Chairman respectively.

The Council unlike the Assembly is not subject to dissolution but one third of its members retire every two years.

As the Constitution embodies a parliamentary system of government the Legislature exercise control over the political Executive the Council of Ministers.

In matters of Legislation, the respective powers of the two Houses envisaged in the Constitution are also somewhat after the pattern of other parliamentary democracies. The Constitution recognises the pre-eminence of the Legislative Assembly over the Legislative Council. All bills other than the money bills, however, can be introduced in either House of the Legislature and before presentation of the Governor for his assent, are required to be passed by both the Houses.

A bill pending in Legislative Assembly does not lapse by reason of the prerogation of the House or the Houses thereof. A bill pending in the Legislative Council, which has not been passed by the Legislative Assembly does not lapse on the dissolution of the Assembly. But a bill which is pending in the Legislative assembly or which, having been passed by the Legislative Assembly is pending in the Legislative

(Next page, please)

STATE	NO. OF MLCS	SCAMS
Bihar	96	No.1 in corruption
Karnataka	75	Mine scam
Maharashtra	78	Adarsh Society Scam
Uttar Pradesh	100	NRHM scam, ration scam
J&K	36	No.2 in corruption

J&K Secretariat, Kashmir

Council lapses on the dissolution of the Assembly.

The framers of the Constitution have so devised the Legislature procedure that the Legislative Council cannot veto bills passed by the Legislative Assembly. It cannot claim equal and coordinate Legislative powers with the Assembly. It can only delay the passage of hasty and ill considered legislation by the Assembly and in certain circumstances invoke the judgement of the electorate. the Council can be a centre of resistance to the abuse of Legislative powers.

The Council does not exercise any control over the ministers. But it has a right to keep itself fully informed of the policies and functions of the government.

The Legislature exercises control over the finances of the State. No tax can be levied without the consent of the Legislative Assembly.

As far as money bills are concerned the Constitution provides that no money bill can be introduced in the Legislative Council. After the Legislative Assembly has passed such bills they are to be transmitted to the Council for its recommendations to be made within fourteen days of its receipt. The Legislative Assembly is free to accept or reject recommendations. If the bills is not returned within the said period, it will be deemed to have been passed by both the Houses in the form in which the Legislative Assembly has passed it.

The Constitution, thus, recognises the pre-eminence of the Legislative Assembly over the Legislative Council.

Alas! over the last decade or so, the upper House has become populated by moneybags, carpetbaggers, opportunists and folks who see it as an exclusive club and a venue to rub shoulders with important ministers and politicians. Legislators from small districts have become the target of unscrupulous people with ready cash. It has become common for money bags to pay for votes to enter the upper House, sit on Assembly standing committees dealing with subjects of interest to them and try and fix policy in their favour. The Legislative Council was supposed to be the dignified House of Elders which would moderate the more populist instincts of the Assembly through reasoned debate. Today, it has become an arena populated by businessmen and fixers. The idea of the Legislative Council has failed. It could be fixed in two ways. One, directly elect its members; or two, scrap the Legislative Council and add seats to the Legislative Assembly.

It is not as if the leadership does not know these things. Every state subject and Indian is aware that large scale scams are adding shame for the nation. It has increased enormously in the last three scams which has rocked the whole country. It is Pertinent to mention here that most of the scams came to surface mainly in the states where members of Legislative Council have been nominated. Bihar and J&K achieved dubious rank of being No. 1 and 2 corrupt states of India as per transparency international.

The time has perhaps, come to think honestly for the future of Jammu and Kashmir State Legislative Council.

Let the corridors of power do some spade work and find out whether the seats are filled by deserving persons or not. Top politicians, high and mighty should not way it with money and muscle power but try to search Navratnas to make Jammu and Kashmir a living paradise on earth.

(The ideas expressed are the author's own and concurrence of the editorial stance is not necessary)

MAY, 2012 STREET VOICE 35

Original plan for colony of defence personnel flouted

EXPRESS NEWS SERVICE
JAMMU, JUNE 10

FLOUTING all norms, the purpose of raising a planned colony for the defence personnel at Jammu was affected as the respective management committee of Sainik Cooperative House Building Society Limited over the period had failed to stick to its original master plan.

According to resident members, the actual plan outlay of the colony is not followed by the management during construction. They said that according to the plan, there was a plot meant for the hospital site, but the managment allotted the same land for 36 shops.

The residents said that original plan of the colony over the period of time had been amended by the management without taking into confidence the general body of the society.

Maj (retd) B.D.Pangotra, resident of the colony, said that a huge self-financed shopping-cum-commercial complex on 60 kanals of land consisting seven storeys at a cost of Rs 25 crore was envisaged in 1997 by the management committee. He said that the execution of project started immediately thereafter without seeking any prior approval either from the general body of this society or the Registrar Cooperative Societies.

He said that management committee was not competent to undertake such a huge project. But it allotted the contract to a firm from Delhi, without floating any tenders, he said and added that the construction of shopping complex was carried on the prime land of the colony, which was specially earmarked in the original plan outlay for hospitals, school, college and community hall.

Another resident member of the society, Kuldeep Sharma said that even the parking place had been allocated for the construction of shops by the management committee. He said that the master plan had totally been neglected and all the utility places were being used for commercial purposes.

Pangotra said that over a period of time, map no. 36A had completely been violated by the respective management committees. He said that in orginal plan, there was provision of 64-f00t wide roads, but in most of the areas the width was curbed according to the will of management committee.

Surender Kumar Raina, another resident, said that the management committee asked all those interested members to deposit certain amount to own a shop in the multi-storey shopping complex being constructed. He said that after collecting the money, the manmagement committee stopped the work for the reasons best known to it.

He said that the management committee decieed to construct the shopping complex without seeking prior permission from general body of the society.

Further, these residents said that despite their repeated complaints to the Registrar Cooperative Societies and Additional Registrar Cooperative Societies, no action had been taken so far. They said that due to violation of original master plan, unplanned structures are coming up in the colony.

However, when contacted, Registrar, Cooperatives J&K G.N.Qasba, expressed his ignorance that the matter was ever brought to his notice. He said that whenever the residents complained in his notice, he would definitely look into the matter.

When he was informed that in 1995, an enquiry conducted by Additional Registrar Cooperatives had indicated tempering with the plan outlay of the colony, Qasba expressed his ignorance by saying that the matter was too old as he had assumed the office after this.

, NOVEMBER 18, 2013 12 PAGES PRICE RS. 2

JUNGLE RAAJ IN SAINIK COLONY-XII

Biggest multi (700) Crore Scam in Asia; Sainik Colony Co-op Society Jammu; surpasses Adarsh Society Scam

S.GURJEET SINGH

JAMMU, NOV 17: The Jammu and Kashmir Government vide Notification RD No. 240 of 1970 published in the J&K Gazette published on July 23, 1970/Ist Sravana, 1892 said, "Whereas land is required by the Government for a public purpose, namely for construction of Sainik Cooperative Housing Colony, it is declared that the undermentioned land is so required. This declaration is made under section VI of the Land Acquisition Act 1990 Svt as amended upto date and under section VII of the said Act, the Collector is directed to take order for acquisition of the said land.

District Jammu, Tehsil Jammu, Mouza Sunjawan, K.M. 2013-19 Khasra No. 389-396, 672, 673, 675....."

The J&K Government vide its another notification No. 7/RD of 1972-73 said, " In exercise of the powers conferred by section...., I JP Kesar, IAS Collector, Additional Deputy Commissioner, Jammu hereby notify that the land particulars mentioned below are required for construction of Sainik Cooperative Housing Colony,...... Village Chowadi, tehsil Jammu, district Jammu, Khasra No. 126/M, 127, 128.,.....837/M."

The land was awarded by the J&K Government to Sainik Cooperative House Building Society in 1972-73 for and by ex-men.

The Colony was meant for Ex-servicemen belonging to Army, paramilitary forces and its Managing Committee was also supposed to be of the ex-men. But as the land-mafia, politicians, corrupt bureaucrats and businessmen developed their vested interest in the colony, the Management Committee was infiltrated by such unscrupulous elements who became the Directors and even Chairman of the Managing Committee of Sainik Cooperative House Building Society.

The issue was left to be untouched as the corrupt bureaucrats heading the Cooperative Society department and the masters in political circles managed to stay in the managing Committee and influence many issues concerning the residents of the area.

The government has, however, remained indifferent to the matters of the Sainik Colony and corrupt and land mafia have flourished like anything.

A list of Managing Committee members of Sainik Colony HBS is reproduced herewith.

Period wef Jun 1995 to May 1998

Hav VK Majotra	Chairman
Lt Col SS Chib	Joint Chairman
Col KS Jamwal	Director
Col Inder Raj	-do-
JWO Mohan Singh Jamwal	-do-
Hony Capt Awatar Singh	-do-
Hony Capt Charat Singh	-do-
Shri JS Jamwal	-do-
Shri KS Samyal	-do-
Hony Capt Sodagar Singh	-do-
Hony Capt. SL Sharma	-do-

Period wef [illegible] 1998 to May 1999

[illegible]	Chairman
[illegible]	[illegible]
Col KS Jamwal	Director
Col Inder Raj	-do-
Capt GL Sharma	-do-
Hony Capt Sodagar Singh	-do-
JWO Mohan Singh Jamwal	-do-
[illegible]	-do-
Hony Capt Awatar Singh	-do-
Hony Capt Charat Singh	-do-
Hav VK Magotra	-do-

Period wef [illegible] to Jun 2002

[illegible]	Chairman
[illegible]	Joint Chairman
[illegible]	Director
[illegible]	-do-
[illegible]	-do-
[illegible]	-do-
[illegible]	-do-
[illegible]	-do-
[illegible]	-do-
[illegible]	-do-
[illegible]	-do-

Period wef Jun 2002 To Jun 2008

[illegible]	Chairman
[illegible]	Joint Chairman
Lt Col [illegible] Singh	Director
Sub Narinder Singh	-do-
[illegible]	-do-
[illegible]	-do-
[illegible]	-do-
[illegible]	-do-
Col Inder Raj	-do-
[illegible]	-do-
[illegible]	-do-

Period wef Jun 2008 To 18 Aug 2012

Col KS [illegible]	Chairman
JWO MS Jamwal	Joint Chairman
Maj Gurdeep Singh	Vice Chairman
Sub Narinder Singh	Director
Hony Capt Gandharb Singh	-do-
Col Inder Raj	-do-
Lt Col SS Chib	-do-
Maj [illegible] Singh	-do-
Hony Capt Suraj Bhan Choudhary	-do-
Nb Sub Daulat Ram	-do-
Lt Col OD [illegible]	-do-

This is only the tip of iceberg

.... to be continued

A PAPER WITH FOLLOW UP

EST

Email:- thelatest.newspaper@gmail.com

ESDAY, DECEMBER 25, 2013 12 PAGES PRICE RS. 2

JUNGLE RAAJ IN SAINIK COLONY-XXX

NO PROBE, NO ENQUIRY SAINIK SOCIETY GOING TO DOGS

Biggest Multi (750) Crore Scam in Asia; Sainik Colony Co-op Society Jammu; surpasses Adarsh Society Scam

Who is stalling the probe...?

S.GURJEET SINGH

JAMMU, DEC 24: Despite serious observations raised by the Audit team during the audit of records of Sainik Co-operative House Building Society Ltd., Jammu for the year 2012-13 Cooperative department seems to be in deep slumber and no action against the defaulter till date has been taken.

One such observation raised by the Audit party pertaining to Defence Colony at Thandi Khui is that an amount of Rs 8,15,94,000/- has been paid to the brokers for purchase of land at Defence colony Thandi Khui. As per the statement furnished by the Society only 30.5 kanal land has been registered in the Court of Law in the name of society with physical possession of 22 kanal land against the amount paid. The possession of land is devoid of any registry in the court of law. The amount has been paid on Agreement to sell attested by the Notary only. This clearly indicates nexus between brokers and Board of Directors who paid such a huge amount without any possession of land.

Initially the land was purchased at the rate of Rs. 1,47,000/- per kanal from one Rattan Lal against an agreement between Rattan Lal and the Society. thereafter the rate was enhanced to Rs. 2,10,000/- per kanal and again enhanced to Rs. 2,96,000/- per kanal. Finally another agreement with Balkar Singh, Secretary, Jammu Cooperative House Building Society, R.S. Pura at the rate of Rs. 2,50,000/- per kanal was made. How the rate has been different from time to time and why the land has been purchased on higher rate without going to complete the legal formalities required remains a mystery to Audit team also. Moreover, the agreement between the parties and the Society since has expired. The Society has failed to take the possession of the land from the brokers. The detail of payment made against purchase of land from the brokers is:- Rattan Lal, Rs. 60,25,000/-, Anil Chopra Rs, 22,72,000/-, Sunil Chopra Rs. 22,72,000/-, Balkar Singh Rs. 7,10,25,000/-, Total Payment Rs 8,15,94,000/-. The payment of Rs 8,15,94,000/- paid against the purchase of land measuring 383 kanals 02 marlas from the brokers. As per the letter

contd on page 2

A PAPER WITH FOLLOW UP

Est

Email:- thelatest.newspaper@gmail.com

DECEMBER 27, 2013 12 PAGES PRICE RS. 2

JUNGLE RAAJ IN SAINIK COLONY-XXXI

NO PROBE, NO ENQUIRY SAINIK SOCIETY GOING TO DOGS

Biggest Multi (750) Crore Scam in Asia; Sainik Colony Co-op Society Jammu; surpasses Adarsh Society Scam

Is 'M' stalling the probe...?

S.GURJEET SINGH

JAMMU, DEC 26: Besides serious audit observations some other frauds came to fore during the course of investigation by The Latest team. It is alleged that the ex-management without consulting Revenue authorities or representing the government about setting up of defence colony, at Thandi Khui directly entered into frivolous and fraudulent contract/ agreements, accumulated about Rs 41,78,15,900 (Rupees Forty One Crore Seventy Eight Lakhs Fifteen Thousand and Nine Hundred only) from 2676 members with a promise with the plots shall be delivered to them within an year's time, however, with no land in hand, it seemed an impossible job.

Pertinent to mention here that on 14th of May, 2013, the Additional Deputy Commissioner, Samba vide public notice DCS/ADC/13-14/81-85 declared that the land over which various people and societies claim to be setting up colonies on is an agricultural land the nature of which cannot be changed. In the said notice, reference has been made of earlier notices and it was informed that any land purchased in violation of law void.

It is amply clear that the ex-management unmindful of the law governing the cooperative societies, without concurrence of AGM and thereafter bringing into the notice of the Registrar Cooperatives about the establishment of Defence Colony, dishonestly extracting the hard earned money of the prospective buyers when not even an inch of land was acquired. To hoodwink the public and the government, fake agreements were forged and deposits were misappropriated that about Rs 7,35,38,560 (Rupees Seven Crores Thirty Five Lakhs

JUNGLE RAAJ IN SAINIK COLONY-XXXII

NO PROBE, NO ENQUIRY SAINIK SOCIETY GOING TO DOGS

Biggest Multi (750) Crore Scam in Asia; Sainik Colony Co-op Society Jammu; surpasses Adarsh Society Scam

Pot calling the Kettle Black; Balkar's Society threatens Secretary SCHBSL; Mr. 'M' remains MUM

S. GURJEET SINGH

JAMMU, DEC 28: It is the POT AND KETTLE CALLING THE Administrator, Sainik Cooperative House Building Society BLACK for writing him to return the money and not allowing him to further loot the gullible members of the Sainik Society waiting for allotment of "never" to be developed 'Defence Colony' at Thandi Khui.

> **"Oho!" said the pot to the kettle;**
> **"You are dirty and ugly and black!**
> **Sure no one would think you were metal,**
> **Except when you're given a crack."**
> **"Not so! not so!" kettle said to the pot;**
> **"'Tis your own dirty image you see;**
> **For I am so clean - without blemish or blot -**
> **That your blackness is mirrored in me."**

The Secretary, The Jammu Co-operative Rural House Building Society Ltd. (R.S. Pura) in a strongly and 'wrongly' written letter to The Secretary, SCHBSL threatened him of launching defamatory proceedings. He also accused him of 'selling' the information to whistle blowers of the multi crore Sainik Society Scam being published exclusively in The Latest.

In his letter Ref No. JCRHBSL/2013-14/95 dated 13/12/2013, Secretary JCRHBSL led by ex-Sepoy Balkar Singh writes to Secretary Sainik Society reproduced verbatim below.

"The Secretary, Sainik Co-op House Building Society Ltd. Sainik Coloney Jammu

Subject: Development of Land Earmarked for the Sainik Cooperative House Building Society Ltd. Jammu REF: Your letter no. SCHB/PC-VOL-I dated 30- Nov 2013

Sir, It is strange that you being a Secretary of the society is writing letter without any basis, you have no knowledge about your society and its working. Your language of the letter is unparliamentary and defacematery in nature, therefore we reserve the right to proceed against you as per law. However Para wise reply of your letter is as under:- In reply to Para2. of your letter, please refer your letter no SCHBS/DC dated 17-10-2012. It has been stated and confirmed by the above said letter that your society has acquired 316 kanals and 07 Marla of land from our society. It was also intimated that agreement already signed has since expired and our society was asked to renew the agreement for further acquiring of land for you society. I have gone to your office a member of times and met Sh. Udam Dass, the then administrator, who asked me to go ahead

CHAPTER – 7

In 2014, Sainik School Nagrota, Jammu welcomed three new officers, and their arrival sparked a flurry of activity for three months. Principal Colonel K D Kaushal initiated numerous changes and development projects in the school, transforming its appearance. In my 14 years at the school, I had never witnessed such extensive improvements. The school's Registrar, Squadron Leader VK Sharma, and our Officer Commanding, Lieutenant Colonel Deepak Thakur, were honest and upright officers who were dedicated to providing quality education and an efficient system for the students. The Principal and the Registrar also exposed a long-running scam in the Accounts Department, particularly concerning the security fees of cadets. Despite the fact that security fees should have been refunded to cadets upon completing the 12th gradc, accountants BK Sood and SS Charak had evaded returning these funds for 20-25 years. Additionally, the computer department faced numerous issues. The computer assistant, who had been promoted to the role of a master grade without any vacancy, monopolized the department and prevented other primary teachers from teaching computer classes. This created discontentment among the teachers. The computer master, along with students and their parents, would file complaints against other teachers. He had even conspired with a student to falsely frame Subedar Naresh Singh and subsequently had that student expelled to avoid getting exposed. Subedar Naresh Singh managed to retain his job with difficulty, the computer master remained on my radar. I had been gathering evidence against him since 2001 and was awaiting the right opportunity.

Lab Assistant JN Sharma, TGT Maths NK Sharma, and PGT English AS Rana approached me regularly, seeking a solution to the computer master's misconduct. This teacher had a history of presenting inappropriate material to please the school's officers. One day, NK Sharma informed me that the school administration was attempting to forcibly retire AS Rana and NK Sharma and also planned to terminate another female chemistry teacher from the school, similar to what happened with Sangeeta Choudhary. Rana fell into depression upon hearing this news, and his wife became seriously ill as a result. The school had already initiated a process of searching for new teachers to replace these three educators. While NK Sharma and AS Rana had only two years left before retirement, the female teacher had only been employed for three years. In response, I submitted a complaint under the Whistle Blower Act to the Defense Ministry, prompting an investigation into the matter. As soon as the investigation began, these three officers shifted their focus away from expelling teachers and began attempting to uncover as to who had initiated the investigation against them. To teach these officers a lesson, I used to file a complaint against them once a month.

During that period, the school's atmosphere had deteriorated to such an extent that diligent and truthful employees were struggling. Out of the 39 cadets who participated in the NDA written exam, only 2 had passed. These three officers were actively looking for chances to torment the employees. With the exception of a few sycophantic workers and four military personnel, everyone else endured daily mistreatment. Even the employees were ordered to wear uniforms. To identify those who reported against the officers, the staff were subjected to such relentless intimidation that some teachers began informing on the officers and even used false identities with each other. People like JN Sharma, CL Pandita, NK Sharma, AS Rana, Rajwinder Singh, Babu Ram, and Miss Salona Bansal were aware that I was the driving force behind all of this. Despite this knowledge, they bore the officers' oppression but didn't disclose my identity because they had trust in me. My objective was to root out corruption from the school, allowing these individuals to perform their duties honestly once more.

Our Officer Commanding, Lieutenant Colonel Deepak Thakur also started applying unnecessary ways and means to harass me. Initially, he prohibited Babu Ram, who was working with me for computer works, believing it would increase my workload. However, I had managed to get Babu Ram appointed as the Junior Assistant Incharge from the NCC Group Headquarters, and I received instructions from the Headquarters that Babu Ram would work as my assistant. When Colonel Deepak Thakur's strategy failed, he began monitoring my office hours. Consequently, I became more punctual and consistently arrived at the office on time. Despite these maneuvers, I held deep respect for Colonel Deepak because he had an unblemished character and was not involved in corruption. My objective, if anything, was to have the computer teacher and the accountant dismissed from their positions.

During tea breaks, we would all congregate in a circle outside for tea. When I engaged in light-hearted conversations, few army personnel would shadow me, eavesdropping on my discussions. Any school employee who interacted with me would face unwarranted harassment from the officers. Similarly, driven by suspicion, they subjected Clerk Mangal Singh to harassment who eventually threatened to take his own life, after which he was left alone. However, NK Sharma and AS Rana remained undeterred by their actions. Occasionally, just to taunt the officers, both would give me hitchhike rides to Jammu.

During this period, I had to take a one-month leave for some important matters. Upon my return, I discovered that Jyoti Prakash Verma's father, a bright 12th-grade student, had passed away from a heart attack while he was at the school. I was acquainted with this student as he was an NCC cadet who frequently visited my office. It appeared that the school authorities had requested the student's parents to come to the school within three days regarding some issue. They had even threatened to expel their son if they didn't comply. However, the student's father, Subedar Om Prakash Verma, an Army Subedar stationed in Assam, was deeply concerned about his son's upcoming 12th-grade exams and the potential repercussions of his expulsion on his future. Fearing these consequences, the student's parents came to the school and were engaged in a conversation with these three officers and teachers. The specific details of their discussion remained undisclosed, but during the conversation, Subedar Om Prakash Verma suffered a heart attack. Realizing the severity of the situation, the Principal instructed the school's Medical Assistant, Rajinder Singh to promptly transport Subedar Om Prakash Verma to the 166 Military Hospital in Satwari,Jammu. Rajinder Singh drove the student's parents to the military hospital, but unfortunately,he did not survive. The Military Hospital then sent the body to the Government Medical College and Hospital in Bakshi Nagar for a postmortem examination. No one from the school accompanied them. Meanwhile, Jyoti Prakash Verma was in the midst of his 12th-grade exams and was not allowed to leave the hostel. Consequently, his mother was left alone to manage the hospital visits. The student's family originally hailed from Uttar Pradesh and were not familiar with Jammu. However, fellow students and their parents from the school managed to gather some funds and arranged for a Tata Sumo to be rented for the student's mother, allowing her to transport her husband's body to their home in Uttar Pradesh.

Jyoti Prakash was an exceptionally bright student, and his father had high hopes of seeing him become an army officer. Consequently, he enrolled him in the Sainik School Nagrota. However, following his father's demise, Jyoti Prakash was compelled to join the Air Force as an airman. His mother, lacking in education and burdened by the financial responsibilities of her son's education, found herself unable to take any action against the school administration. Upon being informed of this incident, I reached out to my friend, Ashok Kalra, who was serving as DSP in the CBI, seeking his guidance. He proposed that if directives were to come from the High Court, an investigation into the matter could be initiated. To this end, I had a phone conversation with the widow of the late Subedar, but she declined suggesting that perhaps it was meant to unfold this way. The question that lingered in my mind is whether any competent authority would initiate an inquiry in this matter.

In the aftermath of this incident, all three officers were apprehensive and eager to leave the school at the earliest opportunity. However, before that could materialize, I orchestrated an audit of Sainik Schools across the country by the CAG, resulting in the compulsory retirement of the computer master, who had 15 years of service remaining, and the accountant, who had 4 years of service left. Both of them were granted pensionary benefits. Additionally, it was revealed that the NCC Subedar and Havaldar, who used to report to the officers and needlessly harass Babu Ram, had been using counterfeit doctor's stamps on their ACR every year. When Babu Ram discovered this, he confronted the Commanding Officer, Lieutenant Colonel Deepak Thakur, who requested that this matter should not be disclosed to anyone. Although we never learnt whether action was taken against them, they had stopped harassing Babu Ram. Another female teacher, Salona Bansal was also subjected to relentless targeting. Salona's younger son was severely ill, and he could not bear to be separated from his mother. Despite this, the school administration detailed her to go to Karnataka for teacher training with the hope that this will force her to either resign due to her child's illness or be expelled from the school. However, fortune smiled upon Salona Bansal, and her teacher training trip was canceled.

Amid these developments, Brigadier G Rambabu, the inspecting officer from the Sainik Schools Society of New Delhi, arrived at Sainik School Nagrota to conduct an inquiry. During his visit, he was accompanied by the computer master, who had been proven guilty of all charges, on a trip to Vaishno Devi using the school vehicle. However, while at Vaishno Devi on a Saturday, he received a call from Delhi, summoning him to appear before the CAG at 10 am on Monday. Consequently, the inspecting officer returned to Delhi on Sunday. On the third day, the school administration dispatched his gifts to Delhi via NCC Subedar Bachittar Singh.

The impact of my crusade against corruption in Sainik Schools across the nation led to the management of student admissions in Sainik Schools being taken over by the National Testing Agency. This effectively put an end to the illicit activities of corrupt individuals, marking the pinnacle achievement of my life.

By this juncture, I had gained recognition in Jammu as the editor of Street Voice magazine, where I exposed significant scams and irregularities pertaining to NCC, Sainik School, and Sainik Colony. I had established a prominent presence in Jammu and had become acquainted with influential figures. However, there remained a threat to my life from those I had exposed. Consequently, I ceased riding a motorcycle since 2009 and avoided traveling alone. Whether I was on duty at Sainik School or undertaking journalistic assignments outside, my cameraman was always by my side like a constant companion.

In 2017, Sainik School had three new officers: Principal Captain A Muthuraman, Vice Principal Lieutenant Colonel Mithali Madhumita, and Major Angad Singh serving as Administrative Officer. All three were known for their integrity and dedication. The new Accountant, Computer Teacher, and Quarter Master had also joined the school, and Sainik School Nagrota was now headed in the right direction.

The fear of arbitrary expulsion or any kind of misconduct had dissipated, and all the staff members were enthusiastically performing their duties. During tea breaks, I frequently engaged in discussions with the teachers, particularly NK Sharma and Sandeep Rana. Occasionally, during tea breaks, Rajwinder Singh would invite me to his residence. Overall, I started finding satisfaction in my work at the office, and time appeared to pass smoothly.

In the interim, Vice Principal Lieutenant Colonel Mithali was promoted and subsequently transferred. On the other hand, Principal Muthuraman was also reassigned to Sainik School Goalpara. Once more, a new principal and vice-principal had arrived at the school.

Brigadier Rajan Jamwal, who served as the Group Commander at NCC Group Headquarters in Jammu, initially appointed a fourth-class employee in 1999 based on recommendations from ministers and officers. However, Lieutenant Colonel VK Khullar wrongly promoted them to the position of senior clerks and now, Brig Jamwal promoted them to Head Clerks without Secretariat Class Course. When we raised a complaint with the Directorate, they ordered the cancellation of their promotion. But he managed to obtain a stay order from the High Court. Brig Jamwal retired and in his place Brig MS Gill took over the command of NCC Group Headquarters, Jammu. As time passed, Brigadier M S Gill, who had been promoted to Major General, was transferred to NCC Assam, and he was succeeded by Brigadier Satish Kumar as the new Group Commander at NCC Group Headquarters, Jammu.

Among the officers under Brigadier Satish Kumar's command was Lieutenant Colonel Masood Ahmed Mufti, who had previously held a lower-ranking position as a

Havaldar Clerk but later became an army officer and was now serving as the training officer. With the retirement of the administrative officer Colonel Jagjit Singh, Mufti assumed his role, and the saying "*Bandar ab pansari ban gaya* (The monkey has now become a grocer.)" seemed to be a fitting description. Mufti's actions appeared tainted with corruption, and his conduct did not reflect the qualities expected of an officer, maybe it was due to his background as a clerk. Being a Kashmiri, he had close ties with clerks in the Civil Secretariat. Moreover, he had control over the NCC canteen.For a period of two years; he indiscriminately sold canteen liquor to the civilians. Mufti personally collected all the funds received from the Civil Secretariat. These three officers, Major General NK Airy, Brigadier Satish Kumar, and Lieutenant Colonel Mufti, engaged in ruthless corruption within the NCC. Brigadier Satish Kumar and Lieutenant Colonel Mufti relocated the NCC Group headquarters from Gandhi Nagar to Trikuta Nagar and misappropriated Rs 20-25 lakh in the process. The entire NCC was under a state of lawlessness, and anyone who dared to speak out against these officers was labeled as "dead wood" and forcibly made to retire.

In response to witnessing these corrupt practices, I gathered evidence spanning from 1986 to 2018 and submitted it to the Honorable Prime Minister Shri Narendra Modi through official channels. Consequently, my complaints were forwarded to the PMO Complaint Centre, and a response was sought.But they repeatedly delayed addressing the serious matter. In light of this, I composed another letter to the Prime Minister this time, including an affidavit and expressing my willingness to serve as a government approver. This prompted the PMO to reprimand the DG NCC, subjecting everyone from Delhi to Jammu to the PMO's scrutiny. In a state of panic and at the urging of Brigadier Satish and Lieutenant Colonel Mufti, a class IV employee named Laskar Satish Chaudhary was labeled as "dead wood" and forcibly made to retire. Additionally, another employee named Laskar Sunil Kumar was transferred from Jammu. When General Airy harassed lady clerk Saroj Jamwal with the intention of appointing one of his own men as a clerk, Saroj filed a complaint with the Defense Ministry.

One day, Brigadier NR Babu and Lieutenant Colonel Mufti Masood paid a visit to Sainik School and had a meeting with our Officer Commanding, Lieutenant Colonel Pawan. During this meeting, they conspired against me, alleging that I had left the office without obtaining permission. On that particular day, I was on authorized leave but Subedar Rakesh informed me that these three officers were pressuring him to provide a written statement against me, a request that Subedar Rakesh had declined. Interestingly, Lieutenant Colonel Pawan along with Major Angad Singh was involved in a financial irregularity amounting to Rs 5.5 crore at Sainik School, a matter that had been brought to my attention by teachers and clerks at the school. In fact, I had already filed a complaint against these two officers, a fact that Colonel Pawan had become aware of. Upon my return from leave, Colonel Pawan summoned me to his office, admitted his mistake. He explicitly conveyed to the other two officers, Colonel Mufti and Brigadier NR Babu, that they were at liberty to transfer me to Jammu Group Headquarters if they so desired. However, Colonel Pawan had unwittingly set in motion a series of events that would ultimately harm his own reputation.

Colonel Pawan took a one-month leave from November 18, 2020, while Principal Prashant Kishore was providing instructions from home due to the COVID-19 pandemic, and online classes had commenced at the school.

On December 15, 2020, I fell ill and took a month's leave. During this time, at the behest of Lieutenant Colonel Pawan, Brigadier Satish, Brigadier NR Babu, and Lieutenant Colonel Mufti attempted to coerce me into withdrawing my complaint lodged with the PMO by transferring me to Jammu Group Headquarters. Upon learning this, I submitted my resignation to the PMO on January 14, 2021. Subsequently, I publicized the injustices suffered by Sunil Kumar, Satish Chaudhary, and Saroj Jamwal in the newspapers and filed a complaint on their behalf through an NGO. Sunil Kumar was recalled from Poonch to Jammu, and Saroj's case was resolved with a warning. While Brigadier NR Babu and Major General NK Airy retired, an investigation was initiated against Brigadier Satish Kumar and Lieutenant Colonel Mufti. Concurrently, an inquiry was launched against Lieutenant Colonel Pawan at Sainik School Nagrota. Brigadier Satish Kumar and Lieutenant Colonel Mufti managed to evade the consequences as they had done previously, but the investigation placed significant strain on Lieutenant Colonel Pawan. The investigating officer of Sainik Schools Society, Brig PK Sharma, spoiled Colonel Pawan's ACR and cautioned him that any future action could jeopardize his eligibility for promotion.

Upon my complete recovery, I submitted my joining report to the NCC Group Headquarters Jammu on July 12, 2021. Colonel Surjit Singh assigned me to work with the SO, and Lieutenant Colonel Mufti avoided eye contact with me. Exactly one month later, in the absence of Colonel Surjit

Singh, I was sent back to Sainik School Nagrota. Upon my return, NCC Group Headquarters, in an attempt to rectify their faults, filed a response to the long-neglected arms and ammunition inspection case which had not been conducted for the past 21 years. Failing to do so would have exposed all the officers at Group Headquarters to serious consequences.

प्रधान मंत्री कार्यालय

Prime Minister's Office

नई दिल्ली- 110011
New Delhi- 110011

Sub:Petition of SHRI RAM GOPAL SHARMA
JD I COY NCC
SAINIK SCHOOL NAGROTA
JAMMU
JAMMU AND KASHMIR

A letter/gist of oral representation dated 30/09/2019 received in this office from SHRI RAM GOPAL SHARMA is forwarded herewith for action as appropriate. Reply may be sent to the Petitioner and a copy of the same may be uploaded on the portal.

[MUKUL DIXIT]
SECTION OFFICER

SECRETARY,DEPARTMENT OF DEFENCE

PMO ID No.:PMOPG/D/2019/0383382 Dated: 11/10/2019

Copy for information to :
SHRI RAM GOPAL SHARMA
JD I COY NCC
SAINIK SCHOOL NAGROTA
JAMMU
JAMMU AND KASHMIR

Note:- Status of the grievance can be tracked through internet at https://pgportal.gov.in/status by entering registration no. PMOPG/D/2019/0383382

Details for registration number : PMOPG/E/2020/0817813

Name Of Complainant	Ram Gopal Sharma
Date of Receipt	08/09/2020
Received By Ministry/Department	Prime Ministers Office

Grievance Description

Grievance Status for registration number : PMOPG/D/2019/0383382 Grievance Concerns To Name Of Complainant Shri RAM GOPAL SHARMA Date of Receipt 03/10/2019 Received By Ministry/Department Prime Ministers Office Grievance Description PRT.........PETITION IS NOT FULLY SCANNED ACTION THERE UPON MAY BE INITIATED ON RECEIPT OF HARD COPY ALONG WITH ITS ENCLOSURES WHICH IS BEING SENT SHORTLY. Grievance Document Current Status Under process Date of Action 18/12/2019 Remarks A grievance received from PMO on 05 Dec 2019 with the subject matter - Appeal for Justice, Enquiry and action by Shri Ram Gopal Sharma of your Dte. You are requested to consider the matter and reply to us as soon as possible with copy to complainant. Officer Concerns To Officer Name Col R S Bhati Officer Designation Director Contact Address Canal Road Jammu Email Address ddgncc-jk@nic in Contact Number 01912100134 Reminder NO-1 Dated-06/01/2020 with due regards I would like to inform you that my grievance was forwarded by Mr Rohit Singh of NCC HQ New Delhi to Col R S Bhati DDG NCC JK at email ddgncc-jk@nic.in but as per my information the said officer Col R S Bhati has been posted out since last three years and the said email is not in use since long time. thus it is very sorry to say that the officials at the helm of providing justice are either trying to mislead the higher authorities or not aware of the changes at the subordinate level due to non timely updating of the information leading to delay in justice and suffering of common people on large scale. Reminder No-2 dated30/07/2020 refer my petition appeal for justice, request for inquiry and action registration no pmopg/d/2019/0383382 received by your office. It is very sorry state of affairs that after lapse of 10 months no action has been taken so far and delaying tactics are being adopted by NCC organisation at every stage. you are therefore requested to look into the matter as justice delayed is justice denied. Reminder N0-3 dated 04/09/2020 refer my petition appeal for justice, request for inquiry and action registration no pmopg/d/2019/0383382 received by your office. It is very sorry state of affairs that after lapse of about an year no action has been taken so far and delaying tactics are being adopted by NCC organisation at every stage. It is developing a strong sense of feeling that there does not exist the rule of law in the country as the concerned department has not responded to the grievance even after the lapse of about a year. It also shows there exist no accountability and the authorities at the helm think themselves over and above the law of the land. I am at the verge of retirement and hope immediate action will be initiated to provide me with justice and relief at the earliest possible. Honorable sir You the last ray of the hope. I have deep faith that you will provide me with justice and bring the corrupts to the book. Regards Ram Gopal Sharma Senior Assistant NCC organisation Jammu,Jk

Current Status	Under process
Date of Action	18/09/2020

Remarks

Kindly take necessary action.

Officer Concerns To

Officer Name	S.GOPAL KRISHNA
Officer Designation	DS TRAINING
Contact Address	
Email Address	gopal.chris@gov.in
Contact Number	01123794126

MOST URGENT

The Hon'ble Prime Minister of India,
PMO, New Delhi.

Subject: Submission of documentary evidence/proof along with affidavit duly attested by Public Notary in complaint registered under Nos PMOPG/D/2019/0383382 and PMOPG/E/2020/0817813.

Reference: Your letter dated 12.11.2020.

Hon'ble Sir,

Kindly find enclosed herewith copies of documentary evidence/ proof along with affidavit duly attested by the Notary in respect of complaint filed by me and subsequently registered under Nos. PMOPG/D/2019/0383382 and PMOPG/E/2020/0817813 respectively for favour of information and further necessary action in the matter on priority at your end please.

Thanking you,

Yours faithfully,

Ram Gopal Sharma
S/o Lt Sh. Mangat Ram Sharma
R/o 254 Sector G, Sainik Colony
Jammu
Mob 94191 57741

Encls: 11 Pages

Dated: 20.11.2020

Copy to the:-

1. Group Commander, NCC Group HQs, Jammu
2. Additional Director General, NCC Directorate, Jammu, Kashmir and Ladakh.
3. Director General, NCC Directorate, New Delhi
4. Personal copy.

INDIA NON JUDICIAL

Government of Jammu and Kashmir

e-Stamp

सत्यमेव जयते

Certificate No.	:	IN-JK00292097437631S
Certificate Issued Date	:	20-Nov-2020 11:10 AM
Account Reference	:	NONACC (BK)/ jkjnkbk02/ SHASTRI NAGAR/ JK-JM
Unique Doc. Reference	:	SUBIN-JKJKJNKBK0200487105484675S
Purchased by	:	RAM GOPAL SHARMA
Description of Document	:	Article 4 Affidavit
Property Description	:	APPLICATION TO PMO
Consideration Price (Rs.)	:	0 (Zero)
First Party	:	RAM GOPAL SHARMA
Second Party	:	PMO OFFICE NEW DELHI
Stamp Duty Paid By	:	RAM GOPAL SHARMA
Stamp Duty Amount(Rs.)	:	30 (Thirty only)

The J&K Bank Ltd. Shastri

AFFIDAVIT

Please write or type below this line

I, Ram Gopal Sharma S/o Lt. Sh Mangat Ram R/o 254, Sector G, Sainik Colony, Jammu presently working as Senior Assistant, JD(I) Coy, NCC,Sainik School, Nagrota, Jammu do hereby solemnly affirm and declare as under:-

1. That I am working as Senior Assistant, JD(I) Coy, NCC, Sainik School, Nagrota, Jammu.

NOTARY VIJAY S. JGOTRA Advocate J&K High Court Regd. No. 176 Date of Exp. 20-4-2022 Govt. of Jammu & Kashmir India

RS 0002982918

Statutory Alert:
1. The authenticity of this Stamp certificate should be verified at 'www.shcilestamp.com' or using e-Stamp Mobile App of Stock Holding. Any discrepancy in the details on this Certificate and as available on the website / Mobile App renders it invalid.
2. The onus of checking the legitimacy is on the users of the certificate.

2. That I have been subjected to undue harassment, mental agony as well as victimization owing to successive exposure of scams/scandals involving siphoning off crores of rupees in NCC organization of J&K since 1986 onwards to till date.
3. That I have been even denied promotion by the officers/officials of NCC organization of J&K purely on the ground that I have exposed their misdeeds from time to time in public domain being upright, honest, dedicated and responsible employee of the organization.
4. That I have not only been subjected to worst kind of victimization by both former as well as present officers/officials of the NCC organization of J&K, but also willfully made junior to all officials in the said organization just to cow down me. This is despite the fact that I am possessing higher qualification as well as better merit as compared to those given promotions by sheer abuse of official position/authority by both former as well as present officers/officials just because of the fact that I successfully exposed their misdeeds in the past and also highlighting the same in the present times.
5. That being a dutiful, vigilant and responsible citizen of India, I am doing my best to expose the loop holes in the system to end corruption which has permeated to such an extent that if fair and reasonable enquiry is being ordered through only men of impeachable integrity then the facts and figures would automatically come out in public domain in order to nail down the culprits involved in the past and present in the various acts of omissions and commissions in the said organization since the year 1986.
6. That whatever documentary evidence, which I am enclosing as annexures with this affidavit are a matter of record and nothing has been concealed therein.
7. That I am apprehending my transfer from the present place of posting i.e. Sainik School, Nagrota, Jammu to somewhere other unit as the officer namely Lt Col Mufti Masood Ahmad, presently working as Training Officer (Trg), NCC Group HQs, Jammu is threatening as well as intimidating me of dire consequences since long for achieving some ulterior motive. The said officer is pressurizing me to withdraw the complaint related to expose of corruption, favouritism, nepotism as well as high handedness of officers of NCC organization, J&K, of case No PMOPG/D/2019/0383382.

8. That the above named Lt Col may kindly be shifted /attached to some other place as he is incapable of conducting impartial enquiry to unravel the truth in order to benefit the officers who were/are involved in creating mess in the NCC organization, J&K. So much so, the said officer even failed to submit the satisfactory reply to the office of PMO of complaint bearing No. PMOPG/D/20190383382 and also PMOPG/E/2020/0817813.
9. That I am also apprehending danger to my life, personal security and service at the hands of such irresponsible officer who is hell bend to pressurize me to take back the aforesaid complaints lodged against the NCC Organization, J&K.
10. That I do undertake to become approver of the case if my services are required for exposing/targeting knee deep corruption in the said organization. Further, whatever kind of assistance is required, I am willing to provide in order to expose the truth for the betterment of society and the National cause at large.

Deponent

Verification

Verified by me the deponent named above at Jammu today on 3-of of November, 2020 that the averments made hereinabove are true and correct to the best of my knowledge and belief and nothing has been concealed therein.

Deponent.

Solemnly Affirm and Declare as

VIJAY SAJGOTRA
Notary Jammu Distt
20/11/2020

MOST URGENT
(Kind Attention Please)

To

Shree Narindra Damoder Dass Modiji,
Honourable Prime Minister of India,
PMO, New Delhi

Subject : Application for grant of volunteer retirement (VRS) from service as a mark of strong protest for inept handling of affairs by PMO Office, New Delhi related to action/probe into massive corruption / malpractices committed by NCC Officers/officials of Directorate of NCC, J & K, Jammu despite submission of documentary evidence/proof along with affidavit duly attested by Public Notary in a complaint registered under Nos PMOPG/D/2019/0383382 and PMOPG/E /2020/0817813 respectively and loud appeal for stringent action in a time bound manner against officers / officials involved in rampant corruption in Directorate of NCC, J & K, Jammu and ensuring of justice to me thereof – regarding.

Esteemed Sir,

Kindly refer to the subject cited above. In this connection, your kind attention is invited towards the inapt handling of affairs by PMO Office, New Delhi related to action /probe into massive corruption / malpractices committed by NCC Officers / officials of Directorate of NCC, J & K, Jammu despite submission of documentary evidence / proof along with affidavit duly attested by Public Notary in complaint registered under Nos PMOPG/D/2019/0383382 and PMOPG/E/2020/0817813 respectively. If such is the state of affairs as well as working style of the office of PMO, New Delhi, then one can really wonder the state of affairs being prevalent in Directorate of NCC, J & K, Jammu. Sir, you may be surprised to know that I am virtually fighting crusade against corruption, nepotism and favoritism indulged in /shown by the officers / officials who were / are working in the Directorate of NCC, J & K, Jammu since long and all my efforts to expose the nexus / cartel prevalent in the said Directorate have virtually gone in vain. There is no concept of time bound Inquiry, fixing accountability and responsibility against those who are blatantly abusing their official position and has resultantly causing enormous loss to the state exchequer by flouting norms, rules / regulations to suit their vested interests.

It is to be noted here that I have been totally fed up with the prevalent system and despite making the PMO office aware of undue harassment, victimization as well as mental torture caused to me by the actions of such notorious officers / officials of Directorate of NCC, Jammu, nothing tangible has happened in the matter in this regard and the said officers / officials are working with impunity. On the other hand, I being a lone bread earner for my family is being subjected to undue harassment and mental agony with no sign of relief visible in near future. Already I had apprised you that the nexus in the NCC Directorate is so strong that one officer namely Mufti Masood Ahmed, presently working as Training Officer (Trg), NCC Group HQs, Jammu is threatening as well as intimidating me of dire consequences since long for achieving some ulterior motive. Moreover, the said officer is pressurizing me to withdraw the complaint related to exposure of corruption, favoritism / nepotism as well as high handedness of officers of NCC Organization, J & K on innocent subordinate employees also.

Sir, I have been deliberately transferred from JD (I) Coy, NCC, Sainik School Nagrota to NCC Group HQs, Jammu to work under the same officer who is hell bent to harm me in every possible manner. Presently I am working as Senior Assistant and have been deliberately denied promotions and other allied benefits because of the fact that I always refuse to toe their line of action which is against my morals and ethics and also conscience.

Sir, I am here by submitting all relevant documentary proof /evidence and also my representations submitted in the PMO Office and also Mininstry of Defence from time to time in the matter but in the end got totally disgusted with the working style of your office as since more than one and half years ago, I had approached the PMO office but till date nothing happened, thereby, I became a soft target and also have been virtually left alone in my crusade against corruption.

In view of extra ordinary urgency involved in the matter, I again earnestly appeal to your good self to personally intervene and kindly do something concrete in the matter, otherwise, I am hereby tendering my application for volunteer retirement (VRS) from the said organization as nowhere action against corruption /misdeeds of officers /officials of Directorate of NCC, J & K, Jammu in sight. Besides, kindly ensure me justice by granting promotion due to me since long despite being well educated and senior most official in the organization and also direct the concerned authorities to keep my present transfer order in abeyance till outcome of findings of inquiry in the matter in future for the sake of my personal safety and also that of my family.

Hoping for your prompt action / kind intervention into the matter please on urgency basis.

Thanking you Sir.

Yours faithfully

Ram Gopal Sharma
S/o Lt. Sh.Mangat Ram Sharma
R/o 254 Sector G, ~~Saiik~~ Colony, Sainik
Jammu
Mob No 9419157741

Dated 14.01.2021

Encls :

Copy to the :-

1. His Excellency the Lt. Governor, UT of J&K - His Excellency is also requested to kindly intervene and ensure action and justice in the matter please.
2. Group Commander, NCC Group HQs. Jammu
3. Additional Director General, NCC Directorate, Jammu, Kashmir and Ladakh
4. Director General, NCC Directorate, New Delhi.
5. Personal copy.

Vol. 09 No. 01 RNI NO. JKENG/2013/50660 Postal No. L-29/JK-502/19-21 JAMMU, JANUARY 04, 2021 Pages-16 Rs. 2.00

Samarkand Express

WEEKLY NEWSPAPER

Enormous And Unprecedented Scale Of Corruption In J&K NCC

LG, Anti- Corruption Bodies Need To Take Action

BY SANDEEP SINGH

Controversy and corruption charges ranging from exploiting scheduled caste employees, harassing women, receiving kickbacks from contractors, misuse of official position and favoritism in appointments/promotions cloud J&K NCC in the trouble torn state.

According to reliable sources, NCC Directorate J&K, figures in a few last position in the national tally, when it comes to rating its performance despite receiving best of the support from the UT (State) as well from the centre. "Our Directorate has been keeping the last position in the national level competition as if it were monopoly of NCC Group Headquarter Jammu," said the sources.

The sources further said that it was due to the independent command and lackadaisical attitude of the Group Commander and the Training Officer posted in the NCC in addition to supply of substandard materials to the cadets. Some of its officials in the past and present are alleged to be on the pay role of the contractors supplying equipment's including uniforms, refreshment and kits for the cadets.

It is alleged that officials who are involved in this racket enjoy the patronage of the higher officials in the NCC Directorate, New Delhi, especially Col. Jagat Singh who is coordinator of NCC Directorate, New Delhi and PMO for dealing the cases of corruption.

During the course of investigation by Samarkand Express Team it was revealed that one Sen Asstt (Smt. Saroj Jamwal) of NCC Directorate Jammu was so much harassed by the ADG that she lost her baby due to pre-mature delivery. The victim is running from pillar to post to get justice but DG NCC Delhi is silent and the accused officer is retiring on 31-Jan-2021. This is the height of harassment to women at work place.

Another startling fact that comes to light is that scheduled caste employees are exploited by the Training Officer and Group Commander, NCC Group Headquarters Jammu. One will be surprised to know the case of Sunil Kumar, a scheduled Caste employee of the NCC Group Headquarter, Jammu was not allowed to work a single day in office but was forced to work at the residences of officers for the last Nine Years. When the poor class 4th employee refused to do menial work at the residence of Brig. Satish Kumar, he was attached at Poonch office which is 300 KM away from his home in Jammu. The case is lying with the office of National Commission for Scheduled Castes, New Delhi. It is worthwhile to see how the Commission takes note of this issue.

(See in box A)

A

Similarly, another class 4th employee who refused to do menial works at the residences of these officers was also transferred to Poonch but he approached the Honorable High Court of J&K and got the transfer order stayed.

(See in box B)

B

Class 4th employees are compelled to go courts, Govt. exchequer is wasted on litigation unnecessary. No one is there to bell the Cat. Wrong information is being sent to DG NCC, New Delhi. Social activists, advocates and SC organizations have demanded probe complaints of this whole scam.

During our in depth investigations much more came to surface. Two contractors viz Bhushan Prasher and Sourab Panchaliya have allegedly gave crores of rupees to ADG and NCC Group Headquarters Jammu as commission for getting the tenders. Mr. Bhushan has been getting the tenders for the last 15 years. Mr. Sourabh is said to be the relative of PA to ADG.

From April 2020 to till date NCC directorate J&K has got Rs 30 crores as office expenditure from the UT of JK and centre and looted the funds in the name of building constructions through these contractors.

Corruption has not plagued NCC J&K today but it also did Yesterday.

(See Detail in Box C)

C

When the whole world was lock down due to Covid-19 NCC J&K was conducting camps. In 2009 and 2010, when Kashmir was burning and shut down by the stone palters, NCC Directorate J&K conducted the camps on papers only.

A Col. (Retd.) on the condition of anonymity said that violations of rules is very common in NCC Group Headquarters Jammu. A class 4th employee who died in 2003 was basically from Himachal Pardesh, throwing all the norms of SRO-43 to wind, his son was appointed as a Junior Asst. thus, setting the crude example of

"Patwari Kaa Beta Tehsildar Baan Gyaa."

Not only this, the said Junior Asst. was simultaneously promoted to Head Asst. without any Assistant Secretariat Class. These so called Head clerks were getting the promotions by pulling the right string in NCC Directorate J&K.

Our sources in NCC Directorate, New Delhi revealed that corruption in NCC is not limited to JK only but has plagued the other states too. In one such case, Col.Shah Ji John Group Commander, NCC Group Headquarters Guntur, Andhra Predesh was the Chairman of Unit Run Canteen with annual turnover of near Rs 45 crores. The officer dealt with dealers directly ignoring the quality and popular brands of groceries. He was also in direct contact with liquor dealers.

He carried out this practice for two years i.e 2018 to June 2020. Col. John was thickly involved in misappropriation and writing off as losses due to breakages. The matter was reported by the CSD Manager to all concerned including the Chief of Army Staff and DG NCC, New Delhi. Court of Inquires were ordered every now and then but Col. Shah Ji used his influence to get away.

DG NCC Court of Inquiry convening order copies were not made available to essential prosecution witnesses. Convening order was modified by the Court to help the accused and essential documentary evidences burnt down by the officer recorded in CCTV. Bank account transaction in the Officers saving account obtained by the prosecution witness clearly shows misappropriation and deposit of funds by the dealers. The Group Commander tried to influence the CSD Manager Shri Nivas Rao through mobile/whats Calls.

Mobile calls recorded by the Manager prove beyond doubt about the complexity of the officer, trying to influence the CSD Manager.

Whats App messages directing the Manager to demand only few particular brands ignoring the popular brands shows his involvement in favoring the selected few dealers. Call records and record of messages maintained by the CSD Manager .... a CD prepared and forwarded by the Manager to all concerned along with the complaint but no concrete action taken against the accused officer clearly shows the hollowness of the DG NCC Organization.

Infect, NCC has become a White Elephant for superseded Army Officers who are posted to NCC and loot the Cadets Money.

Sources in NCC Directorate, New Delhi told "Samarkand Express Team" that a senior clerk from NCC Group Headquarters, Jammu has filed the complaint of corruption before PMO. It is worthwhile to watch how PMO takes stern action against the corrupt officers.

News of J.K.

Enormous And Unprecedent Scale of Corruption In J&K NCC

LG, Anti-Corruption Bodies Need to Take Action

-Sandeep Singh

Controversy and corruption charges ranging from exploiting scheduled caste employee, harassing women, receiving kickbacks from contractors, misuse of official position and favoritism in appointments/ promotions cloud J&K NCC in the trouble torn state.

According to reliable sources, NCC Directorate J&K, figures in a few last position in the national tall, when it comes to rating its performance despite receiving best of the support from the UT (State) as well from the centre. "Our Directorate has been keeping in the last position in the national level competition as if it were monopoly of NCC Group Headquarter Jammu, "said the sources.

The sources further said that it was due to the independent command and lackadaisical attitude of the Group commander and the Training officer posted in the NCC in addition to supply of substandard meterials to the cadets. Some of its officials in the past and present are alleged to be on the pay role of the contractors supplying equipment's including uniforms, refreshment and kits for the cadets.

It is alleged that officials who are involved in this racket enjoy the patronage of the higher officials in the NCC Directorate, New Delhi, especially Col. Jagat Singh who is coordinator of NCC Directorate, New Delhi and PMO for denling the case of corruption.

During the course of investigation by Samarkand Express Team it was revealed that one Sen. Asstt. (Smt. Saroj Jamwal) of NCC Directorate Jammu was so much harassed by the ADG that she lost her baby due to pre-mature delivery. The victim is running from pillar to post to get justice but DG NCC Delhi is silent and the accused officer is retiring on 31 jan. 2021. This is the height of harasment to women at work place.

Another starting fact that comes to light is that scheduled caste employees are exploited by the Training Officer and Group Commander, NCC Group Headquarters Jammu. One will be surprised to know of the case of Sunil Kumar, a scheduled caste employee of the NCC Group Headquarter, Jammu was not allowed to work a single day in office but was forced to work at the residence of officers for the last Nine years. When the poor class 4th employee refussed to do menial work at the residence of Brig. Satish Kumar, he was attached at Poonch office which is 300 KM away from his home in Jammu. The case is lying with the office of National Commission for Scheduled Caste, New Delhi. It is worthwhile to see how the Commission takes note of this issue.

Class 4th employees are compelled to go courts, Govt. exchequer is wasted on litigation unnecessary, No one is there to bell the Cat. Wrong information is being sent to DG NCC, New Delhi Social activists, advocates and SC organizations have demanded probe complaints of this whole scam.

During our in depth investigations much more come to surface. Tow contractors viz Bhushan Prasher and Sourab Panchaliya have allegedly gave crores of rupees to ADG and NCC Group Headquarters Jammu as commission for getting the tenders. Mr. Bhushan has been getting the tenders for the last 15 years. Mr. Sourabh is said to be the relactive of PA to ADG.

मास संदेश, फरवरी 2021 30 ISSN 2454-9843

From April 2020 to till date NCC directorate J & has got Rs. 30 crores as office expenditure from the UT and JK and centre and looted the funds in the name of building constructions through these contractors.

Corruption has not plagued NCC J & K today but it also did Yesterday.

When to whole world has lock down due to Covid-19 NCC J&K was conducting camps. In 2009 and 2010, When Kashmir was burning and shut down by the stone palters, NCC Dirctorate J&K conducted the camps on papers only.

A Col. (Retd.) on the condition of anonymity said that violations of rules is very common in NCC Group Headquarters Jammu. A class 4th employee who died in 2003 was basically from Himachal Pradesh, throwing all the norms of SRO^43 to wind, his son was appointed as a Junior Asst. thus, setting the crude example of

"Petwari Kaa Beta Tehsildar Gyan."

Not only this, the said Junior Asst. was simultaneously promoted to Head Asst. without any Assistant Secretariat class. These so called Head clerks were getting the promotions by pulling the right string in NCC Directorate J&K.

Our sources in NCC Directorate, New Delhi revenled that corruption in NCC is not limited to JK only but has plangued the other states too. In one such case. Col. Shah Ji John Group Commander, NCC Group Headquarters Guntur, Andhra Pradesh was Turnover of near Rs 45 crores. The officer delt with dealers directly ignoring the quality and popular brands of groceries. He was also in direct contact with liquor dealers.

He carried out this practice for two years i.e. 2018 to June 2020. Col. John was thickly involved in misappropriation and writing off as lossess due to brakages. The matter was reported by the CSD Manager to all concerned including the Chief of Army Staff and DG NCC, New Delhi Court of Inquires were ordered every now and then but Col. Shah Ji used his influence to get away.

DG NCC Court of Inquiry convening order copies were not made available to essential prosecution witnesses. Convening order was modified by the Court to help the accused and essential docummentary evidences burnt down by the officer recorded in CCTV. Bank account transaction in the Officers saving account obtained by the prosecution witness clearly shows misappropriation and deposit of funds by the dealers. The Group Comander tried to influence the CSD Manager Shri Nivas Rao through mobile/whats calls.

Mobile calls recorded by the Manager prove beyond doubt about the complexity of the officer, trying to influence the CSD Manager.

Whats App messages directing the Manager to demand only few particular brands ignoring the popular brands shows his involvement in favoring the selected few dealers. Call records and record of messages maintained by the CSD Manager ... a CD prepared and forwarded by the Manager to all concerned along with the complaint but no concrete action taken against the accused officer clearly shows the hollowness of the DG NCC Organization.

Infect, NCC has become a White Elephant for superseded Army Officers who are posted to NCC and loot the Cadets Money.

Sources in NCC Directorate, New Delhi told "Samarkand Express Team" That a senior clerk from NCC Group Headquarters Jammu has filed the complaint of corruption before PMO. It is worthwhole to watch how PMO takes stern action against the corrupt officers.

•••

JD (I) COY NCC, SAINIK SCHOOL NAGROTA, JAMMU

STATEMENT OF THE CASE FOR WAIVING OFF THE PERIOD FOR WHICH THE INSPECTION OF ARMS/AMN AND COMPASS PRISMATIC WAS NOT CARRIED OUT

INTRODUCTION

1. JD (I) NCC Coy was established in 1970 at Sainik School Nagrota. The Coy has been imparting NCC training to the cadets of the School and has the distinction of sending many cadets to RD parade, Youth Exchange Programme and other prestigious camps. Presently this Coy is holding 06 x .22 type Rifles, 02 x .22 Deluxe type Rifles, 1313 x live cartilage of .22 Ball type ammunition, 137 x fired cases along with 10 x Compass Prismatic. The Last Inspection of Arms/Amn was carried out in the year 1999. Thereafter, no record of detailment to carryout the Arms/Amn inspection of this Coy by NCC Group Headquarter is held.

PROPOSAL

2. It is proposed that sanction may be accorded to waive off the period for which Arms/ Amn Inspection was not carried out i.e from 1999 to till date and AI inspection for the Arms, Ammunition and Controlled stores may be carried out at the earliest.

JUSTIFICATION

3. JD (I) NCC Coy was established in 1970 at Sainik School Nagrota. The Coy has been imparting NCC training to the cadets of the School and has the distinction of sending many cadets to RD parade, Youth Exchange Programme and other prestigious camps. Presently this Coy is holding 06 x .22 type Rifles, 02 x .22 Deluxe type Rifles, 1313 x live cartilage of .22 Ball type, 137 x fired cases along with 10 x Compass Prismatic. The Last Inspection of Arms/Amn was carried out in the year 1999. On scrutiny of the records, no record of any correspondence/Inspection carried out is available at this office. However, in 2016, OC JD (I) NCC Coy vide letter No. 0011/Q/NCC-01 dt 24 May 2016 (copy Att.) requested NCC Directorate, JK&L to carry out the AI Inspection of Arms, Ammunition & controlled store.

4. In response to the above mentioned letter NCC Directorate, Jammu Kashmir & Ladakh vide letter No. 305/12/Adm(i) dt 01 June 2016 directed 14 EME Bn(Comd) to carry out the AI inspection of Arms, Ammunition & Controlled Stores(Copy att). Further NCC Dte, JK & L vide letter no. 305/12/Adm dated 13 Jul 2016 has requested HQ 16 Corps (EME) to carry out the AI Inspection of Arms, Ammunition and controlled stores

(copy att) by detailing an armourer, wherein it is clearly mentioned that the AI Inspection wrt JD(I) NCC Coy was not carried out since 1999.

5. In addition to this, NCC Dte JK&L vide letter no. 305/12/Adm dated 19 Aug 2019 sought information from NCC Gp HQs Jammu about the unit which was carrying out the AI Inspection of this Coy prior to 1999. Wherein, it was again clearly mentioned that no AI inspection was carried out at this Coy since 1999.

6. As per the record held in this Coy, the last quarterly Inspection was carried out by armourer of NCC Dte JK&L, Jammu on 28 Sep 1999 under the dependency of 197 FD workshop EME C/O 56 APO and ammunition Inspection was carried out by 10 INF DOU on 01Jan 2001 and the same was intimated to NCC Gp HQs Jammu and NCC Dte JK&L vide our letter No.510/Q/NCC-06 dt 07 Oct 2016. But till date no Inspection has been carried out. However, it is brought to the notice that, the name of JD(I) NCC Coy has not featured in the Annual Technical Inspection Programme given out by NCC Group Headquarters. The record of same since 2009 is attached for your perusal.

7. In view of the above, it is requested that the sanction may be accorded for waiving off the AI Inspection for the above mentioned period and AI of the above mentioned Arms, Ammunition and Compass Prismatic held with this Coy may be carried out at the earliest.

FINANCIAL EFFECT

8. There is no financial expenditure involved.

CONCLUSION

9. In view the justification made above, there is an inescapable requirement of waiving off the period for which Inspection was not carried out that is 1999 to till date and also nominating a workshop to carry out the AI Inspection at the earliest.

Station: C/O 56 APO

Dated: 2021

Sd/
(Pawan)
Lt Col
Officer Commanding

RECOMMENDATION OF GROUP COMMANDER

सेवा में ,

श्री राजनाथ सिंह
माननीय रक्षा मंत्री
रक्षा मंत्रालय, भारत सरकार
104 दक्षिण ब्लॉक नई दिल्ली ।

विषयः **मेजर जनरल एन.के. एरी, अतिरिक्त महानिदेशक राष्ट्रीय कैडट कोर निदेशालय जम्मू कश्मीर और लेह द्वारा दी गई मानसिक उत्पीड़न हेतु और जानबूझ कर की गई आर्थिक तंगी से मेरे बेटे के इलाज न होने के कारण मृत्यु हेतु पत्र ।**

श्रीमान महोदय,

मेरा आपसे विनम्र निवेदन है कि मैं सरोज जम्वाल जोकि मुख्यालय उत्तरी कमान से 21 सितंबर 2017 को राष्ट्रीय कैडट कौर निदेशालय जम्मू कश्मीर और लेह में स्थानातरण हुई । मैंने आपको 30 सितंबर 2020 को पत्र लिखा था जिसका जवाब 26 नवंबर 2020 को इस कार्यालय में पहुँचा । श्रीमान जी मैं आपकी आभारी हूँ कि आपने एक निम्न कर्मचारी द्वारा भेजे गए पत्र का संज्ञान लिया । मैं आपका आभार प्रकट करती हूँ कि आज भी सच्चे और निष्ठावान प्राधिकारी उपलब्ध है जिन्हें हम अपने ऊपर हो रहे अत्याचार या दबाव से अवगत करा सकते हैं इस उम्मीद के साथ कि वो सच्चाई के साथ खड़े होंगे । जब मैंने आपको पत्र भेजा था मैंने उसकी कॉपी अन्य उच्य अधिकारियों को भी भेजी थी। जोकि शायद उनकी फाइलो में दब कर रह गई । क्योंकि मेजर जनरल एन.के. एरी. जैसे उच्चकोटि के अधिकारी के खिलाफ कोई भी बोलना नहीं चाहता । मुझ जैसी निम्न कर्मचारियों की आवाज़ कौन सुनेगा। एक महिला कर्मचारी जोकि सच की लड़ाई लड़ रही है उसका साथ कौन देगा । लेकिन मैं खुश हूँ कि सच्चाई की कभी हार नहीं होती है कहीं न कहीं कोई न कोई सच्चाई की जंग में जरूर साथ देता है । इस देश से सच्चाई एवं ईमानदारी कभी खत्म नहीं हो सकती । 26 नवंबर 2020 को आपके द्वारा भेजा गया पत्र प्राप्त होने के उपरांत मेजर जनरल ने सभी सेना के अधिकारियों और सिविल अधिकारी एवं कर्मचारियों को बुलाया और मेरे ऊपर झूठे

~~Office~~ Pers copy

2

आरोप लगाने शुरू कर दिए । मैं आपको महानिदेशक मेजर जनरल एन.के.एरी.की रिकॉडिंग भेज रहीं हूँ । मेरे ऊपर लगाए गए झूठे आरोपों पर प्रकाश डालना चाहूँगी ।

1. महानिदेशक मेजर जनरल ने कहा, कि उन्होने मेरे इंटरव्यू की रिकॉडिंग की है। सर कहते हैं, कि मैं हर रिकॉडिंग और दास्तावेज को राष्ट्रीय कैटेड कौर महानिदेशालय दिल्ली में भेजता हूँ मेरी आपसे विनती है कि आप वो रिकॉडिंग मँगवा कर सुने। क्या मैंने कभी किसी अभद्र भाषा का प्रयोग किया या कभी कोई दुर्व्यवहार किया किसी भी कर्मचारी एवं अधिकारी के साथ। फिर क्यों मुझे निशाना बनाया जा रहा है। लेकिन मुझे दुख है, कि इतने असभ्य भाषा का प्रयोग करने वाले उच्चकोटि के अधिकारी पर अभी तक कोई कारवाई क्यों नही हुई। ऐ.डी.जी सर के द्वारा दी गई permission के तहत ही की हुई रिकॉडिग मै आपको भेज रही हूँ क्योंकि ऐ.डी.जी सर बार बार बोलते हैं, कि मै किसी से नहीं डरता।

2. ऐ.डी.जी सर ने कहा, कि बलजीत इस औरत ने आपके खिलाफ लिखा है। ए.डी.जी. सर एक ऐसे उच्चकोटि के अधिकारी हैं जो अपने हर बयान को थोड़ी थोड़ी देर बाद बदल देते हैं मेरी आपसे विनती है कि मेरा पत्र दिनांक **30 सितंबर 20** को पढ़ने का कष्ट करें जिस पत्र में मैने बलजीत सर जो कि अकाउंट ब्रांच में हैं उनके खिलाफ कुछ नही लिखा है मैंने सिर्फ वो लिखा है जो सच्चाई है। सर आप मेजर ज़नरल द्वारा बोले गए शब्दो को कृप्या करके सुने। इस औरत का मेडिकल रिम्बर्समेंट क्लेम जो **रू0 7.00** लाख का नियंत्रक रक्षा लेखा कार्यालय सी.डी.ए. ने पकड़ा। सर क्या उच्चकोटि के अधिकारी को ऐसे असभ्य भाषा का प्रयोग करना चाहिए किसी महिला कर्मचारी के बारे में तमाम अधिकारियों एंव कर्मचारियों को इकट्ठा करके जैसे उन्होंने क़िसी मुजरिम को पकड़ा हो। मेरा सिर्फ **रू 20,730/–** का मेडिकल रिम्बर्समेंट क्लेम जो नियंत्रक रक्षा लेखा कार्यालय (सी.डी.ए) ने स्थापना शाखा में भेजा था। मेरे क्लेम पर (सी.डी.ए) कार्यालय में बोलेकर observation लगवाई गई जैसा कि मैने पहले पत्र में भी लिखा था वो सारी observation मैनें clear करवा दी और उससे संबधित सारे दस्तावेज सलंग्न करके अपनी स्थापना शाखा में दे दिए मेडिकल क्लेम को द्वारा प्रस्तुत करने के लिए परंतु मेरा

3

मेडिकल क्लेम अभी तक इसी कार्यालय में पड़ा है जो कि मात्र रू0 **20,730/–** का है **जिसे अतिरिक्त महानिदेशक रू0 7 लाख** का बता रहें हैं मेरा **रू0 5,72,718/–** मेडिकल रिम्बसमेंट क्लेम के दस्तावेज जो कि अभी तक सी.डी.ए में नही भेजें हैं और न ही उस क्लेम पर कोई observation लगी है सर ने रू0 **5,72,718/–** मेडिकल क्लेम के दस्तावेज दो साल से अपने पास ही रख लिए हैं उन्होने मेरे बिमारी डेगूं का **रू0 20,730/–** का क्लेम observation clear करने के बाद भी नहीं भेजा। और दूसरा रू0 5,72,718/– का क्लेम भी दस्तावेज सहित अपने पास ही रख लिया । मैनें 2019 में अपने बेटे के उपचार के लिए रू0 5,00,000/– अपने GP Fund से निकलवाये थे।

3. ADG ने कहा कि **previous Major General Nailender Kumar and previous Director Shailender Singh** डरते थे । और कुछ देर के बाद उन्होने खुद बोलना शुरू कर दिया कि वो चोर थे । previous Col.Shailender Singh Dir ने 20–20 लाख रूपये खाए हैं और Transport Allowance का claim भी करते रहे । सरकारी वाहन को इस्तेमाल भी करते रहे । लेकिन Col Shailender Singh (Dir) तो ADG NK Airy के tenure में भी इस कार्यालय में थे । तो उनके झूठे claim का certificate ADG Sir, क्यों sign करते रहे और Baljit Sir जो एकाऊंट ब्रांच में थे उनके Medical Claim का certificate क्यों sign करते रहे । इसका मतलब है कि claim sign करवाने के पैसे लगते हैं तो शायद इसलिए ADG Sir, ने मेरे claim का certificate नहीं दिया जबकि मैंने उनको Undertaking लिख कर दे दी थी। मैं उसकी कॉपी आपको भेज रही हूँ। **ADG** सर ने काफी वार **Bansi, JSA** जो राज्य का लेखा **(Accounts)** संभालते हैं उनका नाम लिया। **ADG** सर को सारे अकाऊंट ब्रांच के कर्मचारियो से खास लगाव है । क्योंकि उन्होने खुद कहा कि जब बंसी मेरे घर आता है तो मैं बंसी को **Drawing Room** में बिठाकर चाय पिलाता हूँ

4

और फिर **discuss** करता हूँ **ADG Sir** ने कहा कि तुम्हारी औकात नहीं है कि मुझे समोसे खिला सको। मुझे उनकी बात समझ नही आई और **ADG** सर ने कहा कि उन्होने मेरे लिए **trap set** किया है और मैं उसमें फंसती जा रही हूँ। सर आपसे निवेदन है कि यह कौन सा **trap** है कि जो उच्चकोटि के अधिकारी एक निम्न कर्मचारी के लिए पिछले दो साल से बना रहे हैं । मुझे जाल में फंसाने की कोशिश की जा रही है ।

4. ADG सर ने सभा में यह भी कहा कि सरोज ने इस समय मेरी शिकायत की जबकि Medical Reimbursement claim High Court में pending हैं परंतु मुझे यह समझ में नहीं आ रहा कि जब ADG सर जानते थे कि मेरा Medical claim Court में pending है तो उन्होने मेरे विरूद्ध charge sheet क्यों लगाई। क्योंकि जब case court में लांवित है तो मेरे विरूद्ध Deptt. enquiry क्यों उच्च न्यायालय की प्रतिष्ठा का मान क्यों नहीं रखा गया ।

5. Rules & Regulation की बात करने वाले उच्चकोटि के अधिकारी ADG सर जो हमेशा सिर्फ Rules & Regulation को तोड़ते नजर आए हैं। ADG सर ने अपने आपको ईमानदार और सच्चा दिखाने के लिए हजारों झुठ का सहारा लिया है और ले रहे हैं और अभद्र भाषा और दुरव्यवहार का प्रयोग भी कर रहे हैं । ADG सर ने कहा कि मैं इस कार्यालय में 2019 को आया हूँ जबकि सच तो यह है कि 2018 में आए थे।

6. एक महिला कर्मचारी को यातनांए दे देकर उसका मानसिक सन्तुलन खराब करने की कोशिश की जा रही थी इन मानसिक यातनाओ के चलते मै **21 दिसंबर 2018** को गिर पड़ी । जिससे मेरे गर्भस्थ शिशु को गंभीर चोटें आई और उसका जन्म निर्धारित समय से पहले हो गया। 22 दिसंबर 2018 को जन्म लेते ही उसका इलाज चलने लगा जिस पर मेरी जमा पूंजी जोकि GP Fund के रूप में मैनें जमा की थी । उसे निकाल कर मैनें अपना और अपने बेटे का उपचार करवाना

5

शुरू किया। मेरे रू0 20,730/– के क्लेम को लेकर ही मेरे कार्यालय अधिकारियों ने परेशान करना शुरू कर दिया था। मेरे बेटे का रू0 5,72,718/– का मैडिकल क्लेम आगे पास होने के लिए भेजा ही नहीं और अपने पास रख लिया । जिससे मुझे आर्थिक तंगी होने लगी और पैसों के अभाव में मेरे बच्चे की जान चली गई। मैं अपने बच्चे को अस्पताल से घर ले आई क्योंकि इतने बड़े अस्पताल का बिल का भुगतान करना मेरे लिए मुश्किल होने लगा। क्योंकि मेरे पति भी सर्विस में नहीं है । मेरी दो और बेटियाँ भी है। वह इस बच्चे से बड़ी है। परन्तु मेरे लिए आर्थिक तंगी का भी चक्रव्यूह बन गया था। जिसमें Authorities मेरे हक का पैसा मुझे वक्त रहते दिलवा सकती थी। परन्तु उन्होंने ऐसा नहीं किया। मेरे बिल को झूठा कहके रोक लिया गया। जबकि आजकल Online payment होती है। Max Hospital की साइट पर अब भी हर एक मरीज (Patient) का तमाम डाटा उपलब्ध होता है। परन्तु मेरे पास आपके आगे अपील करने के सिवाय कोई दूसरा साधन नहीं बचा । **इसलिए मेरे केस में स्वयं हस्तान्तरण करें। और मेरी Authorities को बताएं कि किसी निम्न महिला कर्मचारी पर इस प्रकार अपनी सत्ता के जौहर न दिखाएं।**

7. **ADG सर ने कहा अब खेल खेलने का मजा आएगा श्रीमान महोदय जी मैं सरोज** जम्बाल आपसे पूछना चाहती हूँ कि क्या यह कोई खेल चल रहा था पिछले दो साल से कि एक महिला कर्मचारी को कार्यालय मे मानसिक यातानाएँ दे देकर एक माँ से उसका बेटा छीन लिया। आज पता चला की एक उच्चकोटि के अधिकारी **ADG** सर ऐसे खेल खेलते है इसलिए मेरा और मेरे बेटे के उपचार को झूठा साबित करने की कोशिश कर रहें हैं बल्कि डाक्टर, **Max Hospital** वहाँ की Official साइट पर जो **bill** का विवरण है उनका भी।

8. अगर मै ADG सर के आगे खामोश रही तो इसका मतलब यह नहीं की मैनें उनकी द्वारा बोली गई झूठी बातों के आगे झुक गई या मैं डर गई।

6

कृप्या सर आप हस्तान्तरण करें मेरे मुद्दे में और न्याय प्रतिक्रिया को सक्रिय बनाने मे मेरा साथ दें यदि मै सही हूँ तो। प्रार्थिनी आपकी सदा आभारी रहेगी।

आपकी आज्ञाकारिणी

सरोज जम्वाल

सरोज जम्वाल
JSA
राष्ट्रीय कैडेट और निदेशालय
जम्मू कश्मीर एण्ड लेह
जम्मू ।

दिनांक 05 दिसम्बर 20

संलग्न– Undertaking recording , Max Health Care bill, CGHS List, Emergency Certificate (5 leaves)

प्रतिलिपिः

1. जनरल मनोज मुकुंद नारावने
   चीफ ऑफ आर्मी स्टाफ **(COAS)**
   रक्षा मंत्रालय भारत सरकार
   दक्षिण ब्लॉक– आर के पुरम
   नई दिल्ली – 110001

2. लैफ्टिनैंट जनरल राजीव चौपड़ा
   राष्ट्रीय कैटेड कौर महानिदेशालय
   रक्षा मंत्रालय भारत सरकार
   पश्चिम ब्लॉक – 4 आर के पुरम
   नई दिल्ली – 110066

3. श्रीमती रेखा शर्मा
   राष्ट्रीय महिला अध्यक्ष
   राष्ट्रीय महिला आयोग,
   नई दिल्ली –110025

4. एन.सी.सी. डॉयरेक्टोरेट
   जे.के. एण्ड एल, केनाल रोड,
   जम्मू –180001

CHAPTER – 8

Back when I was in the ninth grade, our school organized a cultural program to commemorate Republic Day. During this event, a group of twelfth-grade students performed a qawwali. The leading vocalist of the ensemble was Shri Subhash Chandra Ji, who has since retired as a principal. The lyrics of the qawwali were as follows:

"यह हिरसो-हवस की मंडी है, अनमोल रत्न बिक जाते हैं।

बिकती हैं सुहाग की रातें भी, दुल्हन के चमन बिक जाते हैं।"

(This is a marketplace driven by insatiable desires. Here, you can find precious gems for sale. They trade on wedding nights, and even the bridal attire is on display.)

Back then, I couldn't fully comprehend the meaning behind the lyrics of this Qawwali. However, as I ventured into my career as a crime reporter, delving into topics related to prostitution, particularly during my 2004 trip to Nepal, I realized that every word of this Qawwali seemed really accurate. Corruption had deeply infiltrated the political landscape to the extent that awards meant to honor deserving individuals were now being bought and sold. As a matter of fact, only 10 percent of these awards were actually bestowed upon deserving recipients. An honest observer witnessing this manipulation in the political sphere could only sigh in disillusionment while watching the annual news broadcasts announcing the list of award recipients.

Time passed, and the trend of corruption in award allocations persisted. A few years later, in 2015, I had a discussion about this issue with Kuldeep Nayyar. We lamented how deserving journalists were overlooked on Republic Day, with individuals having political connections receiving the Best Journalist Award instead. I was deeply frustrated by this and Kuldeep Ji proposed a course of action. He suggested that I apply for the Padma Award nomination that year,even if I personally believed that I wasn't entirely worthy of it. His reasoning was that this would provide me with firsthand insight into the extent of corruption within the Padma Award selection process and reveal how the list of awardees was predetermined.

Agreeing with Kuldeep Ji's perspective, I submitted a nomination application for the Padma Award, providing comprehensive documentation related to my work spanning from 1987 to 2013. I hoped that even if I didn't receive the Padma Award, the committee would at least take the time to review my application and acknowledge the work I had dedicated my life to. Another reason for my filing for the nomination was the recognition I had received from then-President Abdul Kalam in his address to the nation in 2006.

The Hon'ble President had mentioned one of my books that delved into the principles of Sheikh Abdul Qadir Geelani. The information was conveyed to me by RK Prasad who served as the Secretary to President Abdul Kalam at the time. This held significant personal meaning for me because my lucky number is 11. Abdul Kalam Ji was the 11th President of India.

My intent in pursuing the Padma Bhushan Award was not solely to receive the accolade but to shed light on the corruption embedded within the Padma Award selection process. I firmly believed that the award committee was overlooking deserving candidates while dismissing valuable documents representing a lifetime of diligent work. There was a substantial possibility that I wouldn't receive the award, primarily because, unlike others, I had refrained from engaging in corrupt practices or seeking recommendations from the influential politicians.

Finally, the awaited day arrived when the list of Padma Award recipients was unveiled, one evening before Republic Day in 2016. The outcome was as anticipated.It was time to take action that Kuldeep Ji and I had discussed. On Independence Day, Kuldeep Ji's article was published in the media.A few days later, on February 6, 2016, I made a robust appeal to the Home Secretary, urging a reconsideration of the award decision and the return of all the original documents and photographs I had submitted. After receiving no response for an extended period, I penned another letter to the Hon’ble Home Secretary on March 28, 2016, demanding a reply and cautioning of potential legal action in the absence of nonresponse. My warning ultimately spurred a response.On June 2, 2016, I received a letter from the Home Secretary firmly declining any reconsideration of the decision. The letter clarified that the Padma Award process had transitioned to a fully online system starting that year. While I initially felt disappointed by this news, I later realized that my efforts had succeeded in advocating for a more transparent selection process, which held greater significance for me than receiving the Padma Award.

This narrative encapsulates my journey with the Padma Award which I did not attain but ultimately triumphed in drawing attention to the imperative for transparency in the selection process. Meanwhile, corruption continued to permeate Jammu and Kashmir, extending its roots deeper into every facet of society. It was rumored that on every Republic Day and Independence Day, the Chief Minister would bestow awards upon individuals who had excelled in various domains. However, the criteria for selection and the identities of the awardees remained shrouded in secrecy. By this juncture, I had assumed the role of editor of a magazine called Street Voice. The magazine's owner was approached by an individual who had previously served on the Railway Board and had faced legal trouble in a railway ticket black-marketing case. This individual proposed to contribute political journalism to the magazine without any salary or remuneration, in exchange for an identity card and having his name mentioned in the magazine's imprint line. His motives were questionable from the outset, and once he secured the press identity card, he began exploiting it.

Within the secretariat, he disseminated rumors that he was the actual proprietor of Street Voice and leveraged this influence to cultivate acquaintances with prominent politicians. In a bid to win over the genuine owner, he conducted interviews with politicians and published them in the magazine. His political connections grew so potent that during the Darbar Move of J&K state capital, he resided in the MLA Hostel in Srinagar for six months at their expense.

The magazine owner's son was residing overseas, necessitating the owner's annual and biennial visits to be with him. During these visits, I took on complete responsibility for the magazine as all our dedicated employees appreciated working under my guidance. It felt like a close-knit family where everyone collaborated effectively. The particular individual in question avoided any interaction with me because he lacked journalism knowledge and writing skills. Consequently, none of his articles were published in the magazine during the owner's absence.

This arrangement persisted until the CBI apprehended the individual in connection with an old case and took him to Delhi. This development garnered significant media coverage. In the aftermath of this incident, I strongly advised the magazine owner to distance himself from someone with such a tarnished reputation. However, the owner's response was sympathetic towards him. The owner stated that despite the individual's checkered past, he had provided evidence related to substantial corruption cases including the JKBOSE scandal and another involving Ghulam Nabi Azad. This individual had also furnished evidence implicating Azad.

As time passed, owing to his political affiliations and influence, this individual returned to Jammu a few months later. Ironically, he received the Best Journalist Award from the then-Chief Minister Omar Abdullah the following year, leaving seasoned journalists bewildered. At this juncture, it would be unjust to solely hold senior politicians at the Centre accountable because award decisions are made by committees as I had previously highlighted. After this incident, I refrained from applying for journalism-related awards. I was engaged in my role in NCC at the time, which necessitated postponing my aspiration of pursuing journalism as a full-time profession. Nonetheless, my outspoken and satirical writings left a strong impression on senior officers, bureaucrats and others. As far political journalism, it had never held any allure for me.

EE 898334395IN

1273

From: - R Gopal Sharma
House No. 254, Sector-G
Sainik Colony Jammu-180011
Mobile: 09419157741
E-mail: rgopalsharma11@yahoo.com
09 Sept. 2015

To,

The Home Secretary
Government of India
Ministry of Home Affairs
North Block, New Delhi-110001

Public

CITATION: PADMA AWARDS 2016

Sir,

Refer your advertisement of 1st May 2015. I take this opportunity to submit the following documents for your kind perusal and sympathetic consideration please.

1. Citation- Two pages
2. Book- Abode of secularism
3. Articles on women Empowerment, Bureaucratic reforms, Human rights, Investigative stories related to scams and corruption in defence and civil administrations.
4. Photo copy of certificate of **"Rashtriya Gaurav Award"** and original photo of felicitation by people of Sainik Colony, Honorable Member of Parliament and J&K Industries and Commerce Minister Chander Parkesh Ganga for excellence in free and fair Journalism.
5. Although, I don't believe in self praising but highlighting the factual position leads me to trust the documents shall find me the most suitable person for Padma Awards 2016.

Thanking you

गृह मंत्रालय
Ministry of Home Affairs
नई दिल्ली/New Delhi
14 SEP 2015
के.र.सं. 600985
C.R. No.

Yours faithfully

R Gopal Sharma
(Journalist)

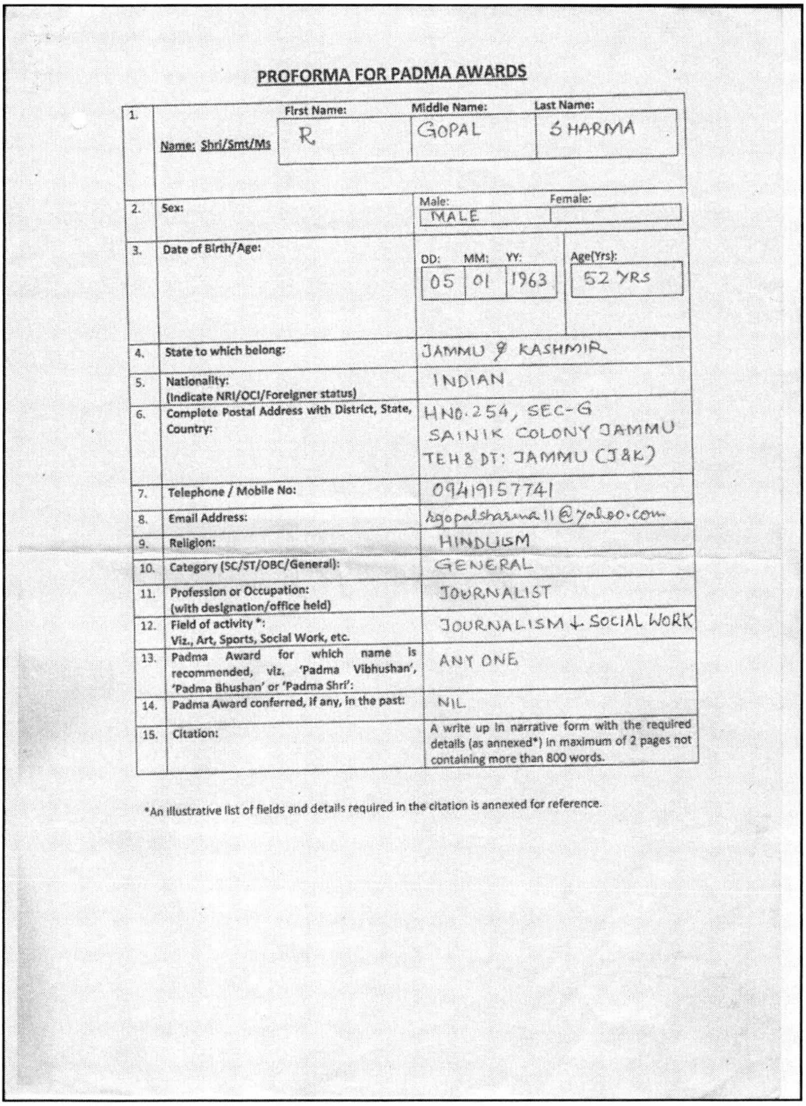

PROFORMA FOR PADMA AWARDS

1.	Name: Shri/Smt/Ms	First Name: R / Middle Name: GOPAL / Last Name: SHARMA
2.	Sex:	Male: MALE / Female:
3.	Date of Birth/Age:	DD: 05 MM: 01 YY: 1963 / Age(Yrs): 52 YRS
4.	State to which belong:	JAMMU & KASHMIR
5.	Nationality: (Indicate NRI/OCI/Foreigner status)	INDIAN
6.	Complete Postal Address with District, State, Country:	HNO. 254, SEC-G SAINIK COLONY JAMMU TEH & DT: JAMMU (J&K)
7.	Telephone / Mobile No:	09419157741
8.	Email Address:	rgopalsharma11@yahoo.com
9.	Religion:	HINDUISM
10.	Category (SC/ST/OBC/General):	GENERAL
11.	Profession or Occupation: (with designation/office held)	JOURNALIST
12.	Field of activity *: Viz., Art, Sports, Social Work, etc.	JOURNALISM & SOCIAL WORK
13.	Padma Award for which name is recommended, viz. 'Padma Vibhushan', 'Padma Bhushan' or 'Padma Shri':	ANY ONE
14.	Padma Award conferred, if any, in the past:	NIL
15.	Citation:	A write up in narrative form with the required details (as annexed*) in maximum of 2 pages not containing more than 800 words.

*An illustrative list of fields and details required in the citation is annexed for reference.

विचार

JAMMU • TUESDAY • 26.1.2016 6

'पुरस्कारों के महत्व' पर देश में बहस होनी चाहिए

कुलदीप नैय्यर

From: - R Gopal Sharma
House No. 254, Sector-G
Sainik Colony Jammu-180011
Mobile: 09419157741
E-mail: rgopalsharma11@yahoo.com
06 Feb 2016

To,

The Home Secretary
Government of India
Ministry of Home Affairs
North Block, New Delhi-110001

Appeal for reassessment of Citation and return of original Articles:-

Sir,

Refer your advertisement invited citation / applications for Padma Awards 2016. I have applied for the same vide my application dated 09 Sep 2015. But my name was not there when the list of awardees was declared. I apprehend that it was all due to lack of political connections which a free and fair journalist worth to his salt should not maintain at any cost (Article written by Kuldip Nayar published in a section of the press is attached). If you reassess my bio-data then each and every thing will be crystal cleared.

Sir, what will be the position of this country where awards are bestowed to incapable persons who have only *chamchagiri*.

Keeping in view the above mentioned, your good self is requested to reassess my all documents attached with citation and return of the same at the earliest.

Thanking you

Yours faithfully
R Gopal Sharma
Journalist

Copy to:-

1 His Excellency The President of India - For information and further necessary action please.

2 Leader of Opposition - To have comments on your role in the selection committee

Encls: [illegible]es

REMINDER-I

From: - R Gopal Sharma
House No. 254, Sector-G
Sainik Colony Jammu-180011
Mobile: 09419157741
E-mail: rgopalsharma11@yahoo.com

28 Mar 2016

To,

The Home Secretary
Government of India
Ministry of Home Affairs
North Block, New Delhi-110001

APPEAL FOR REASSESSMENT OF CITATION AND RETURN OF ORIGINAL ARTICLES:-

Sir,

1. Reference is made to letter dt 06 Feb 2016.

2. It seems that no action has been taken at your end.

3. Therefore, your good self is requested to let me know the present position of the case and return my articles and photographs at the earliest. Failing which I shall be compelled to take legal remedy for getting back my articles and photographs, which will be entirely at your cost and responsibility

Thanking you

Yours faithfully
R Gopal Sharma
(Journalist)

Copy to:-

1. His Excellency The President of India- For information and further necessary action please.
2. Leader of Opposition- -do-

No. 01/27/2016-Public
Government of India/ Bharat Sarkar
Ministry of Home Affairs/ Grih Mantralaya
****

North Block, New Delhi.
Dated the 02 June, 2016

To,
Shri R Gopal Sharma
House No. 254, Sector-G,
Sainik Colony,
Jammu-180011
Jammu & Kashmir.

Subject: Reassessment and returning of original articles regarding.

Please refer to your letter dated 28.03.2016 received in Public section on 31.05.2016 regarding appeal for reassessment of your citation for Padma Awards and returning of your original articles and photographs.

2. It is informed that all the nominations received during the prescribed period are submitted before the Padma Awards Committee, which makes its recommendations for the Awards. There is no mechanism for reconsideration of the same nomination. Every year fresh nominations are considered. You may send your nomination afresh. The nomination has to be sent through online mode. The details are available at www.padmaawards.gov.in

3. Your original articles and photographs are returned herewith.

Yours faithfully,

Encl.: As above

Sunil
02/06/2016

(Sunil Kumar)
Section Officer (Public)
Tel. No.23092421

From: - R Gopal Sharma
House No. 254, Sector-G
Sainik Colony Jammu-180011
Mobile: 09419157741
E-mail: rgopalsharma11@yahoo.com

30 June 2016

To,

The Home Secretary
Government of India
Ministry of Home Affairs
North Block, New Delhi-110001

APPEAL FOR REASSESSMENT OF CITATION AND RETURN OF ORIGINAL ARTICLES REGARDING.

Sir,

1. Reference is made to your letter No.01/27/2016-Public GOI/ MHA dt 02 June, 2016.

2. It is to inform you that I have received only eight pages (Application, Performa for Padama Award's, Citation, Rashtriya Gaurav Award's Certificate of Excellence, acknowledgement of Rashtrapati Bhavan etc) and four photographs but not the original articles which are 1000 in number of my research work duly numbered by me. The articles have been written mainly on corruption, militancy, women empowerment, bureaucratic reforms, human rights and investigative stories related to scams, corruption in defence and civil administrations. Besides these, original copy of my book titled "Abode of Secularism" has not been returned by your good self.

3. It is surprising that either my papers have not been put-up before the Padma Award's Committee or the Committee did not even bother to check my papers for the evaluation of the merit objectively and impartially as it is crystal clear from the eight pages and four photographs returned by you. From this entire, one can easily apprehend that Award's were not in honour of excellence but it was a totally exercise in futility to give benefits to few blue eyed and favourities of the politicians.

4. The research work / articles written be me are a golden treasure and a source of inspiration for those who want to follow the path of truth and honesty in journalism as a career.

5. Therefore, your good self is requested to return my original articles at the earliest, failing which I shall be compelled to take legal remedy for getting back my articles, which will be entirely at your cost and responsibility

Thanking you

Yours faithfully
R Gopal Sharma
(Journalist)

Copy to:-

1. The Hon'ble President of India - For information and further necessary action please.
2. Leader of Opposition- -do-
3. The Hon'ble Prime Minister of India - A separate letter in detail is being sent to you.

From: - R Gopal Sharma
House No. 254, Sector-G
Sainik Colony Jammu-180011
Mobile: 09419157741
E-mail: rgopalsharma11@yahoo.com

10 Dec 2016

To,

The Home Secretary
Government of India
Ministry of Home Affairs
North Block, New Delhi-110001

APPEAL FOR REASSESSMENT OF CITATION AND RETURN OF ORIGINAL ARTICLES REGARDING.

Sir,

1. Reference is made to your letter No.01/27/2016-Public GOI/ MHA dt 02 June, 2016 and my letter of dated 30 June 2016.

2. With great regret it is to inform you that nothing has been done so for at your end.

3. Therefore, your good self is requested to return my original articles at the earliest, failing which I shall be compelled to take legal remedy for getting back my articles, which will be entirely at your cost and responsibility.

Thanking you

Yours faithfully

R Gopal Sharma
(Journalist)

Copy to:-

1. The Hon'ble Prime Minister of India - You are requested to please analyse my case and direct Home Secretary to put up my original document before Padma Award committee.

CHAPTER – 9

When NCC officers in Jammu and Kashmir, including Major General NK Airy, Brigadier NR Babu, Brigadier Satish Kumar and Lieutenant Colonel Mufti, failed to achieve their goals against me, they eventually reassigned me to JD (I) Company NCC where I was attached to Sainik School Nagrota. On August 16, 2021, I visited Kol Kandoli temple in Nagrota, submitted my joining report to Sainik School, and resumed my duties. When I entered the the staff room, I was warmly welcomed by everyone, as if I was a returning family member.

Juggling responsibilities, for fighting against corruption in NCC Directorate Jammu Kashmir and Sainik School Nagrota, along with all the associated challenges, was certainly no easy feat. However, with the immense grace of Guruji's blessings, I managed to overcome the obstacles that came my way. Additionally, I was in the process of constructing a new house for which I had invested all of my life's savings. Building a house in today's times presents its own set of challenges. When I needed additional funds, I contemplated selling some ancestral land in Poonch. Nevertheless, my elder sister and her husband created obstacles in the process, and even some other family members sided with her. Coping with such behavior from loved ones was a profound disappointment. My family was well aware of the individuals I was fighting against and the threats to my life that were involved in this task. Colonel Javed Mir was the sole person who supported me during these situations; everyone knew that a misstep could lead to legal troubles. Despite being fully aware of these circumstances, my family's conduct was a significant letdown for me. This emotional shock had a noticeable impact on my memory, and I started experiencing lapses in memory which made it challenging to retain information.

In less than two months since I had joined Sainik School Nagrota, the Officer Commanding, acting on Lieutenant Colonel Mufti's directives, began subjecting me to unnecessary harassment. The pressure they exerted on me reached a breaking point, leading me to request a CBI raid in the school on October 22, 2021. During the CBI investigation on that day. While officers were conducting the raid, the Officer Commanding, visibly nervous and smoking a cigarette, entered my room and inquired about the ongoing situation. I firmly declined to provide any information regarding the matter. On one side, the CBI raid was in progress, and on the other, there was a palpable sense of relief among us in the staff room. Jamwal and Gupta were also present with me at that time. Jamwal was a trustworthy individual, while Gupta served as an informant for the Officer Commanding. As soon as news of the raid reached the media, apprehension spread among all the officers. Subsequently, Lieutenant Colonel Mufti also received a warning, further intensifying his unease. Colonel Pawan Kumar on the other hand, realized the gravity of his mistakes in confronting me.

Following this incident, the atmosphere at the school became notably more harmonious. The reason for this was the appointment of Captain AK Desai and Administrative Officer Lieutenant Colonel Meena Joon, both known for their honesty and integrity. With Colonel Pawan Kumar going on leave, the additional responsibility of NCC also fell on Meena Ji. My tenure was nearing its end, with only one more year remaining,my room lacked air conditioning or even a cooler. Upon learning of this, the Principal suggested that I work from the staff room. During breaks in the staff room, we often engaged in discussions and shared our thoughts. I had a colleague there, Sandeep Rana Ji who was particularly close to me as we had known each other since 2004. He frequently expressed his belief that my departure would be a significant loss to the school because I consistently raised my voice against corruption within the school and the mistreatment of staff members. Similar situations had arisen with Sangeeta Chaudhary and Sister Messi. Due to these issues, I had taken the initiative to usher Captain SB Ray and his colleagues out of the school. From 2006 to 2014, the school was on a positive trajectory. However, between 2014 and 2017, I had to get another inquiry started, leading to the termination of a computer teacher and an accountant who were found guilty and subsequently expelled from the school. Following this, the school once again began moving in the right direction.

In November 2021, I came across Ms Meenu Sharma, a teacher in Sainik School. During our interaction, I discovered her impressive educational background. In addition, she also was NCC 'C' certificate holder. She was married to an army officer, and her educational achievements and demeanour clearly reflected her capabilities. I came to know that Ms Meenu was going through discord in her married life and she was involved in a legal dispute with her husband. She was currently residing with her mother and son in the school staff quarters, separated from her spouse.

As mentioned earlier, I had become a little more forgetful, but I persevered in my studies and diligently maintained my diaries. During the COVID era, winter holidays were non-existent in the school and teachers were conducting online classes. One day, while enjoying a cup of tea in the staff room, Sandeep Rana Ji casually remarked that had I not initiated an inquiry in the school and requested a CBI raid, Ms Meenu too could have met a fate similar to Sangeeta Choudhary. His comment served as a stark reminder of the unfortunate situation that befell Sangeeta Choudhary.

My research work was nearing completion and I was preparing for my final assignment abroad. Our interactions were limited due to my role as an NCC staff member. One day Ms Meenu's husband forcibly entered the school premises with some soldiers in an army vehicle, attempting to take custody of their son. It was only through the intervention of Colonel Meena Joon that he was prevented from doing so despite his threats. Eventually, he was forced to return. Regrettably, I was on leave on that particular day. Upon my return the following day, I heard everyone discussing the incident.

I made an effort to obtain the registered number of the army vehicle and photographs of the armed soldiers who accompanied her husband, through a colleague at the school. The remaining information was gathered from the local police station where she had filed a formal complaint against her husband. With her consent, I decided to initiate action against the army officer for the misuse of a government vehicle. To deter any future attempts, the school administration displayed a photograph of the military officer on the notice board near the gate and instructed the gatekeeper to not allow him if he tries to enter the school premises again.

Although her husband did not turn up in the school, he had plotted a different plan. He had filed a custody case for their son in the family court of Jammu. After consulting with senior police officers, he also lodged a complaint against his wife, with instructions to take legal action against her. All of this was carefully orchestrated with the guidance of his lawyer. Understanding that no mother would willingly part with her child, he sought to intimidate her into agreeing to a divorce. As a result, on March 7, 2022, she received a court summon, directing her to appear within a week. Ms Meenu, who had no acquaintances outside the school, attended court alone, secured legal representation and appeared as required. She was then scheduled to make another court appearance on March 23, coincidentally; it was her son's birthday.

She had just returned from her court appearance on March 16 when she received a call from the SDPO office in Nagrota, informing her that she must visit the office, or else a warrant would be issued against her. This news intensified her anxiety. Since she didn't have anyone she could rely on outside the school, she approached several individuals at the school but none was willing to accompany her. They feared getting involved with the police unnecessarily. Fortunately, one teacher, also an ANO, contacted me to meet and help her. When I approached her, I noticed that she appeared visibly nervous. Given that we hadn't been formally introduced yet, she may have been uncertain if I would accompany her. Recognizing the seriousness of the situation, my first course of action was to reach out to some female police officers to explain the situation and then arrange for them to accompany us at 3 o'clock.

I provided her with reassurance, much like one would console a distressed child assuring her that everything would eventually improve. Together, we made our way to the SDPO office where we met Deputy SP Pradeep Kumar who was quite courteous. We discussed the matter with him over a cup of tea. Deputy SP Kumar offered words of comfort and absolved Meenu of any wrongdoing. He initiated legal proceedings against her husband and alerted his unit. After this meeting her life gradually started to improve as the police cleared her of any charges. On our way back, she informed me about her upcoming court appearance on March 23. I assured her that I would accompany her.

On that particular day, Meenu's husband submitted a request to the court to celebrate his son's birthday, which was approved. In the evening, he arrived with the soldiers in army gypsy, celebrated his son's birthday and then departed. Little did he know that trouble awaited him too. Perhaps he believed that the reputation of the Indian Army, being one of the world's finest, would shield him from repercussions for the misuse of a government military vehicle. I had other commitments that evening but had requested DSP Pradeep

Kumar to send some police officers to the restaurant to ensure that he didn't indulge in any rude behaviour..

Meenu had now felt quite comfortable and had become an integral part of our family. My wife and I entrusted her with the task of guiding our daughter, a responsibility she fulfilled exceptionally well. Our daughter had an upcoming university entrance exam. Meenu helped her prepare for the exam.

Winter had settled in at the school and Meenu had gone to her home in Punjab with her son during winter vacation. In the meantime, I departed from the school to undertake my final assignment. Upon my reaching Jammu, I learnt that she had emerged victorious in the lawsuit. The court had directed her husband to provide child maintenance allowance to her.

Colonel Javed Mir frequently emphasized that performing acts of kindness and aiding those in need is akin to embarking on a pilgrimage. However, in my view, this time Meenu's case was a pilgrimage for me. By the time this book of mine is published, I will be engaged in research on Sufism in the sacred city of Baghdad, Iraq!